The Truth About Melissa

A Soul Mate Experiment

LISA MAYME CORBIT

outskirts press

The Truth About Melissa
A Soul Mate Experiment

v3.0

Outskirts Press, Inc.
http://www.outskirtspress.com

ISBN: 978-1-4787-1457-6

PRINTED IN THE UNITED STATES OF AMERICA

For Mom and Dad

Disclaimer

This book is a combination of facts about Lisa Mayme Corbit's life and certain embellishments. Names, dates, places, events, and details have been changed, invented, and altered for literary effect. The reader should not consider this book anything other than a work of literature.

PROLOGUE

The night was advancing brilliantly. Jonathan had always found it difficult to plan an evening with his dad Richard and brother James. Just the three of them. No women to interfere with their conversation. But tonight they were enjoying a decadent dinner, marveling at the view from Jonathan's First Hill condo as the sunset faded just beyond the Space Needle.

As they lounged in what the sales brochure called 'the well-appointed living area', Jonathan reflected and readjusted his assessment. In reality, the night was a bit short of brilliant. The dinner was Chinese takeout, the penthouse really belonged to Richard, and quite honestly, Jonathan missed the company of James and Richard's significant others, their soul mates. Which led Jonathan to lament for the umpteenth time about his loneliness and longing to be united with his own soul mate. Even though he knew Richard and James were sick of hearing about it, he brought it up anyway.

"Why don't you just create her?" James's exasperation oozed boredom.

"What? Like a blow-up doll? Not what I had in mind." Jonathan hugged the couch pillow.

"No. Not that. Although—" James laughed.

"Shut up." Jonathan chucked the pillow at him but missed by a good two feet.

"No. You're supposedly an author. Create her." James leaned back and clasped his hands behind his head. "You know, from fiction. Write what you want in your perfect soul mate."

Just as the dismissive thought, *he really thinks he's some kind of genius*, entered Jonathan's mind, Richard chimed in.

"Wait a minute." Richard slowly processed a thought as James and Jonathan waited patiently for the next wonderful idea that would spew from their father's mouth. "Manifesting," he continued. "You know, visualize and put an abundance of effort into your dreams."

"Like you daydreamed of finding your soul mate?" Jonathan prompted. He was excited that Richard was offering advice about his life; any advice was a nugget.

"Yeah. But be even more serious about it. I had thoughts of finding my soul mate. But I didn't actually write specifics down. You should really commit to it. Even write her letters."

"And have her write letters to you," James added.

"Write a whole fictional biography." Richard pulled a small notebook from his pocket and jotted a few notes.

Jonathan leaned toward the notebook and absently remarked, "Sounds a little like the blue feather experiment."

Richard abandoned his scribbles. "I guess I do believe a lot of what I write." He continued, quoting, "It takes zero faith. What it takes is imagination." His eyes twinkled with the familiar phrase from *Illusions*.

James was into it now, "Imagine this: start with her physical appearance, then her education, and her family background, and her personality—"

"—and job, and past loves, and goals, and dreams. And then simulate a story through a series of letters and responses. Create the whole essence of this woman," Richard finished.

"She needs a name," James said. "Katrina. Create your Katrina."

Jonathan took the first bite. "Why Katrina?"

"I don't know," James spat. "Why not Katrina? Do you have another name for your soul mate?"

"I really never thought about her name."

"Well, there's your problem. You need to start believing that she is real and out there and getting ready to join your life." James' enthusiasm always overshadowed his ideas, even when his ideas lacked substance.

But Jonathan actually found himself absorbed with this pitch and decided to toy with the idea. "Yeah, it might be worth a shot," he mumbled. Sitting up straight, he announced, "But her name is Melissa."

As soon as his guests left that evening, Jonathan spent the entire night creating his Melissa.

August 1988---Melissa

- *Starting college this month—graduates in 1992, then moves to Seattle! to be with me!*
- *From Iowa*
- *Majoring in some kind of art, but will switch before graduating*
- *Good student; honor roll*
- *Middle name same as grandmother's*
- *Worked while going to college—waitress??*
- *Involved in a long-term relationship throughout college*
- *Went to small high school; played sports*
- *Wrote for her school newspaper*
- *Brown hair, brown eyes, 5'7", hwp, in shape, athletic*
- *Independent, feisty, sarcastic, funny, smart*
- *Does not wear a lot of makeup; hair in pony tail*
- *Doesn't drink a lot*
- *Original parents are still together*
- *Youngest in family. 3 older siblings; 10 years older; 1 brother, 2 sisters.*
- *Had dogs growing up*
- *Spiritual, but not religious*
- *Will be new to Seattle; not know a lot of people*
- *Will have a red, older car*
- *Will be continuing education rather than a career; but have a part-time job*
- *Likes to read, write*
- *Will teach me things that I cannot do; sports*
- *Will learn things from me; mentally, chess*

- *Can shoot pool*
- *Does not smoke*

As the first morning light reflected across Elliot Bay, Jonathan wrote his first note to Melissa:

Dear Melissa,

You are my soul mate. I look forward to meeting you in four years!

Till then,
Jonathan

CHAPTER 1

Bulging plops of rain streamed down the outside of the phone booth and Lisa's patience washed away with them. "I'm not an idiot. I'm just lost."

"Mercer Street Exit. You can't miss it," Cathy said.

"I took Mercer Exit, but I didn't see Westlake where you said it should be."

Cathy tried again, slower this time. "Mercer Street Exit."

Lisa's jaw clenched as she spoke more slowly than Cathy. "I took Mercer Exit and took a left at the light. I've gone about three miles and no Westlake Avenue. I—"

"Wait! What? You've gone three miles?"

Lisa could feel that some drastic mistake had been made. "Yes, but there's no Westlake here."

"You must be on Mercer Island!"

"I guess. It says Mercer Island Exit."

"No, no, no. You need Mercer *Street* Exit."

Island? Street? Was there a difference? "Remember, Cathy, I've never been to Seattle before. Where am I supposed to be?"

Cathy started laughing. "Well, little cousin, you haven't even made it to the right freeway yet."

Lisa did not find this humorous. Cathy backtracked Lisa to I-90 and explained she needed to take the I-5 North and Mercer *Street* Exit, finishing with, "You'll be here in fifteen minutes." Not a moment too soon.

The last five hours driving west across Washington State had been filled with apprehension and these last thirty minutes of being lost almost had Lisa headed back to Idaho to rethink her plan.

What was her plan anyway? She was moving in with a cousin she had only met once. She wasn't even sure how they were related. She was moving to a city she had never been and where she knew no one. She was starting Court Reporting school when she thought her schooling was over. Lisa knew her plan should be to find a job since she had finished her BA, but even in Idaho that had been impossible: no experience, no job. And a degree in English didn't really provide experience...or qualify you for any place to get experience.

On the other hand, Lisa had found her cousin to be quite entertaining when she met her at the family reunion a few months ago. She had always been intrigued by the big city and made it her destiny to move there. Court Reporting could be exciting, right? At least an opportunity to make a good salary.

Lisa's thoughts were as tumultuous as the rainy weather outside. However, she felt more adventure than anxiety and was ready for this next step in her life.

Through the smudged windshield, she strained to see the final street sign of her destination. Turning left onto Dravus Avenue at the north end of Lake Union, Lisa saw Cathy and her sister, Tammy, waiting under the covered patio. Seeing the pair bundled together against the damp night air brought a smile to her face. Tammy stood tall and stiff and Cathy had her arms wrapped tight around Tammy's middle. Cathy was about a foot shorter and when she started jumping up and down at the sight of Lisa, it forced Tammy to time her own body with little jumps. Her rolling eyes and tight lips suggested this was something she put up with often. Lisa could hear through her closed window Cathy calling out, "She's here. She's here."

Lisa parallel parked into the only open spot. She gathered her coat off the passenger seat and dashed across the street to the cover of the building.

Cathy's greeting was accompanied by a smothering hug, pinning Lisa's arms to her side. "Ah little cousin, you made it. You Mercer Island adventurer, you."

"My first lesson learned in the big city is who *not* to get directions from."

Tammy, looking toward Cathy, said, “And in just one conversation with you, she learned that. Smart girl.”

With the banter, Lisa’s feelings easily slid from frustration to comfort. She kind of liked being called ‘little cousin.’ And the way Cathy said it with the emphasis on the Ts made it endearing. This was the right choice. She was definitely feeling good about her new journey as a single, career-focused girl in Seattle.

CHAPTER 2

Sauntering into Jillian's Billiard Club—oh, who was he kidding? He had never sauntered in his life. But as an almost-published author, Jonathan was always searching for the right word. So, sauntering into Jillian's, Jonathan prepared to dazzle the good-looking front desk girl, Tawnya, with the greeting he had perfected over the last few days. Perhaps the fact he saw her every day boosted his confidence to try his new lines on her. Or maybe he really was getting more comfortable around the ladies. Either way, he was more than ready to find someone and settle into a relationship.

The combination of wood oil and ammonia barely masked the lingering cigarette odor of Jillian's. Jonathan took a swift glance around the club. The gold banisters beamed against the backdrop of the pale wood floors and green felt pool tables. Seeing as it was not yet five o'clock, only two of the ten tables were in use. The crisp connection of billiard ball on billiard ball echoed around the cavernous room. Beyond the pool playing area, the lingering rays of the afternoon sun shone through the high windows that surrounded the Algonquin Bar and met at a point at the back of the club. Jonathan loved the idea of the Algonquin Bar, learning a few months back that it had been moved here from New York's Algonquin Hotel where a bunch of famous writers liked to hang out. Their names were etched behind the bar, and he often had the thought maybe someday after his book was published the manager at Jillian's would add his name.

He bounded—another word he thought would perfectly describe his anticipation of impressing Tawnya–up the carpeted stairs. "Hey Tawnya, how about checking me out some balls." His elbow barely missed the counter as he leaned against it. He recovered quickly.

Tawnya smiled. It was her job. Make the regulars feel special. "Sure, Jonathan. Just need your ID."

"Seems as a regular I shouldn't have to give you my ID every time." Jonathan attempted to be flirtatious.

"You know the routine. Want balls? Gotta leave your ID. Hell, I had to take Gary Payton's ID the other day. You should have seen the attitude I got from him. You're not going to give me attitude are you, Jonathan?"

"No, no. I was just kidding." He fumbled to remove his wallet from his back pocket as he pushed upright from the counter and tried to balance his pool cue without knocking himself in the head. "Here you go. One ID for one rack of balls."

"Great. I even have your favorite table open. Nineteen."

"Nice. I'll come down and keep you company later if you're bored." He knew she would like that. Everyone seemed to enjoy his company here. He almost had enough courage to ask her out. Even though he knew she was off the 'Melissa' watch—she smoked—it wouldn't hurt to go out on a dinner-and-a-movie date.

"Sounds good." Tawnya barely glanced in his direction as she greeted the next regular.

Jonathan struggled to the top of the stairs trying not to drop his rack of balls, pool cue, and wallet that he had not returned to his pocket. "Hey, Greg," he called. Greg had become more than his waiter over the last few months. Greg invited him twice to Sunday night dinners at his mom's house. It was a social gathering Jonathan hoped he would be invited back for. Even though there were no women prospects, he enjoyed the company, and Greg's mom always made a great meal. Jonathan thought of Greg as a friend.

"Hey, Jonathan. The usual?" Greg's uniform was proof of his mom's good cooking. The buttons struggled to hold his vest together and his arms bulged against the white cotton shirt as he reached to toss a coaster on Jonathan's bar table.

"Of course." Damn, he loved being 'known.' And it was only going to get better now that his book was almost published.

Around the corner, Greg punched in Jonathan's usual—a Shirley Temple with extra grenadine. His coworker, Steve, said, "Ooh, you got the big spender today. Bring him a plate with extra cherries with his drink. Save you an extra trip. That guy's weird."

"He's not bad. Just lonely. And a little socially challenged, and—" Greg paused as he glanced over toward Jonathan and saw him miss the side of the pool table with his cue box sending it crashing to the hardwood floor, "—and definitely a bit clumsy. But a good guy. I like him. Plus, he might be famous some day. He just wrote a book."

"Yeah, yeah, we've heard all about that book. Haven't seen it yet, just heard about it," Steve mumbled as he lifted his tray to deliver his drinks. "I, on the other hand, get to wait on these young punks from Microsoft who think they're going to rule the world some day in a technologically enhanced society. As if we'll all communicate through a computer some day. God help us."

Greg chuckled as Steve sauntered off and delivered the drinks.

"Hey Jonathan, how ya doin' today?" Greg set Jonathan's Shirley Temple and side plate of cherries down and laid his tray on the chair. He wasn't busy. Jonathan was his only table.

"Good man, good, real good." Jonathan always made sure his life seemed better than it was. After all, *he* wasn't working for tips. "Got the book back from my editor and have some work to do this week, but real good, man. How 'bout you?" Jonathan was being polite asking. He knew Greg was frustrated, still waiting tables with a Bachelor's degree fresh in his possession. But within their friendship they had developed a mutual respect: Greg was happy for Jonathan that he didn't have to wait tables, and Jonathan was happy for Greg that he had a permanent girlfriend. They both wanted a little of what the other had.

"You know, same ol' same ol'. Just trying to pay the bills. When will your book be in print?" Greg asked.

Ah, the important stuff, Jonathan thought. His fingers greedily picked a fourth cherry from the plate and his lips plucked it from the stem. He murmured through the thick red juice, "Soon, soon." After squishing the fruit with his tongue and swallowing, he took a quick sip from his straw and continued, "Just have the final changes, then I get my galley copy. That's pretty much finished and ready to go to print. I got my first check the other day for thirty grand."

Jonathan loved saying that. Thirty grand. His thoughts raced to how he'd already spent it: computer, fax, copier, printer, desk, furniture, car and big screen TV. All a tax write-off because he could connect it to his home-based business of being an author. Taxes. The thought sprinted through his head. He'd think about setting some aside for that with the next thirty grand or the final thirty grand. Anyway, he would soon be a published author. The money would pour in for the rest of his life. Hell, his dad *still* got checks for a book he wrote twenty-five years ago.

Greg responded exactly as Jonathan wanted. "Man, thirty grand. That would be so cool."

Jonathan sat up straighter. "Yeah it's a trip. I—"

Greg jolted off his stool as a couple claimed a table in his section. "I'll be back. You want your usual sandwich?"

Disappointed he couldn't continue, Jonathan's shoulders drooped. "You know it. Thanks, man." He immediately straightened as he called out, "I'll leave you a big tip." People like rich. These people at Jillian's like rich.

Jonathan grabbed his drink, headed to the pool table and opened his long, narrow box. Oh yes, and the thirty grand had also paid for a brand new custom pool cue. He carefully removed both ends of the cue stick and clumsily screwed them together. He loved the smooth texture; the shiny mother of pearl had been a priority when he had it made.

Removing the balls from their rack, he arranged them in the plastic triangle and plodded to the other side of the table. This was his workout for the day. Shirley Temple, greasy fries, juicy burger and shooting pool. Yes, he had it all. He returned to his upright bar table, rested one thigh against the stool and pulled the cocktail napkin toward him. He slipped the ever-ready pen from his chest pocket and scribbled:

Oct. 15, 1992
Dear Melissa,

I am lonely tonight. I wish you were here. But I know you're just getting settled into your new city. You'll be here soon.

Till then,
Jonathan

Jonathan ignored the urge to write the reply. He knew she would say she missed him too and was coming soon. His fingers fumbled the napkin into awkward folds and he stuffed it into his shirt pocket. Maybe he'd write the reply later—before adding it to the shoebox full of notes from her already. Right now, he was ready to shoot some pool.

CHAPTER 3

"What do you want to do first in the big city, little cousin?" Cathy and Tammy hadn't even got Lisa through the front door of the apartment complex and Cathy was already filling her head with changes that were soon to become her every day reality. "Sushi?"

"What?" *Isn't that raw fish?*

Cathy continued, "Dim Sum?"

"Huh?" *Not even ringing a bell.*

"Bon Thai?"

Is she even speaking English anymore?

"Capital Hill? Pioneer Square?"

They crossed the foyer and Cathy pushed the call button for the elevator. Lisa finally got in a question. "I'd like to join a gym. Do you go to a gym?"

"Didn't see that one coming, did you?" Tammy said to Cathy.

"I'd kinda like to get that set up before I start school on Monday, so I'll have a place to work out." Lisa quickly explained.

"Sure I have a gym—"

Tammy interrupted her. "Not that she ever goes."

"I do too, fat head."

Lisa looked from Cathy to Tammy. Fat head? How could she call Tammy fat head? Tammy was tall, blond and skinny. And Cathy was, well, short, red-headed and kind of frumpy.

Tammy guessed Lisa's confusion. "She calls everybody that. Not just me."

The elevator dinged and the doors slid open. The three of them stepped inside and Cathy put the bag she was carrying down to push the "2" button. She faced Lisa and cupped her hands around her head. She carefully tilted it from the left to the right and then back to the left again. Then Cathy rubbed the top of her head, actually rubbed her head. "Except not you, my precious. You're going to be little cousin. My little cousin," she enunciated. "What do you want to do *besides* find a gym, little cousin?"

Lisa made a mental note to ask her parents exactly how they were cousins. "I don't know. I'll leave that up to you since I've never been here. I have two days before I start school full time."

"Then we'll have to do as much as possible in these next two days. Fun, fun, fun." Cathy mimicked a little kid, rubbing her hands together and bouncing around.

"How old are you again?" Lisa asked. They reached the second floor and exited the elevator.

"I know. She acts twelve, huh?" Tammy said.

"Maybe even younger than that." Lisa quickly recognized the smell in the hall as the fermented vegetables used in kimchee. It reminded her of her Korean neighborhood friends from childhood. Two pairs of slippers placed outside a front door exposed the source of the familiar scent. The non-reaction of the odors by Tammy and Cathy also revealed to her that she would be welcomed by these aromas everyday. It was a thought that comforted her, bringing forth a rush of memories of her younger days.

Ahead of Lisa, Cathy reached for her sister with her free hand and rubbed Tammy's head this time. "Not as old as fat head."

Tammy corrected her immediately. "That is totally not true. She's older than I am, even if she doesn't act it. She's going to be thirty-three next month."

"Looks like you're eleven years older than me, fat head." Lisa waited, not sure if she was allowed to use the endearment.

"Ah, poop. Anyway—" Cathy opened the door to her apartment and the three of them, loaded with bundles from Lisa's car, entered. "You can put your stuff in here." She led the way to a room where two beds were on opposite sides. "I told you, it's small, but it's free."

The room was dark. Heavy, maroon velvet curtains draped across the entire far wall and an oriental rug covered the floor. There was a small single bed on one side of the room and a slightly larger bed on the other side. A floor lamp adorned with hanging tassels and beads stood between the two beds. Pictures on the wall were framed, different from posters taped at the corners that Lisa was used to in her college apartment.

Lisa set her duffle bag on the bed she assumed was hers, because it was neatly made. It was close quarters, but not as close as the dorm room where she'd spent her first two years of college. She was adept at adapting and she knew that for her, it would be sufficient. However, she was a bit uncomfortable about the intrusion into Cathy's life. "Are you sure this is going to be okay?"

"Absolutely. You just have to help me clean the building on Sundays and help with clean up outside too. Sometimes we have to plant flowers and pretty-up the grounds. That's how we get the apartment for free." Her sentence ended in a sing-song and she threw her arms high as she swirled around. It sounded like a sweet set up. How did she get such a great arrangement?

Again, Tammy answered Lisa's unasked question. "You will learn that Cathy is the queen of great scams. If there's a scam, Cathy's first in line." Lisa looked at her curiously and she added quickly, "Oh nothing illegal. Just unbelievable breaks and sweet-talking deals. She's lucky like that."

"That's right, little cousin. And someday my ship will come in and I will never have to work again."

"She's been saying that since she was five. Problem is, her ship isn't even close to shore and she still doesn't get a real job."

"You don't work?" Lisa asked.

"Of course, I work." She wasn't very convincing. "In fact, these clients of mine just discovered a ship off the coast of Japan from the Yuan Dynasty. We're waiting for the typhoon season to be over and then I'll be going to help them recover the treasures. That's why I'm learning to scuba dive right now. It's an amazing find. But don't tell anyone, because they haven't filed the claim yet. I'm working on securing a story with National Geographic also."

Ships? Yuan Dynasty? Discoveries? Treasure? National Geographic? Lisa could not keep up with this girl. She glanced to Tammy whose eyes were rolling to the top of her head as Cathy's story simmered. Tammy winked at Lisa and muttered, "As I said, her ship, blah, blah, blah." Tammy grabbed Lisa's wrist and pulled her forward. "Let's go to the living room."

They left the bedroom, Cathy at Lisa's back continuing, "It's going to be cool. She just doesn't get it. But someday—"

The living room was the same size as the bedroom. Another large oriental rug swallowed the floor. Three or four framed paintings hung around the room. Wooden masks—kind of creepy—were situated in open spots on the wall. Ornamental fish were swimming up the wall and onto the ceiling. A purple—yes, purple—leather couch and a wicker chair were the sitting furniture and in front of the couch, where Lisa had always seen a coffee table placed, lay a five-foot black obsidian naked woman.

"That's Jacquie."

"Huh?" Lisa looked at Cathy and she was pointing to the figure sprawled before her.

"She's one of very few sculptures that was successfully carved out of a solid piece of obsidian. Usually something that large will crack during the sculpting phase. But not Jacquie, she made it. I got her for sixteen thousand."

"Sixteen thousand dollars?" Lisa gasped.

"She would have been sixteen thousand dollars," Tammy interrupted. "But Cathy got her on a whim from a guy closing his gallery who didn't want to move her. I'm telling you, scam queen. Right place, right time. Tell her about the Dali."

Cathy pointed to a painting on the wall. "Do you know Dali?"

Lisa recognized the genre from an art history class she had taken a few years before. "Yeah, Salvador Dali, the Spanish surrealist artist. I don't know if I've seen that one, but I can tell it's him."

"The guy from the gallery gave me that too. I have papers; it's an original drawing with charcoal pen and crayon on paper. May be worth a hundred thousand."

"What? And he just gave it to you? I don't get it," Lisa exclaimed.

"I guess he thought I was cute." Cathy lifted her eyebrows, smiled, shrugged her shoulders and laughed. "Cute gets you stuff."

"I need to learn that cute stuff," Lisa said. Cathy and Lisa sat on the couch and Tammy took the wicker chair.

"Okay, enough of that. We need to talk to you about some things." Tammy instantly pulled the mood to serious.

Lisa figured this for the catch. There had to be a catch. Two days ago, Lisa had received a call from Cathy and Tammy telling her they thought she should live with Cathy. They had heard of her plans to live in Gig Harbor and immediately decided it would be much better for Lisa to live in Seattle. They convinced Lisa only old people lived in Gig Harbor and at twenty-two years old she needed to be in Seattle if she was going to have any kind of a social life.

Cathy had explained to Lisa she could live rent-free with her if she didn't mind the small apartment; which she didn't, considering she would probably never be there. Lisa had figured she would have to leave at 7:00 in the morning to get to school on time and she would be there until 3:30. And soon enough, within a month, she would have to work a few nights a week somewhere. Lisa's thoughts stopped abruptly as she realized they were both looking at her. "What?"

Tammy looked at Cathy. Cathy looked at Lisa, then back at Tammy. "You say it."

"Say what?" Lisa didn't like this.

"Okay," Tammy started slowly. "We thought we should have a talk with you."

"About what?" Lisa was hovering at the stage where she wanted to hear what they had to say but hoped it would be stalled as long as possible. The way the conversation started assured her it would be something awkward. *Just rip the band-aid off already*, she thought.

"We know you're from Idaho and things are a lot different here in the city," Tammy started.

"I know that. I did live in Huntington Beach until I was thirteen." Lisa didn't want them to think she was a total hillbilly.

Cathy straightened. "You lived in Huntington Beach?"

"Yeah. I—"

"Cathy." Tammy interrupted Lisa's answer with a look to her sister.

"Sorry. Go on."

"What we're trying to say is, well, I'm just going to say it. If you're going to be, you know, out and about, and well, having sex, you need to take precautions."

Lisa's laugh broke the awkward silence. "What?"

"We're serious. This is serious. AIDS is becoming such a big deal and we don't want you to be naïve about it. Especially now that you are in a big city. It's not Idaho."

Lisa was embarrassed. She laughed again. She did not know what to say.

"Lisa, this is not funny. It's serious. You need to be careful."

"I'm not laughing because it's funny. I laugh when I'm uncomfortable." Lisa was definitely uncomfortable. Sex was not a conversation that was natural in her upbringing. Her family did not talk about it. She certainly did not talk about it with strangers. And these were strangers. *Hell*, Lisa thought, *I've only been here half an hour*. Yet she still tried to seem informed. "I know all about AIDS. Our professor talked about it in Biology class. But only gay people and drug addicts get it, so I'm pretty sure I'm fine."

"Oh, God," Cathy blurted. "Do you really think that?"

Lisa didn't reply. She tried to remember what the professor had said, but honestly couldn't. It seemed such a meaningless lecture at the time. She didn't have to worry about AIDS.

"Lisa, do you really think that?" Cathy repeated.

"I don't know. I've never really thought much about it, I guess. My college boyfriend, Jason, and I were together for three years and didn't even, you know, have sex the last year we were together because we wanted to see if we were compatible without that."

Tammy and Cathy offered nothing.

Lisa continued, "I guess it's never been a concern for me."

They still said nothing.

Lisa moved to lighten the mood. "You guys get right to the point, don't you? I have three older sisters and in my entire life, I have never had any conversation about sex with any of them. And here you are, known me for about forty-five minutes and BAM... with the heavy stuff."

Tammy was still serious. "We want to make sure you're not stupid."

Lisa was slow to respond. "Not stupid, but not a slut either. So if I do decide to become one, I will remember your words of advice. How's that?"

"Fair enough. Let's get you unpacked."

CHAPTER 4

Jonathan was well into his fourth Shirley Temple and pondering if he should order one more plate of the famous Jillian's fries when his thoughts were interrupted. "Hey, Jonathan."

Jonathan turned toward the approaching short Asian man. "Yo, Keith, whassup?" He wasn't sure if 'Yo' was still hip, but he knew the slow, drawled 'whassup' was. He had practiced getting the inflection perfect.

"Not much, man. Mind if I shoot a few games with you?" Keith had already begun to open his cue case.

Jonathan didn't mind. He was never waiting for anyone to join him. Jonathan just shot pool by himself until one of the waiters got off work or Keith showed up.

"Not at all. Cool man. I was just hanging out, having a bite to eat, not doing much."

The phrase sounded familiar to him. Was that what he always said? He'd have to scribble out some new dialogue to use. He didn't want to appear dull. He decided to spice up his life. "I just have time for a few games tonight, though. My editor is calling later to go over some last minute changes on the book with me." He hoped Keith wouldn't ask why his editor would be calling at night.

"Sounds good. How about best two out of three?"

"Okay. I'll rack 'em." Jonathan rounded the table, rolling the balls toward one side. He grabbed the rack and shuffled the balls into place stuffing his fingers in the back to tighten them. It took three times to make sure they were absolutely perfect before eliminating the rack.

Keith finished assembling his cue and took his place at the opposite end with the cue ball. "What kind of work is left on the book?" He took the first shot and scattered the balls on the green felt table. Two stripes and a solid fell.

"Nice shot." Jonathan hurried on to respond to Keith's question. "Not much left now. A few changes in the next couple days and then in about two months, I'll get the galley copy. That's the last stage before print."

Keith sank one more stripe and then missed. "You're solids. That's cool, man. Are you going to let me read the galley copy?"

"Of course." Jonathan lined up his first shot. "I'll reserve you a personal copy." He sank his shot and moved to his second.

"Then what happens? When it gets published, I mean?"

Jonathan was on a run, but it didn't bother him to talk while he was shooting. "Then the fun starts. I get to go on a tour that my agent will set up. She's talking Chicago, New York, Larry King, Paula Zahn. Maybe some interviews with my dad."

"That's big time," Keith said. "You're, like, gonna be famous."

"It's pretty exciting." Jonathan finally missed, leaving two of his balls on the table.

Keith chalked his cue to take his turn. "Why your dad? I mean, why your dad in the interviews? Is the book about him?"

"In a way, I guess it is. It's kind of a reconciliation. I didn't really know him growing up." Jonathan tried to condense the version, but leave it open enough so Keith would continue asking him questions. He liked this part of someone getting to know him.

Keith proceeded perfectly. "Why didn't you know him?"

Jonathan thought, here goes the first punch. "After having six kids, he decided he didn't want to be a father."

"What?" The typical incredulous reply Jonathan was used to. "It took six kids for him to figure that out?"

Jonathan liked that reaction. "Yeah, most people would probably have that figured out after one or two, eh?"

"You'd think." Keith missed his shot at the eight ball. "You're up."

Jonathan rechalked and sized up his next moves. He still had two balls to make before he had a chance at the eight ball.

Keith pushed for more information. "You had no contact with him at all? Not even phone calls?"

Jonathan sank the first of his two balls. "Nope, nothing. Not after he became rich and famous." He nonchalantly delivered the second punch.

"Famous? Famous for what?"

Jonathan tried to sound casual, but this was when the adrenaline rush kicked in, revealing to people who he *really* was. "He's a pretty well-known author and made a lot of money." He tried to slow his response by shooting his last ball. He missed.

"Would I know anything he wrote?" Keith asked as he strategized his next shot.

Now the knock-out punch that Jonathan loved to deliver. He tried to make it sound unimportant, knowing that it wasn't. "He wrote one book that was pretty big back in the '70s. *Jonathan Livingston Seagull*."

"No way," Keith exclaimed. "I love that book. Richard Bach's your dad? Of course. Jonathan Bach. Richard Bach. *Jonathan Livingston Seagull*. Wow, that's something."

Jonathan let the amazement of what he said register for Keith. He reveled in the awe. Keith would now know how significant he was. Keith did not disappoint.

"Did he name the book after you?"

The most frequent question, and the one he liked least. He wished his dad had named it after him. Maybe that would have given him a strand to hold onto while growing up. Some sort of my-dad-was-proud-of-me medal to cling to. "Nah, I was actually named after the book. It was rejected seventeen times by publishers and right around the time it was accepted, I was born. So they decided to give me the name Jonathan, after the seagull. Imagine being named after a seagull."

"That's some seagull to be named after." Keith sank the eight ball and reflexively called, "Rack 'em."

Stepping aside for Jonathan to grab the rack, he asked, "How come you couldn't see him growing up? Didn't he have visitation rights?"

"Didn't want 'em." Jonathan knew how the rest of the conversation would go.

Sure enough. "What do you mean, he didn't want 'em? Richard Bach abandoned six children? That doesn't sound like something he'd do."

It always amazed Jonathan that people had this ideal of his dad just because he wrote some profound book that was required reading material in many English classes twenty years ago. Richard Bach was just a man. With a lot of flaws. "Nope, I'm telling you, he didn't want 'em."

"So you never knew him?"

"Only what I heard when he had some new book on the best seller list. He was a stranger to us. A stranger to the ground," Jonathan added to see if Keith would get it. He didn't. It wasn't one of his dad's more popular books.

"That's just bizarre. I always thought he was this amazing guru that everyone should learn something from."

As he racked the balls, Jonathan's mind raced. He still wasn't sure if he liked or hated this part. The part when he revealed to a Richard Bach fan that Richard Bach was kind of an ass of a man. He liked that after all these years he could finally tell his story about his dad deserting him and his family. But he also noted the irony that he was now trying to get along with his dad and get to know him after all these years.

He still wasn't comfortable defending him fully. He felt he was betraying his brothers and sisters, who had not reconciled with him as he had while he was writing his book.

He tried an explanation to Keith. "He's okay. Growing up, my mom kept us from him. She was pretty bitter. She told us only the things about him that would make us hate him as she did."

"That's understandable, I guess, after he abandoned her with six children." Keith lined up his shot.

Jonathan mulled over how to respond to this empathy for his mother, whom he still resented for lying to him for years. "Turns out, she wasn't exactly honest. That's what my book is about. Uncovering some of the clouds of confusion that I was brought up believing about him and finding out the truth for myself."

Keith broke and ran his first six balls before responding. "It sounds fascinating and an interesting read. I will definitely buy a copy when you get it done."

"Thanks, man. I hope you and a few others buy it so I can live the easy life and be rich and famous too." Jonathan missed his shot, but wasn't sore. "I'll even sign your copy so you can sell it for lots of money some day."

Keith ran the rest of the table. "That's two, man. Looks like I got you today." He laid his cue on the table and stretched his hand out for the sportsmanlike handshake. "You better sign it. I'm going to say I knew you when. Better get home so you don't miss that call from your editor."

Huh? Jonathan had forgotten. "Oh, yeah, you're right. Will you return the balls for me so I can check out?"

"Sure. See you soon, Jonathan." Keith gathered his things along with the rack of balls.

"Tomorrow, rematch. I'll get you."

"Sounds good. I'll be here around 5:00. Same as usual."

Jonathan was sorry he made up the lie about his editor calling. He could have hung out with Keith longer. Now he was alone again. He hated being alone. He fumbled in his pocket for the crumbled napkin from earlier and turned it to the clean side.

Dear Jonathan,

I am missing you terribly too. We will be together soon and I will kick your butt in pool.

Love,
Melissa

Jonathan smiled at the feistiness Melissa had and hoped she lived up to his expectations. He liked feisty.

He paid his bill, stuffed the note in his pocket, gathered his cue and headed home. Alone. Lonely.

CHAPTER 5

Tammy and Cathy helped Lisa unpack. She didn't have a lot and they were done except for a miscellaneous bag of things she had packed at the last minute. Lisa unzipped the duffel bag and Tammy pulled out the book on top. "*The Bridge Across Forever*. What's this about?"

Lisa had forgotten she shoved it in there. A leftover during packing that she wasn't sure what to do with, she had just set it in with some clothes. "No idea. Never read it. Some love story, I think."

Cathy snatched the book from Tammy and opened it to the inside front cover. "Ooh. Listen Tammy." She read the hand scrawled inscription in a teasing banter. *"To Lisa, Please read this. It is a great love story. Maybe we can talk about it someday. Keep in touch. I will miss you, Tony."*

God, how embarrassing, Lisa thought as she snagged the book from Cathy and tossed it back on the top of the bag. Both Cathy and Tammy let out a long, "Oooooooh," and Cathy finished it with a saucy, drawled out, "Who's Tony?"

"No one. Just a friend. We went out a few times and he gave me this book before I left. Like it said, he said it was a love story I should read. I haven't even looked at it yet, so I have no idea what it's about." Lisa's words stumbled out trying to convince them how insignificant she thought it was.

Tammy pulled the book from the top again. She read from the back. *"If you've ever felt alone in a world of strangers, missing someone you've never met, you'll find a message from your love in 'The Bridge Across Forever.'"* She turned the book back to the front.

"Richard Bach. Isn't that the same author that wrote *Jonathan Livingston Seagull* back in the '70s?"

"No idea. Never heard of it," Lisa said.

"Hmmm, well, it sounds okay," Tammy said. "Maybe you should read it."

"Nah. Not into love stories right now." Lisa tried once again to dismiss the topic. To no avail.

"What? Why? Everybody likes a good love story. Don't you?" Tammy gushed.

Now what. Lisa didn't want to seem like a total cynic. But, really, she was not into this stuff right now. Not that she wasn't hoping to find a special someone. She loved being in the comfort of a relationship, having dated her high school boyfriend for four years and her college boyfriend for three years. She was lucky she didn't have to do that dreaded dating scene in college. Which didn't really amount to a scene as much as a lot of 'one-night stands' and 'hoping he'd calls.' She'd hated watching her friends' disappointment and then anger when the call never came. "Sure, I do. Just not right now."

"Uh oh, I think she's been burned," Cathy said. "What, little cousin, was a big, bad boy mean to you?"

Lisa tried to organize what she wanted to dispel at this point. "No, not at all. Just a hard break up. Jason and I thought we'd be together forever. Then we realized our lives were going in different directions. It was hard to accept. He wanted to stay in little town Idaho and I wanted to move to the big city." Lisa stood, hoping to get out of spilling all this. "Can I get some water?"

"Sure. Juice and pop in the fridge. I don't drink, so if you want beer or whatever, you'll need to supply that yourself. Grab me a Diet Pepsi. Tammy?"

"Juice, please."

"Guess I'm not company anymore. Anything else I can get for your highnesses?"

"Maybe some—" Cathy started.

"Don't even think about it," Lisa blurted before Cathy could finish. She delivered the drinks and sat back down. "You don't drink at all?" Lisa asked.

"Thank God, no," Tammy answered.

"It's not that bad." Cathy tried to defend herself. "Well, okay, it got a little bad. But I also realized when I needed to stop. So it's all good. But anyway, back to you and Jason."

Lisa thought she had gotten off the hook. "Yeah?" A statement and question in one.

"That was it? You broke up for good?" Cathy prodded.

"We're still friends—"

"Oh no, the kiss of death," Tammy interjected.

"No really. We still talk a lot. Maybe things will work out. We get along well. Never fight. No one would ever say a bad thing about him." Lisa wanted them to know he was a good guy. He was a good guy. She still questioned daily their decision to break up.

"Who loved who more?" Tammy asked.

"What?"

"I said, who loved who more? Like, did you love him more? Or did he love you more?"

"We loved each other the same." Lisa wasn't sure of the right answer.

"Bullshit." Cathy was apparently aware of the meaning of Tammy's question. "There's always one person in the relationship that loves the other more. Like, who was more sad when you broke up?"

"We were both sad." Lisa knew Jason had not wanted the break up. He did not see the need to date other people. But they had both cried.

"Okay. Who was more willing to change their plans for the other?" Cathy pushed more.

"I couldn't change my plans because they don't have a court reporting school in Idaho." She thought this was sufficient.

"So would he have changed his plans?"

"I think he might have, but he's got one more year at Idaho State and he's on scholarship, so it would have been stupid for him to transfer to another college." Lisa repeated to them the same things she and Jason had talked themselves into believing were smart, mature decisions. Lisa still wasn't sure. She had had a taste of dating other guys this summer, Tony being one of them, and she knew it was going to be a challenge to find someone as good as Jason.

"So he loved you more." Tammy said as a statement this time, not a question.

"Maybe." Lisa tried to end the discussion. "But anyway, I'm not into reading a love story right now. I'm here to concentrate on school and work on a career. I want to be young and single and have fun. Right, Cathy? You're not married or attached to anyone. Seems to be an okay plan."

"Absolutely. No stupid boy around to tell me what I can and can't do and when and where I can do it. Speaking of, fat head," she said to Tammy, "don't you need to get home to your hubby wubby before he sends the guards out?"

"I was just thinking that." Tammy rose from her place. "I guess I'll leave you two man-bashers here while I go cuddle up nice and warm in the arms of my love."

Now Lisa felt stupid. That was what life should be about: going home to someone who loved you at the end of the day. She had enjoyed the comfort of that with Jason; choosing nights at home curled up on the couch watching movies over attending the college keg parties. She looked forward to finding that with someone again soon.

"Okay, night." Cathy jumped up and pinned her in a bear hug.

Tammy rolled her eyes toward Lisa and explained as Cathy squeezed her, "This is her thing. Best not to fight it."

"You love it, you love it, you love it." Cathy chanted to her sister as Tammy's arms flailed. Cathy let go and turned to Lisa. "And now you, my little cousin."

"But I'm not leaving," Lisa pleaded as she felt her belly squeezed up by the tight bear hug.

Tammy warned, "Doesn't matter. Any time, any place, be ready for the grips of hell. And here's a hint," she whispered as if Cathy couldn't hear her, "don't struggle, it makes it worse."

"Wuahaha, I've got you now, my pretty." Cathy gave Lisa one more tight squeeze before releasing her.

"I feel like I'm living in an evil fairy tale," Lisa said.

They all were laughing now. Lisa at the absurdity of it all, Tammy, Lisa thought, because now her sister had a new play toy giving herself some relief, and Cathy because she was correcting Lisa's assessment of living in a fairy tale.

"I like to call it La-la Land, little cousin. Welcome to La-la Land. And we are going to have sooo much fun."

CHAPTER 6

Jonathan struggled to hold his pool cue and get his keys into the deadbolt lock of his Queen Anne apartment. The keys slipped from his hand and he hit his head on the doorknob bending over to pick them up. "Shit," he mumbled as the cue slid from under his arm and slammed to the cement walkway.

"Geez, times like these I wish I was deaf, not blind. Good thing you ain't no robber."

Jonathan turned to greet his neighbor. "Man, sorry Jim. Did I wake you?" He realized the ruckus he must have been making.

"Wake me? What the hell? I'm blind, not dead. It's only nine o'clock on a Friday night. Just gettin' ready to head out." Jim smoothly locked his door and slid his walking cane in a preventative arc.

"Sorry about the noise," Jonathan offered, realizing this blind guy had more of a social life than he did.

"No worries, you're usually pretty quiet. 'Cept a few weeks ago when you had that wild little hussy staying with you. Woo wee," he drawled. "Man alive. That thing sure had some lungs, yellin' 'giddyee up' and all." Jim poked Jonathan in the rib cage with his cane. "Ooh, feels like she had quite a bit to ride on there big fella. Best be watchin' the fries and junk food."

Jonathan finally got his door open. "Yeah, well, have a good night, Jim. Nice talking to you." His mood had gone from feeling pretty proud of himself that Jim had noticed he had had a girl staying with him—he wasn't a total loser—to downright sour with the fat joke.

"You have a good night, too. No late night pizza deliveries, okay?" Jonathan closed the door on this retort, but he could hear Jim chuckling as he shuffled down the walkway.

Jonathan stood with his back against the door and assessed the contradiction of his present living quarters: dingy apartment, but great view of downtown and the Space Needle. He had thought for sure he'd be living in his dad's penthouse suite on First Hill forever. It was great there; killer view, doorman that greeted him by name, weight room—not that he ever used it—and best of all, room service. But his dad had gone and sold it and Jonathan had to find what he could in Seattle with a view.

$800 a month got him a view—nothing like First Hill—and a really small apartment. As he reopened the front door to release the odors of tenants past, he stepped outside to the communal walkway that offered the unobstructed expanse of downtown Seattle and reminded himself, *I love the view. It's the view I crave.*

He never really had any visitors anyway, other than Jim. Oh, and of course, his visitor a few weeks ago, an old college girlfriend, Celeste. Jonathan thought about her getup that prompted the 'giddyup cowboy' Jim had referred to.

He had been lying on the couch naked like she requested, or demanded rather, before she went in the bedroom.

When she returned to the living room, it was the red cowboy hat that caught his attention, but that wasn't what started the blood flowing. As his eyes wandered down her body and took in the black lace bra and panty set, the black and red lace garter and the red cowboy boots, his desire boiled.

She coyly slid her hand from behind her back to reveal a lasso and made her way to Jonathan. "Looks like I've got myself a bull to lasso," she remarked, her voice sultry as her eyes slid down his body. She slung one red cowboy boot over his waist and mounted him for just a moment before whooping out the 'giddyup cowboy' and from there Jonathan's hands hungrily grabbed at everything he could.

Coming back to the present, Jonathan took in the twinkling images of the city coming to life and smiled, recalling that night. But as he turned to go back into his small, mildewed apartment, he remembered the end of what had started as a great fantasy.

Of course, it hadn't taken very long. Celeste dismounted as soon as he'd finished and said matter-of-factly, "There, don't you feel better. You needed that."

The remnants of anger he felt now were nothing compared to what he'd felt the moment she said that. Typical Celeste. Turned out she only came to visit because she knew his book was almost finished. She hinted to him she'd be more than willing to be his date on the red carpet if he became famous.

Well, screw that, Jonathan thought. *I'm not a horny college boy who would do anything for a lay. Well, maybe a few weeks ago I was, but I'm not anymore.* He had not called her since and he didn't even care. Let her run off to Hollywood to become whatever it was she thought she was going to become. He *was* going to become famous and she certainly wasn't going along on his ride. The thought gave him satisfaction; thinking of the don't-you-wish-you-had-treated-me-better attitude he couldn't wait to hold in front of her.

Besides, he had Melissa.

He slumped on his garage sale couch and pulled out two shoeboxes from underneath. His pulse returned to normal and a soft calm washed over him as he slid the tops off both boxes. He pulled the napkin from his shirt pocket he had written on earlier at Jillian's and put it in the box that was about three quarters full.

"Ah, Melissa, where are you?" She should be here soon.

He pulled the top letter from the shoebox that was crammed full. He read the date from two years earlier: *August, 1990.* She had written the letter the start of her junior year in college. He skimmed it. She was liking her classes. She had four papers due at the end of September. She was happy with her decision to change her major to English. Her parents had recently celebrated their 38th anniversary. She missed him very much and would get to him as soon as she finished her degree. She finished the letter as she always did; *Love, Melissa.*

Jonathan set the letter aside and grabbed the typed one under it:

September, 1990
Dear Melissa,

I got your letter. Sounds like you have a full load of classes. But I know you'll do well. I hope the papers are going okay. Remember, I was a Journalism major. I can help you if you need it. But I know you won't ask. You never do. You are quite capable on your own.

That is so cool about your parents' 38th anniversary. Not many people these days can say their parents are still together after that many years. I know I can't.

I miss you terribly too. I wish you were here. I want to share Seattle with you. It's so beautiful. And the view from my apartment is incredible. I am sitting in the window looking out at the city lights right now as I type this. I wish you could see it. I hope you are thinking of me too.

Till then,
Jonathan

Jonathan carefully refolded the one-page typed letter and slipped it under the one on top. He liked to keep them in order. He had them dated chronologically from Melissa, but then he always put his response under her letter. He scavenged through the box and did a mental count; about fifty letters from her and the same amount of responses from him in the first box. The second box was almost full also. Some were handwritten on legal yellow lined paper, some were typed, while others were written haphazardly on napkins or cocktail coasters or paper menus or any other attainable writing pad that had been available at the moment.

He found what he was looking for: a little golden nugget about three quarters of the way down in the first box. It was his favorite. It was handwritten on carefully selected stationery with a light pink background and darker pink and red hearts framing the words:

August, 1989
Dear Jonathan,

I love you. I am your soul mate. Wait for me.

Love,
Melissa

It was the first time she told him she loved him. His response was immediate. He pulled out the postcard with his reply. One side was the night view of the Space Needle taken from Highland Park just a few blocks up from his apartment. And on the other side:

Dear Melissa,

I love you too. I know you need to finish school. I will wait.

Love,
Jonathan

He remembered this first exchange of love so well and recalled the exact happenings of the evening that led up to it.

He had moved into this apartment and was feeling particularly low. The extreme change from living like a millionaire in his dad's condo to the slum he could afford had really dampened his spirits. At the age of twenty-five, he was feeling the crunch of "What am I going to do with my life?" He'd written his book and thought things were moving ahead. But then he'd received news the manuscript needed major work to even get accepted by a publisher; at least a year of editing and rewriting awaited him. So he now had to decide, was it worth it?

To get his mind off his latest disappointment, he had decided to drive to his favorite bookstore. The Elliot Bay Book Company was particularly crowded that night and he quickly realized why. Robert Fulgham, a local author, was doing a reading of some love stories that he had been collecting for a new book. Jonathan had decided to sit and listen. It made him feel worse.

Long after the reading—and after the crowds had cleared—Jonathan decided 'what the heck' and went to talk to Fulgham, who was studying a mountain of his own handwritten notes. "Hey, Mr. Fulgham." Jonathan greeted him as he would any of his college professors and held out his hand for a return welcome.

"Boy, do you look glum." Fulgham motioned to the opposite chair. "Sit down. Share a love story with me."

"Ha," Jonathan blurted as he sat across from the small wooden table tucked in the corner.

"Ha? Uh oh. No love story?" His eyes twinkled.

"Oh. I've got a love story. It just hasn't started yet."

"Hmmm. Interesting. What's your name?"

"Jonathan."

"Okay, Jonathan. I'll bite. A love story that hasn't started. Why's that? You afraid to ask her out?"

"I can't ask her out, she doesn't live here yet. We've been pen pals for about the past year." Jonathan was careful proceeding with this. He didn't want to reveal the depths of his obsession to his fictional Melissa.

"Sounds tough. But have you been learning everything about her that you need to know through the letters." Fulgham seemed to be fishing for a new story to add to his collection.

"Of course. She's absolutely perfect. Everything I want in a woman." Jonathan wondered to himself what this man would think if he knew that Melissa was just in his mind. He might find it very interesting. Maybe even interesting enough for a story in his book. But Jonathan wasn't sure how the ending would go. And he didn't want to spoil it for himself, so it was an idea he kept private.

Fulgham's next question caught Jonathan off guard. "Have you told her you love her yet?"

"She'll tell me first," Jonathan said with no hesitation. Mr. Fulgham gave him a quizzical look and jotted down a note on his notepad. Jonathan tried to save himself. "I mean, I think she should say it first."

"Why is that?"

Jonathan strained to see what it was he wrote, but couldn't read it. "I don't know. Then I'll know for sure before I make a fool of myself."

"Are you afraid she won't respond the way you want her to?"

"Oh, no. That's not it. I'm sure she'll respond *exactly* the way I want her to."

"I think it's time you tell her. Make sure she knows. Then you'll have the start of your love story." Mr. Fulgham carefully folded his notepad over and collected his book. "It was nice meeting you, Jonathan. Good luck."

"Yeah, thanks. Nice meeting you too, Mr. Fulgham. I love your books." Jonathan pushed back the chair a little too hard as he got up, and it crashed to the floor drawing the looks of hushed readers. "Oops, sorry," he whispered as he stooped to upright the chair. When he turned to shake his new friend's hand, Fulgham was gone.

Jonathan's mind raced. Really? Was it time to declare love already? It *had been* a year.

Then he saw the sheets of stationery for sale and one particularly interested him; pink with red hearts edging. He held it in his hand and knew it was exactly what Melissa would choose to write these important words to him. He carefully brought the single sheet of paper to the checkout. While he dug in his back pocket to retrieve his wallet, he saw the postcard of downtown Seattle and quickly lifted it from the wire rack, tossing it on the sheet. "This too," he said to the cashier.

He left Elliott Bay Book Company that night knowing Melissa would reveal to him she loved him first. As much as he idolized Robert Fulgham, this love story was his creation and he wanted her to say it first. He would respond quickly and no one would feel rejected or hurt. It went exactly as planned when Jonathan returned to his lonely dark apartment that night.

Returning to the present, Jonathan felt the sheet of paper in his left hand and the postcard in his right and once again read the words that had been written three years ago. It had been what he needed that night long ago to motivate him to keep working on his book.

There was one more thing he wanted to look over tonight. He reached to the very bottom of the first shoebox; *August 1988--My Melissa.*

As he finished reading the original list he had written four years ago, his heart swelled. He was filled with love for this woman he had never met and he wanted to pick up the phone to tell her. But he couldn't. Not yet. The love letters were all he had for now.

He started up his new computer, bought with the advance for his book, and began to type:

October 15, 1992
Dear Melissa,

It is another lonely night for me in Seattle and I have just settled in against the fall chill that skulks outside my window. I went through our letters just now and I am torn. I do love you, but I am ready to give up this crazy idea. I guess I thought that you'd be here by now. I figured you'd come right after your graduation; but that would have been about four and a half months ago.

You are still not here. Or have I met you already and not realized it. I guess you could be the new girl at the coffee shop; but she's blond. Did you dye your hair? Or maybe you are the girl that bumped into me at the grocery store. But you were so short; not even close to 5'7". Perhaps Bertha at Café Ladro that always makes my coffee just perfect. But Bertha? Doesn't sound quite like a soul mate name. Well, not my soul mate anyway.

I guess I'm a little sad, but angry too. Where are you? You have told me for the past four years that you were coming. I have waited. Where are you? I could answer for you, but I want you to tell me in person now. I'm going to stop writing for a while and I want you to stop, too. I don't want to see your words that you miss me and that you're coming soon anymore. I just want you to be here. Now.

Jonathan

He pushed print and the letter was put to ink before his eyes. He couldn't believe it. Was it over? He felt as if he was going to throw up. He hadn't known when he woke up this morning that he would be breaking up with Melissa. But he couldn't wait anymore. Two shoeboxes full of declarations and unmet promises. Over four years. He was done with it. His dad and brother's little manifesting a soul mate exercise had failed. He folded the letter and placed it on top of the second shoebox, replaced the lids to both and slid them back under the couch.

He dialed James. "We broke up." He hung up before his brother could respond, and took the phone off the hook.

Jonathan crawled in bed, curled up in his tattered comforter and brooded into a deep sleep.

CHAPTER 7

"Cathy. Get off me." Lisa sputtered between being bounced up and down on the bed.

"Come on, little cousin, I can't sleep. Get up. Get up."

Lisa had realized in the two months of living with her that Cathy was not only animated, but was also an insomniac. She glanced at her alarm clock and groaned. "It's 11:30. Seriously, get off me. I need to get some sleep."

"Come on, come on, come on, let's go to the bookstore." She had removed herself from Lisa's bed and was tugging relentlessly on her arm.

"Nooooo." Lisa pulled the blanket over her head. "I have to get up at 5:30. I'm not going to the bookstore at midnight." What kind of insane person ran a 24-hour bookstore anyway?

"Fine." Cathy relented, but Lisa knew it wasn't over. Sure enough, within minutes she felt something bound across her legs. "What the hell—" Lisa threw the covers off and looked toward Cathy's side of the room. "What are you doing?"

"Nothing," she giggled.

"Well, stop throwing stuff at me." More giggles. "I'm serious. I have to leave for school early. Do you want me to jump on your head in the morning?"

"No, I do not, little cousin," she replied formally.

"Then knock it off."

"Okay."

Again, not okay. Lisa felt the same bundle fly across her and immediately threw her blanket back. Cathy was sitting up in her bed with a flashlight, but she didn't switch it off in time.

"Jeepers Cripes." Lisa's dad's familiar exclamation sounded in her ears as she reflexively used it. "What in the Sam Hill are you doing?"

"Nothing."

"Nothing, my ass. What're you doing?"

"Kitty games," she squealed.

"Kitty games? And just what are kitty games?" Lisa was pretty sure she didn't want to know.

"Watch." Cathy turned her flashlight on and ran the light quickly across Lisa's bed. Her cat, Pasha, sprinted after the light over Lisa's body and then was left dumbfounded as Cathy snapped the light off.

"Are you kidding me? Is this what you do at night?"

"Yup. Watch." She repeated the action and Pasha flew up Lisa's legs and almost hit her head. When she clicked the light off, Cathy erupted into fits of giggles. "Kitty games, kitty games, they are so fun."

Lisa got up and went across the room and flipped the light on. Cathy was sitting Indian-style with her comforter bundled up around her head and just a flashlight sticking out from the opening. Lisa shook her head in disbelief as she pulled on sweats and a sweatshirt.

"What are you doing? Are you moving out?" Cathy asked.

"Come on. Get up. We're going to the bookstore."

"What?" She stared out from the peephole in her bundled armor.

"You're obviously not going to let me get any sleep. So let's go. Hurry up before I change my mind."

Cathy shed her cocoon and bounced off her bed instantly. "Oh, goody goody. Yeah, the bookstore."

Lisa tried to sound irritated. "You owe me. I'm going to be so tired tomorrow. And I have a job interview at 4:00." She sighed, thinking about her schedule for the following day: school, gym, interview, then about three hours of homework and practice. But Lisa had to admit, she loved the energy and spontaneity of living with this childlike cousin of hers.

"A job interview? What? Where?" Cathy whispered as they scurried through the hall of the building to the garage.

They opened the door to the garage and descended the cement stairwell. "A place right down the street. Jillian's. It's a billiard club."

"I know Jillian's. That's a cool place." She opened the door to her ancient jaundice yellow Cadillac, which she fondly referred to as 'The Boat.' "How'd you get an interview there?"

Lisa couldn't help her sarcastic reply. "Well, Cathy, when most people need a job, they go into the place and ask for what is called a job application. Say it after me....job application." Lisa enunciated slowly and waited for her cousin to respond. Cathy wasn't playing.

"Oh, little cousin, I know what a job application is. It's for people who have to work real jobs." She turned out of the garage and headed for her favorite hill.

"No, Cathy, it's for people who have to make *real* money. Not La-la Land money." Lisa still hadn't figured out how she was living this life. She pulled her seatbelt on, knowing what was about to happen.

"Well, when we get our treasure up, I will make sure to show you a La-la Land gold coin." She took a wide right turn so they were now facing a steep hill leading to the top of Queen Anne. "Now, hold on."

She gunned The Boat, forcing Lisa's body into the seat. "Wheee," Cathy screeched as The Boat flew up the hill. Together, they emitted an "Uggh," as the car hit the flat of an intercepting street. Then one more burst up the remaining five blocks. The Boat crested the top and they both let out the breath they'd been holding. The adrenaline spilled from Cathy. "I love that hill!" she shouted.

Lisa loved it too. However, it was only fun in Cathy's boat. Lisa knew, because she had tried it in her little red stick shift and it didn't deliver quite the effect. "Me too. That was the best one yet, especially not having to worry about traffic," Lisa said.

"So anyway," she said. "The Jillian's thing. How did you get an interview there? And no smarty-tarty remark this time."

"On Friday after school when my friend Emily came to visit, we went there for a beer."

"And?" Cathy was impatient with the pause.

"And. We started chatting with the bartender there and I asked if they were hiring."

"And?"

Lisa looked at her. She thought that explained it. "And. He said they were always hiring. And he gave me a job application. And I filled it out and left it with him." Lisa made sure not to leave anything out.

"And? How'd you get the interview?"

"Saturday morning the manager called and asked if I could come in on Monday and interview." Lisa paused and then quickly added, "And I said yes."

"Really?"

"Yes. Really. Are you serious? Have you never filled out an application and had an interview?" Lisa was amazed Cathy did not get this concept at all.

"I don't think so." She was being serious.

"What do you mean, 'you don't think so?'"

"I don't think so. I've always just started my own business or been asked to work for friends or work for friends of friends."

"Business?" Lisa asked. "Cathy's Business of Scams. Open 24/7. If opportunity knocks and I don't answer, just leave your deposit on the front step." Lisa was pleased with her mini commercial as they pulled into the deserted Tower Books parking lot.

Cathy was pleased too. But Lisa knew it was because it was true. That was her life. She wanted something, BAM, she got it. In fact, the latest 'deposit' left on her doorstep was a brand new pair of K2 skis. From Lisa's dad. Cathy mentioned she would like a pair of new skis and Lisa's dad got them for her as an early Christmas gift. He did it as a nice gesture since Lisa was living with Cathy for free and he felt she was looking out for her. But a new pair of skis? Damn. Lisa had never had a new pair of skis in her life; just hand-me-downs from her sister.

It reminded Lisa. “Can we go skiing before I go to Idaho for Christmas?”

Cathy opened the door to Tower Books and Records and ushered Lisa inside. “I don’t know. Between school and the gym and now, a job,” she sneered the last word, “how are you going to have any play time for me?”

“I have Saturdays and Sundays.” Lisa lowered her voice even though there was only one other person in the whole store at this ungodly hour. “I’ll tell Jillian’s I can’t start until after the New Year.”

“Then we should go this weekend,” Cathy said, then added, “so I can try my brand new skis. Oh my skis, my brand new skis,” she sang. “So shiny and pretty. I love my new skis, K2ooooooh, K2oooooooooh, I love youuuuu.”

Of course, the one person in the store had now labeled them as crazy. And correctly, Lisa thought, with Cathy dancing around hugging an imaginary set of skis. Lisa tried to sneak away, but Cathy followed her to the back corner. “Cool, you’re starting in the travel section. I love it. Let’s see, where to tonight? Tibet? Cancun? Europe?” She pulled Lonely Planet after Lonely Planet off the shelf and carefully returned them. “I think I’ll explore Egypt. You?”

Lisa eyed the Caribbean guide. She pulled it from the shelf and sat down on the floor—it was that kind of bookstore—and dreamily uttered, “I think I’ll go here.” Its cover showed crystal blue waters and white sand and one lone palm tree leaning across the isolated beach.

“Oh yeah, good one. I’ve been there.” Of course she had.

“I wonder if I’ll ever get to go anyplace. Being broke and in school sure isn’t much fun.” Lisa envied Cathy’s life right then, wondering why she thought school was the answer.

“Seems like a waste of time if you ask me. There’s so much more to do with your life,” she said, “outside of a classroom.”

“But it’s a way to make more money. Not now, maybe. But later. It’ll pay off.” Lisa repeated to Cathy the thoughts that had kept her in school so far.

“Or maybe.” Pause. “Just maybe.” Sly look. “You can start looking for the man who will take you there." Cathy pointed to the sunset-strewn Caribbean beach on the cover.

"That sounds like the ticket," Lisa said. "Marry a man just because he can deliver me all the dreams of travel that I want."

"Who said anything about marriage? Man, you're an idealist."

"First of all, you don't even know what that word means. And second, so what...? Just date a man that will take me to these places?"

"Why not?" She was serious.

Lisa turned the page to reveal a man and woman—of course, with beautifully toned and tanned bodies—walking hand in hand across a silk of white sand. "Because if I go see these places, I want to go with someone that I'm planning to spend the rest of my life with. Isn't that every girl's dream? I don't want to experience them with some random guy. And especially not the guys I've dated here. Echhh," Lisa grunted. "No, thanks."

"No doubt. You have dated some winners lately. Especially Derek." She held her hand up and snapped her wrist toward Lisa as she mimicked, "You're such a fox."

This got them both giggling and an ugly stare from only-other-one-here guy. "Oh my gosh. He was such a dork. Um, yeah dude, the '70s called and they want their word back," Lisa said. "Who says that anymore? Fox? Isn't that from, like, your era?"

Lisa got a punch for that one. "Hey, little cousin, no age jokes."

"It was hilarious when you were standing behind him making faces while he was talking to me. I could've killed you," Lisa recalled.

"I know. Your face was saying, 'save me, save me!'" Cathy mimicked the wicked witch. "Bet you wish you would have opted for kitty games that night."

"No doubt. Did I tell you where he took me?"

"No. Where? Let me guess, Neighbors?"

Lisa ignored her and let her think she didn't get her gay bar reference. "To the Seattle Aquarium."

"Oh crap. You should've told him that you were deathly paranoid about the things in the ocean."

"I DID!"

"And he took you to the aquarium? Wow, brilliant."

"That's what I thought."

"And he keeps calling you?"

"Yeah. I haven't called him back. I don't know what to say to him."

"Um, yeah, 'dude, you're an idiot' oughta do it," Cathy said.

"Just a minute ago you were suggesting that I travel across the world with these guys," Lisa reminded her.

"Not a weird one."

"Oh, okay. How about the one you met a few weeks ago that took me to the Puyallup Fair? Nick."

"Yeah, he seemed nice. What's wrong with him?"

"Not sure. He said he'd call me. And it's been like ten days. Is that normal? How long do you wait when they say they'll call?" Lisa's voice revealed she was still irritated by it. She felt he became a bit perturbed when she declined his invitation back to his place after dinner. But he had kissed her goodnight at her door and said he had a good time.

"Ah, little cousin, the first thing you need to learn is boys are stupid heads." Cathy shocked Lisa by being consoling. Usually she was mocking. "The only smart boy in your life is your daddy-o. And they don't get smart until they're like, sixty years old."

"That's a comfort to know," Lisa said.

"That's why you shouldn't worry about finding someone and getting married. Just have fun."

"I'm not thinking of marriage with any of these guys. I just want to travel somewhere." The book was now open to the couple dining on the beach with tiki torches all around.

"You could go with Harry." Cathy dramatized the *Harry* and then lost it. She rolled from her cross-legged upright position to her back and her feet flew high in the air as she howled. Only-other-one-here guy had had enough and he abruptly shoved his book back on the shelf, gave them one more disapproving sneer and hurried out the door.

Lisa punched her this time. "Stop it. You're going to get us kicked out of here." Lisa tried to sound serious.

Harry was the worst of all Lisa's recent dates. She'd met him at a coffee shop and then just kept running into him. They'd become friends in a sort of way. He'd said 'Hi', then she'd said 'Hi', then the next time he asked 'How are you?', and she'd replied 'Fine', then the next time it was 'Have you tried the muffins?', and Lisa replied, 'Ah, muffins; is that what you're here for?' From that, an everyday exchange began and then an invitation to dinner. It had not progressed beyond that.

Harry is the guy girls are continuously warned about. Arrogant and stuck in the throes of his youth. Add in an '80s Tom Selleck mustache and an open-buttoned shirt revealing blond chest hairs and a thick gold chain on an obvious fake tan, and you had Harry.

Cathy lowered her voice. Not a whisper lower, an octave lower. Cheesy bow-chica-wow-wow low. "Hey baby, how's it hangin'? You diggin' me baby?"

Lisa tried to be stern, motherly. But through her laughs, she could not. "Stop."

Still the low voice, "Oh, come on, baby, you know you want me."

"He asked me the other day why I didn't like him." Lisa knew this would send her into another fit of laughter.

"And what'd he say?"

Lisa didn't know if she meant to ask what did she say or really wanted to know what he said. So Lisa lowered her voice like Cathy's and repeated to her what he said, "'Hey, baby, so what's the deal? Why doncha wanna hang with moi?' So I told him. 'One, you are too old for me.'"

"You did not," she said.

"Yes. I did. He's almost forty."

"That had to have shot his ego down a bit."

"Are you kidding?" Here Lisa dropped her voice to cheesy octave again. "'Maybe whatcha need is an older man to show you some good lovin'.'" She waited for Cathy's eye roll and 'Oh God' before continuing. "What the hell does that mean anyway? Good lovin'?"

"Hell if I know. I've never even heard that line. What else did you tell him?"

Lisa didn't know if Cathy was interested at this point or just wanted more ammunition to feed her humorous needs. Lisa decided to feed her need because this was funny shit. "Get this. I told him I could never, and I repeated never, date a guy who wore his shirt buttoned open to the middle of his chest to expose a gold Mr. T chain."

"You did not!"

"Totally did."

"What'd he say?"

"That's the funniest part. Nothing. But the next day at the coffee shop, guess what he was wearing?"

"Shut up!"

"Seriously. He was wearing just a normal T-shirt."

"And the gold chain?"

"Gone."

"No way."

"Yup. Haven't seen it since."

"When was that?"

"Oh, it's been like a week, week and a half maybe. He hasn't worn a buttoned shirt since then. Always a T-shirt or polo shirt with the few buttons."

"And has he asked you out again?"

"Nope. Just changed his look. And it seems that he's not acting as cheesy anymore. You know, he doesn't say, 'baby' or the 'how ya doin' bit anymore. It's funny."

"Yeah, funny. Funny how guys'll do anything to get laid."

"Cathy!" Lisa chastised more loudly than she meant to. "I don't think that's what he's after. He thought about what I told him and decided maybe it was time for a wardrobe update."

"Oh, little cousin." There was that mocking tone.

"No. I'm sure. I'm like half his age. Why would he think that?"

A bit louder this time, "Oh little naïve cousin," along with a head rub.

Lisa ducked from her hand and retaliated, "Well, whatever he thinks he might want, it's not happening. It's gross. He's twice my age."

"All the more challenge for him." Cathy got up and held out her hand. "Come on. Enough traveling for one night."

"Serious. It's not like that." Lisa followed her out the door. And Cathy continued with her "Uh huh, yeah, right, okay," remarks.

"Well, if it's like that, why don't they just say so, rather than these stupid games. I guess it is easier to stay single and not deal with this crap." They loaded in The Boat. "But, I do have a date this weekend with a nice guy," Lisa said.

"That's an oxymoron."

"No, really. I've known him since high school. We went out a few times the summer before I left for college."

"Did you have sex?" Cathy asked.

"God, no. Is that always the first thing on your mind?"

"Pretty much. Did you?"

"No. His dad was a pastor," Lisa said.

"And?"

Lisa ignored her insinuation. "He goes to school in Tacoma and he's going to come up here Friday to go out in Seattle. He'll probably stay the night at our place, if that's okay."

"Are you going to have sex with him?"

"He'll sleep on the couch," Lisa said.

"With you?"

"You never give it a rest, do you?"

"Answer the question. It's not a big deal, you know. Everyone goes through their slut stage. You even said your friends at school are all having a little fun." Cathy winked with the last word. "You might as well start yours."

Cathy made the final turn into the garage and it went quiet in the car. Lisa thought about Trevor. She had liked him a lot and he was very cute; tall with thick, black hair and hypnotic blue eyes. He had gone to a different school and they met at a church camp. It was a relationship that never took flight because of the distance between their homes. Forty miles was a long way in high school. Forty miles now was nothing. Lisa drove it everyday. She thought about the possibility of it going anywhere and decided maybe it could. Even though they had lost touch over the last four years during college, Trevor seemed quite excited to hear from her. She was looking forward to going out with him.

In the elevator, Cathy broke the silence. "Well, are you? Are you ready to rock his world?"

"Who knows? Maybe," Lisa said.

"Atta girl. Just go for it." Cathy whooped and swatted her butt as she stepped into the hall. "Just don't be loud. I will throw up if I hear you. You little slut, you."

"Just shut up." Lisa entered the apartment first and went straight to the bathroom. Her stomach was churning. She just may do this. She was going to do this.

CHAPTER 8

A week before Christmas and it was a typical dull Monday for Jonathan. He rolled out of bed around noon and shuffled to his workspace in the living room. He groaned as he looked at the fax machine. Three months ago when he got it, he eagerly looked everyday to see if he had received any 'important' stuff; which usually consisted of a joke from his brother. But now he knew the fifteen or so pages piled in the receipt box only had to do with making *more* changes to his book. He felt like he had completely rewritten the thing.

Between his editor and his dad's wife, Leslie, the whole thing had been worked over. Sure enough, the fax box revealed copied pages of his book covered with lines and scribbles and notes splattering the margins. He was at the end with his editor. Who did she think she was anyway? His book would have been just fine. He was at her mercy though, because if he didn't make the changes, the book wouldn't go to print. And Leslie, undoubtedly, had spent hours of time she didn't really have to read and reread edits for him. But he knew that she helped his dad out on his books, so it just seemed like part of her job.

He glanced at Cindy's fresh ideas and notes in front of him and sat down at his computer. "*Above the Clouds*; take 582," he said as his computer clicked to life. At least she hadn't changed the name. Yet.

He plucked at the keyboard with his two index fingers; hunting furiously for the correct letters. After cleaning up two pages, he felt he deserved a break and headed for the kitchen. The fridge contained five cans of coke, a pizza box with three slices from a week ago, ketchup, and a bag with rotten apples that was a reminder to Jonathan of his failed health kick he tried to start a few weeks back.

He closed the fridge and pulled a container from the top. He returned to his computer and pulled a Twinkie from the box. He took half of the Twinkie in one bite and escaped morsels fell to his bare chest and belly. He extracted these from around his hairs with his thumb and index finger and returned them to his mouth with the rest of the cream filled sponge cake.

Back to his notes, his thoughts escaped for a moment to Melissa. He glanced at the shoeboxes that he could see just under the couch. He had kept his promise and had not written to her in, *what was it now*? "Just over two months," he said.

Jonathan struggled daily to avoid her. It was hard. He missed her. He missed the love letters and updates. He missed feeling wanted. He missed having *somebody*. But then he'd remind himself of the fact it was her fault. She was the one who didn't keep up her end of the bargain. He would get upset again and then she was easy to avoid.

His brother and dad said he was crazy. Told him he had put too much time into Melissa and he was giving up too easily. He appeased them by telling them he had decided just to take a break from her. But every conversation with them started the same. "How's Melissa?" He would reply, "Hmmm. Haven't heard from her. She must be busy." Then they would get on with other business.

Jonathan grabbed another Twinkie and repeated the process four more times while he tried to clean up his book from the notes. When he finished, he faxed them back and thought, *I've got to get out of here, before she calls or faxes back*. He jumped in the shower and was out the door in ten minutes with his pool cue. As he hurried to lock the front door he heard, "Hey Jonathan. That you?"

Jonathan always pondered the idea of not answering. He knew it was messed up. He knew Jim knew *someone* was there. But really, if Jonathan didn't answer how could Jim ever really prove it was him? And today especially, Jonathan just wanted to sprint out of there. But he replied, "Yeah, hey Jim, what's up?"

"Not much. How's the book going?"

Funny, Jonathan wasn't even in the mood to talk about his book lately. It had become such a pain and so much work, he actually dreaded it. But he would never admit that. "Oh, great. Just a few more tweaks here and there—" He let his stock response fade.

"Cool. Remember I get the first copy."

"Of course. As soon as the mailman delivers them, the first knock I will make is on your door." Jonathan wondered why he wanted it. It wouldn't be in braille. Could it be in braille? Would he make more money if his book were available in braille? He was just about to say goodbye to Jim when his telephone rang. He tried to ignore it, but Jim said, "Hey, man, I think that's you."

"Yeah. I hear it." Third ring. Two more and the answering machine would pick it up.

"Are you going to get it?"

"I'm trying." He shoved the wrong key in the lock on the fourth ring and got the correct key inserted on the fifth. He left the keys in the door and took the three steps across the living room to the phone. "Hello, this is Jonathan." Jim remained in the doorway. He always did if Jonathan didn't close the door.

"Hi, Jonathan. It's Cindy. How are you?"

Jonathan tried to hide his disappointment but wasn't sure he succeeded. "Hey, Cindy. I'm good. Did you get my changes? I just faxed them over about fifteen minutes ago."

Through the headphone, the high-pitched voice of his editor stung his ears. "Yeah, Jonathan, nice work. We got them."

He tried to cut her off before the 'but.' "Good. I tried to get them to you as soon as possible." He was always trying to make this lady happy.

"Well, I just called to give you some news," she said.

For the past three months the news was always the same, so he answered without waiting for it. "Just fax the changes and I will work on them as soon as I can."

"No, Jonathan. This is better news. All the changes are done.

We're printing your galley this week. You should have copies by next Monday; maybe even as early as this Friday."

"What? Really?"

"Really," Cindy said. Jonathan realized she was probably just as sick of the whole back and forth as he was.

"What do I do with the galleys?" He knew this was pretty much the last step, but did not know what happened from here.

"Just hand them out. To friends, to family, anyone famous you know." She let her sentence trail off. Jonathan could picture her winking. "Get some feedback and have them catch any minor edit errors like spelling or such."

"And then what?" Jonathan was beginning to sweat. It was a disorder he hoped would fix itself by the time he went on Larry King.

"I'll send copies to some magazines and other published authors. We'll be looking to get quotes to put inside, you know, like about how great a read it is. That sort of thing. Have you asked your dad if he'll write the prologue? That would be huge." Cindy knew it wouldn't save the book, but it would help. This book had been a monkey on her back since she took it. They had accepted the book because of the name, but excitement had quickly waned after the first reading. It was a disorganized mess that needed a lot of work.

"I'll call him as soon as I hang up and ask. He said he would. But that was a while back." Jonathan already knew he would. Richard still owed him for abandoning him when he was two.

"Okay, then. I'm going to run this down right now to print and you work on your dad. I'll be in touch. And Jonathan?"

"Yeah?"

"Congratulations." It was the best she could do.

"Thanks, Cindy. You too. I couldn't have done it without you." All of a sudden he felt connected to her. He wondered what she looked like, if she was single. "Bye for now."

"Good news?" Jim was still standing in the doorway.

"Yeah. Great news. We're going to print. Not final print, but it'll be in book form by Friday. Man, this is good."

"Congratulations."

"Thanks, man. I need to call my dad real quick." Jonathan had already picked up the phone to dial.

"Okay, catch ya later. And good job and all that." Jim retreated to his apartment.

"Thanks again. Bye. Oh, yeah, hey Dad. Hi." Jonathan switched conversations.

"Hi Jonathan," his father replied.

"Do you have a minute?" Jonathan always asked this of his dad. It made him feel that his dad had to commit to him. A counselor might say it was his way of finally getting assurance after so many lost years of not having it. Jonathan told himself he was being polite because he knew his dad was a busy man.

"Sure, Jonathan. How's Melissa?"

Jonathan ignored the comment today. "Hey, Dad. Cindy just called. They're printing the galleys right now."

Leslie's voice came from another line. "Oh, that's good news, Jonathan. Did you make the changes I sent yesterday before it went?"

"Yeah, I included them this morning." There was a pause. Jonathan still found it surprising Leslie was always on the other line. "Dad, I wanted to ask you again if you would write the prologue. Cindy thought it would be really good to add something from you."

"Of course. I'll get to work on it."

Another pause. Jonathan felt the one-sided conversation pressure he always felt on the phone with his dad.

"Well, okay. I guess that's it. I'll let you know when I get the copies," Jonathan said.

"Okay, Jonathan, sounds good." His dad finished his end of the conversation.

"Congratulations, Jonathan," Leslie added.

"Thanks. I'll talk to you guys later." Jonathan hung up feeling the sting that his dad wasn't as excited for him as he thought he'd be. But it quickly dissolved as he made the decision to change his tie, gathered his cue and rushed out the door. He was going to be a famous author.

CHAPTER 9

Five a.m. came far too soon after the late night excursion to the bookstore with Cathy. Lisa looked at her peacefully sleeping and fought the urge to bop her in the head with her pillow. *Let's see how she likes her sleep interrupted.* But Lisa left her alone, slipping quietly out of the room.

Outside, the latte guy greeted her a little too cheerily on what Lisa had learned was a typical Seattle morning—damp and bite-to-your-bones chill. She tried to match his enthusiasm, but failed miserably. Her greeting came off as a cold can-you-please-not-talk-just-make-my-usual-mocha-and-pretend-I'm-really-a-nice-person?

The mocha addiction Lisa had developed in the two months since moving to Seattle helped thaw her out. But it did little to compensate for the hours of sleep she lost. She gave up being warm and opened the windows to the chill for the last half of her hour-long drive to Tacoma.

The rest of Monday blurred and she was worthless at school. Even through the fog of heaviness in her head on her drive home, she found her thoughts returning to Trevor. Was Cathy right? Should she not give so much weight to this physical stuff? She had been around plenty of people who frequently had one-night stands and so what? Big deal? It wasn't even like Trevor would be a one-night stand. She'd known him since she was seventeen. Holding hands and kissing was the limit of their physical history, but they were adults now. She even thought this could be her next serious relationship if they picked up where they had left off back in Idaho.

Lisa had to put her thoughts on pause when she arrived home. She had just enough time to change and freshen up and make it to her interview at Jillian's by 5:00. She was thankful Cathy wasn't home. Most days, she enjoyed her immensely but Lisa found she always prompted a nervous energy in her—perhaps because of all the new ideas and things she was introducing her to—and she didn't have the time to foster it today.

At five minutes to 5:00, Lisa entered Jillian's with a forced energy. She greeted the pretty redhead at the front desk. "Hi. I'm looking for Patricia. I have a five o'clock interview with her."

"Sure. You must be Lisa. I'll let her know you're here." She was nice enough, but the boredom of her job, or maybe her whole life, seeped through her words and showed in the hunch of her shoulders.

Patricia greeted her with a solid handshake and said, "Let's sit at the Algonquin Bar."

Lisa followed her along the brass rails on the outside of the pool table area to a table that had the last rays of sunlight pouring across it. Patricia started in immediately on the questioning and within twenty minutes, Lisa had a job working two to three nights a week as the front desk hostess starting January 18.

Patricia stood. "I'll introduce you to Tawnya. She'll be training you when you start. We usually do a four-day training."

"Sounds good." Lisa followed her back to the front desk. On the way she smiled. *This is great*. New city, new school, new job. It was all falling into place. Come Friday night, she decided, she was going to be a whole new girl on her date with Trevor.

When Patricia and Lisa reached the front, a different girl had replaced the redhead. Patricia said, "This is Tawnya. Tawnya, Lisa."

"That's me. Hi." Her attitude reeked of short-timer's syndrome.

"Hi. I guess you'll be training me for your position." Lisa made her introduction quick as a customer headed toward the counter.

"Cool. I'm sure Patricia put you on a four-day training schedule, when it takes about half an hour to learn all you need to know." She smiled and Patricia warned, "Tawnya."

"Yes, she did," Lisa said, laughing. "It was nice to meet you."

Lisa dismissed herself as a guy in khaki pants and sports coat and Snoopy tie made his way to the counter.

"Sounds good. See you then." Tawnya said, then turned to her customer.

CHAPTER 10

"Hey, Jonathan. Nice tie." Tawnya's greeting was methodical. Jonathan was excited she noticed the last minute change he had made after getting the news of his galley. He always wore just about the same thing; khaki pants, brown belt, sports coat and tie. But today he had worn a really cool Snoopy tie that he'd bought to benefit Children's Cancer Research. It was his favorite tie and it always opened up a conversation for him. "Thanks. I got some good news today, so thought I would break out the Snoopy tie." He fingered his tie and hoped Tawnya would bite.

She did. "What kind of good news?"

"My editor called and I should be getting the galley copy of my book by the end of this week." He went on to explain. "That's the last step before the final book hits the shelves."

"Sounds exciting. Do you want to play on Keith's table? He's up on 19 as usual." She moved to type a note in the computer.

"Um, yeah." Jonathan was disappointed she didn't fawn over him as he hoped. *Doesn't she get that I'm going to be famous? She could say she knew me when. Heck, she could even go on a date with me*. He had wondered often if he should ask her out. And he was feeling enough confidence today he might do it. But right now he wanted to share the exciting news with someone who would react in awe and support for him.

"Is Greg working today?" he asked as he headed for the stairs.

"Yeah. You and Keith are in his section."

Jonathan took the stairs two at a time, only stumbling once. He greeted Keith and Greg. "Hey, guys."

"Hi, Jonathan," they responded simultaneously. Greg said, "Nice tie, man."

"Thanks. It's my celebratory tie." He waited.

"And what are we celebrating?" Keith asked as he meticulously slid his cue through his fingers and caught the cue ball dead center, sending it reeling across the table, smacking the nine ball near the pocket and curling backwards to set up his next shot on the ten perfectly.

"Whew, nice shot."

"Thanks."

Jonathan continued quickly before the moment was lost. "My book will be in print by the end of this week."

"Wow." Greg slid from the edge of his stool and extended his hand. "That's so cool, man."

Keith came from the other side of the table and reached for Jonathan's hand next. "Fantastic. That's great."

"I know. I got the call right before I came here. I can hardly believe it's really happening."

"Well, this calls for a celebration," Greg said. "I will bring extra *extra* cherries for your Shirley Temple tonight. Be right back,"

"So how does it feel? You're almost there." Keith kept Jonathan's sprits soaring.

"I know. I know. It's so surreal." He bowed his head and thumbed the bottom of his tie, concentrating on the big grin on Snoopy's face. "It's like all this time, I wasn't ever really sure it would happen and then now, I'm like, wow, it's here." Jonathan felt himself gushing, but he couldn't stop. "I feel like I'm on top of the world. Like nothing could go wrong right now."

"That's incredible. Sounds like a good day to invest in a lottery ticket." Keith knew Jonathan was not a gambler, but would give into an occasional whim now and then to believe in the prospect of becoming an overnight millionaire.

"Or ask Tawnya out on a date." Jonathan pushed his luck just as Greg walked up.

"What?" Greg blurted surprise; more interested in the

conversation than Jonathan thought he would be. "Who's gonna ask Tawnya out?"

Jonathan paused, waiting to see if Keith would answer. But when Jonathan looked at him he cast his eyes down to his cue with what Jonathan thought was a hint of a smirk on his face.

Jonathan proceeded nonchalantly. "I was just telling Keith I was feeling like anything was possible now and I might live life on the edge and ask Tawnya out."

This brought an unmistakable smile to Keith's face and a hearty guffaw from Greg. Jonathan thought they were being a little unfair. "What? She might say yes if she knows I'm almost famous. She's not that far out of my league."

Greg and Keith continued to stare at him and chuckled quietly. "Seriously," Jonathan pleaded now. Then questioned, "Really? Is it really that far fetched an idea."

Greg watched Jonathan and then his face turned serious. "Oh, man, you really don't know."

"Know what?" Jonathan was confused.

"Dude, unless you grow a set of boobs and lose everything that God and testosterone gave you, I don't think she'll be going out with you."

"Huh?" Jonathan looked to both of his buddies whose faces were filled with a secret ready to be exposed. "Ah, crap. Are you serious?"

"Are *you* serious? Did you really not know?"

There was an awkward silence as Jonathan decided if he should play it off like a joke or fess up to his ignorance. "Well, how would I know? She doesn't *look* like a, um, a lesbian, or dyke, or dang... what do you even call them?" He was embarrassed; not only because he didn't know the correct term, but because he didn't figure it out on his own.

Greg and Keith both laughed and Keith used the moment to give Jonathan a hard time. "And what does a lesbian look like, according to the great author Jonathan Bach?"

"I don't know. But I didn't think they were hot. I mean, Tawnya is hot!"

"No shit, she's hot," Greg echoed. "You should see her girlfriend; even hotter."

"No way." *What a waste,* Jonathan thought.

As if reading his mind, Keith piped in, "What a waste. Here we are, three fairly good-looking guys—well, except you Greg." The dig was lighthearted. "And two of them lost to the 'other team.' There should be a law against it or something."

"Maybe I will invest in that Lotto ticket." Jonathan was more disappointed than he wanted to admit about the dead end with Tawnya. He thought everything would fall into place once his book was well on its way; and that included an adoring woman on his arm.

Keith and Greg kept his spirits raised the rest of the night, however. With the appropriate amount of, 'congratulations' and 'way to go, man' and 'wow, really, truly unbelievable.'

He was feeling confident and proud by the time the night ended and in a moment alone, he broke his promise to himself. He slowly pulled the cocktail coaster toward him, knowing full well what he was about to do.

December 21, 1992
Dear Melissa,

I know I said I wasn't going to write. But I have some exciting news. My book is going to galley. I wish you were here to share it. If you'd like to show up now, I would give us another chance.

Love,
Jonathan

He pushed the Snoopy tie aside to stuff the coaster in his shirt pocket as Greg returned without his bill. "Hey man, celebratory Shirley Temples and burger on me tonight."

"Really? Cool. Thanks. I owe ya." Jonathan knew this is what fame meant—people sucking up. He had witnessed it many times when fans recognized his dad.

"You bet you owe me. Remember me when you're famous, man. And remember Sunday night dinners at my mom's. She's become quite fond of having you there."

CHAPTER 11

Lisa was enjoying a rare quiet moment in the apartment, curled up on the couch reading and sipping hot almond milk. The pattering of December rain was intensifying and the wind was causing the windows to shudder. She'd returned home from the gym to take a long warm bubble bath, and the after effects had lulled her into a blissful serenity. Her date with Trevor was tomorrow night and her nerves had needed this calming. Several rehearsals of how the evening would go played over and over in her mind. It was going to be a good night and hopefully lead to something significant.

"Hello," Cathy sang before getting through the door. She unbundled from her wet raincoat at the doorway and jumped right on the couch on top of Lisa. "Hello, my precious."

"God. Get off me. You're soaking wet."

"It's raining out."

"You're kidding. I never woulda guessed. Tell me again why you don't just use an umbrella."

"Only tourists use umbrellas in Seattle." Cathy shook her hair and made sure she got Lisa as wet as possible.

"So tourists are the only smart ones?" Lisa pushed her off and she dramatically rolled to the floor.

"Ooh, my leg, my leg."

"You're fine."

"So, whatcha doing?" Cathy sat upright.

"Just sitting here waiting for you to get home to make my evening complete," Lisa said.

Ignoring the sarcasm, Cathy squealed, "Oh, goody. Let's go to Fremont to—"

"No. No. No." Lisa cut her off. "I'm not going anywhere tonight."

"Why such a spoil sport?"

"I'm staying right here and going to bed early so I won't be tired tomorrow," Lisa answered.

"What's tomorr—oh, oh, oh. Your big date with Trevor." She split the name as she said it and shimmied her body.

"Yup. And I don't want to be tired."

"Are you going to do it? Are you?"

"Not that it's any business of yours, but—"

"Oh, but it is my business, little cousin. It is." Cathy grabbed Lisa's ankle and ran her hand up the inside of her sweats.

"What are you doing?" Lisa jerked her leg away.

"You shaved. That means you're going for it."

"That doesn't mean anything. I always shave."

Cathy grabbed Lisa's hand and pulled her from the couch.

"You're so weird. Now what?" Lisa asked.

"Just come here." Cathy led her to the bedroom and opened her side of the closet. There was a small dresser and she opened up the bottom drawer. "Here."

Lisa looked into the drawer. "Oh God." She took a step back.

Cathy picked up four different boxes. "Look. Your choice. There's Extra Large—a girl can hope."

Lisa started out of the room, but Cathy followed her and continued show-and-telling each box. "Ultra thin. Grape flavored—I wouldn't recommend—nice idea, but bad execution, tastes like rotten grapes. And my personal favorite—"

"Stop. I don't want to hear." Lisa had returned to her place on the couch and put her hands over her ears.

"Fine," Cathy said. "But you know where they are." She disappeared into the bedroom and yelled back to Lisa, "My personal favorite. Ribbed for Her Pleasure."

"Please don't be here tomorrow when we get home," Lisa pleaded.

"Are you kidding? I wouldn't miss this for the world." Cathy returned to the living room. "First row tickets."

"Seriously. Please."

"Fine. What time will you be here?"

"We're coming here right from school so I can change, but then we'll be heading out. We'll be gone by 5:00."

"Where are you going?"

"What? Are you going to stalk us?"

"Of course not. Although—" Cathy placed her finger to the side of her mouth and made a thinking face. "I'm kidding. Kidding. Where're you going?"

"He's got some friends in the U District. We're meeting up with them and then going to a place called Dante's."

"I love Dante's," Cathy squealed.

"No. You can't go," Lisa said.

"It's not like you own it. I can go if I want." Carla faked a pout. "Anyway, you'll have fun. Take a cab, so you don't have to drive home."

"We will."

"And, again, don't make too much noise when you get home or I will come out here."

The next day, Lisa picked Trevor up at his house and they caught up on the past four years during their drive from Tacoma to Seattle. He was even cuter than she remembered; the four years had chiseled away his boyish looks and revealed the man he was becoming. She was definitely attracted to him.

She gave him a quick tour of her place "You can sleep there," she said, pointing to the couch. "Just put your bag anywhere."

Trevor dropped his bag on the far side of the couch and took a seat. "Cool sculpture." He pointed to the black naked lady at his feet.

"That's Jacquie."

"She has a name?" Trevor lifted one eyebrow.

"You haven't met my cousin yet. It would all make sense if you had," Lisa said. "Do you want a beer? I'll be a few minutes."

"Sure. I can get it." He went to the kitchen and Lisa went to change and get ready. She heard Trevor turn on the TV while he waited. "Should I call a cab?" He called.

"Good idea," Lisa responded. "I'll be ready in fifteen."

When she emerged, Trevor stood. "You look great." He took the few steps toward her. "And smell great."

"Thanks." Lisa felt the flutter in her stomach as he lightly grabbed her wrist.

"I'm so glad you got in touch with me." He turned and lifted her hand up, running his thumb up the inside of her wrist to the middle of her palm. He pulled it gently to him and kissed the inside of her hand.

Lisa's breath caught and her natural response sent her stepping back and reacting uncomfortably to his close proximity. She looked away from him. Nervous. "We should go downstairs. The cab's probably here."

"Of course." Trevor released her hand and followed her to the door.

Lisa was cursing herself. *That's what you wanted. What's wrong with you?* She didn't understand her actions herself sometimes. She liked him, she was definitely attracted to him. But it's like there was this door that was labeled with all these items/questions that needed to be ticked before moving through it: did he like her, did she like him, what would people think, what would he think, was it too soon, would it last. She was exhausting herself rather than enjoying herself. Trevor seemed unaffected by it all and kept up the conversation of old memories and new adventures he'd had since they had last seen one another. With his infectious attitude, she regrouped and refocused on having a good time.

They met up with Trevor's friends—two guys he went to UPS with and were now in graduate school—at a small Mexican restaurant in the U and then walked to Dante's. Although only 7:00, the place was packed. These college kids liked to start early and end late. There were no tables left, but Lisa immediately eyed a Pop-A-Shot in the back corner by the pool tables. "Hey, me and Trevor against you two for a pitcher of beer."

"You're on."

Lisa and Trevor's score easily won, with Lisa scoring twice as much as the next guy. "You're still athletic," Trevor said. "I remember watching you play our school in volleyball and you reeled off eight straight aces in a row."

"At least now, it's worth something. Look, free pitcher for us." Lisa pointed as the losers brought two pitchers and four glasses over.

Trevor put his hand on the small of her back sending tingles through her. "Looks like we may be on to something."

For the next few hours, Trevor drummed up business, challenging several guys to a pitcher of beer if they could beat her. Their group didn't pay for a pitcher the rest of the night.

"You're awesome." Trevor and Lisa fell into an easy flirtation as the night went on. He hugged her several times and she kissed his neck during one of them. The awkwardness from earlier had disappeared. The beer helped. Lisa was feeling uninhibited and she knew the boys were too, after rounds of tequila started appearing. Lisa stuck to beer keeping a level buzz. It was fun to be in this atmosphere with Trevor. He was laughing and joking; unlike the shy boy he was several years back. He grabbed her hand and pulled her to two tall stools behind a corner table. "Let's sit for awhile."

"Okay. I need a break anyway. My arm is killing me from all this Pop-A-Shot," Lisa said.

Trevor started massaging her arm. "I guess it's the least I can do after you've done all the work to get us free beer the last few hours."

"I'm going to hire you as my manager. You'll have to take on the guys that get pissed also."

"Oh my gosh. I know. That guy wouldn't let it rest. Although, you weren't very fair, asking him how the game was played before starting. Then beating him by twelve points," Trevor said.

"Strategy."

"Good strategy," Trevor said as he pulled her arm gently toward him. With his other hand, he turned her face to meet his and kissed her.

It was a soft kiss and his hand wrapped to the back of her head, massaging the base of her hairline. His tongue gently explored and Lisa responded. Her body exploded as her breath caught emitting a small hum as she exhaled. She felt bold placing her hand on his thigh and kneading the muscles under his jeans.

When they parted, Lisa smiled and said, "Looks like you have some good strategy of your own."

"You ready to go?" Trevor asked.

"Sure, if you are," Lisa said.

On the cab ride home, he continued his affection; rubbing her neck, holding her hand, stealing kisses. It was a good energy. They were both feeling the effects of the alcohol, but not sloppy. By the time she opened the door to the apartment, her body was pulsating.

Flipping the light on, she gasped. Cathy had pulled her mattress from her bed and it was now lying in the middle of the living room. Trevor laughed.

"Oh, she's so not funny," Lisa said.

"Looks like you're sleeping out here," he said. "I'm going to use the bathroom."

Lisa went into the bedroom where Cathy was bundled under her covers not even trying to pretend she was sleeping. Lisa could hear her laughing. Lisa bopped the mound of her body. "You are a piece of work."

Cathy threw the covers back. "You know you love me."

"Like I said, you're a piece of work."

"It was Pasha. Pasha did it." She pointed to her cat in the corner who was ignoring his name being mentioned and licking his paws.

Lisa pulled out shorts and a T-shirt from her drawer and changed while Cathy sat looking very pleased with herself. Once she was changed, Cathy said, "Oh, that's sexy."

Lisa looked down at her oversized T-shirt. "It's comfortable."

"God. No wonder you never get laid. Boys like sexy."

"Cathy, shut up. He'll hear you," Lisa said.

"Not like it matters. He'll only care what it looks like...on the floor." She fell back on her bed and raised her feet in the air enjoying her little joke.

Lisa went to Cathy's side of the closet, slid the door open, and bent down to open the bottom drawer Cathy had exposed her to last night.

"Oh. Oh. Oh." Cathy was now sitting upright again and pointing at Lisa with one hand and covering her mouth with the other.

Lisa retrieved a box, closed the drawer, stood and walked to the door. "Shut. Up."

In the living room, Trevor was in a pair of sweats and T-shirt and sitting on the couch. Lisa went to the TV and hoped he didn't notice her place the box behind it as she grabbed the remote. "Do you want to watch a movie?" Even though Lisa was sure they were going to have sex, she didn't know how to proceed.

"Sure. Sounds good," Trevor said.

"Casablanca?" Lisa held the VHS tape up. "It's the best one we've got."

"Never seen it."

"What? It's my favorite. Here's lookin' at you, kid." She tilted her head and winked at Trevor. He looked confused. "You'll see," she said.

She pushed play and went to the kitchen to get waters. Trevor followed and wrapped his arms around her from the back. "I had so much fun with you tonight," he said.

"Me, too." She turned in his arms to face him and handed him his glass. He kissed the tip of her nose. She left her glass at the counter and wound both arms around him. He felt warm and solid. Their kiss started slowly again and soon Trevor reached to place his glass on the counter in order to use both hands to pull her close. The kiss progressed passionately. He was a good kisser; the perfect combination of playful and serious.

"Let's go watch that movie." He pulled away gently and led Lisa by the hand back to the living room. "You okay laying on the mattress, rather than sitting on the couch?" he asked.

"Okay," Lisa said. Her heart was racing. She needed to sit or lie soon because her legs were weak. She lay down on her side facing the TV and Trevor crawled behind her. Pulling the thick down comforter over them both, he spooned her in his arms. He nuzzled the back of her neck, sending chills through her. She turned in his arms and started kissing him. After only a few minutes, she could feel that he was enjoying it. Her shorts and his sweatpants were a thin barrier.

His hands were caressing her back under her T-shirt and sliding slowly up the side of her body just grazing the side of her breast. Her breath caught and his kiss intensified. Her body reacted, arching into him. All her insecurities and inhibitions were gone. She slid her hand down over his rear and wrapped it around to the inside of his groin. Trevor let out a low moan. She continued up and rested her fingertips right at the waistband of his sweats. His kissing became frenzied, urging her on. She slipped her hand under the band and moved it slowly down.

Trevor snapped his hand down to stop hers. "What are you doing?"

"It's okay. There are condoms on the TV stand," she said.

He pulled her hand out of his underwear. "No. Stop. What are you doing?"

Lisa immediately felt ashamed. "I was—I thought—I—"

"I can't do that. I can't—" Trevor said. "I was just—I thought we were just—"

"This is so embarrassing. I thought—"

Trevor sat up and put his head in his hands. "This—I can't—I just—"

Lisa stood up. She was mortified. Now, the beer hit her in an opposite effect. She suddenly felt queasy. She left Trevor sitting there and went in the bathroom. The first ejection was pure liquid. The smell of the beer and bile provoked the second. Lisa turned the cold water on and soaked a washcloth. She placed it over her entire face trying to quell the tears, the embarrassment. She brushed her teeth and walking from the bathroom to the bedroom, she heard Trevor's quiet, "Lisa," but ignored it. She crawled in bed with Cathy. "Uh, oh. Did little cousin get sick from too much beer?"

"Yeah, that's it," Lisa said and curled in a ball.

The next morning, Trevor's friends picked him up early and he was gone by the time Lisa crawled out of bed at noon. Her experiment of trying Cathy's way was an epic failure. She was so done with this dating thing and trying to figure out how she was supposed to behave. She realized how much easier it had been to be in a relationship and not have to deal with these awkward situations.

CHAPTER 12

Christmas and New Year's flew by as Lisa visited family and friends back in Idaho. She was still reeling from the sting of the rejection from Trevor. She was too embarrassed to even tell Cathy about what happened and let her continue to believe she had drank too much and gotten sick. She spent most of the break snow skiing and snowmobiling with her high school classmates and forgetting all about the mortification of her misjudgment. She was sure she would never hear from Trevor again and so far, that was the case.

Back in Seattle, she was in to her second week of school when her new job at Jillian's started. She braced herself for a consecutive four days of training, knowing the next week she would have her set schedule of just Monday, Thursday and Friday nights.

She was excited to start and showed up fifteen minutes early. Entering Jillian's, she immediately saw Chris, the bartender who had originally prompted her to fill out an application, and Tawnya at the front desk. Without hesitation Chris greeted her. "Even early. Good to see you."

"As my dad would say, 'Lombardi Time.'"

"Good man." Chris got it.

"What time?" Tawnya did not.

"Just on time." Chris winked at Lisa.

"Hey, Tawnya. How are you?"

"Good. You? Are you ready to be amazed by what is the smooth and elaborate operation of the front desk of Jillian's?" Her sarcasm was not lost on Lisa.

"Of course. I hope it's not too difficult. What's first?"

Chris dismissed himself saying, "I'll let the blind lead the blind and catch up with you later."

"Jerk." Tawnya threw a ping pong ball at his back. He picked it up and winged it side arm back, bouncing it off two walls behind her.

"First thing to know," Tawnya said to Lisa. "Learn to duck with quick-like reflexes. The boys seems to have a need to throw things. I think it's a testosterone-releasing mechanism instilled in their tiny little brains."

"Good to know." Lisa joined her behind the counter.

For the next two hours, Tawnya proceeded to talk her way through all of the procedures. It was low stress, elementary work. Most of it involved being friendly and taking care of the customers' needs.

Tawnya ducked into the back room to discuss a matter with the manager and a guy showed up at the desk. Lisa's first solo greeting, "Hi. Welcome to Jillian's."

He stood there looking lost.

"Hello?" Lisa tried to remain friendly while he stared.

"Um, yeah, I uh, um," he mumbled. "I need a table."

"Okay, I just need your ID." Lisa repeated the phrase that Tawyna had declared to every customer so far.

Lisa pulled a rack of balls from under the counter and set it in front of him as he struggled to pull his ID out of his wallet. She grabbed his ID and glanced at the board in front of her to see what table was vacant.

As Lisa stalled waiting for Tawnya to reappear, she watched the guy's hands move clumsily over the rack, placing the billiard balls in perfect order; starting with the upper left hand corner with the solid yellow ball and placing them numerically along the rows.

Tawnya appeared, breaking the silence. "Oh, hey, Jonathan. How's it goin'?"

He looked up and relief washed over his face. "Hey, Tawnya. Wondering where you were. Thought maybe you quit early."

"Nope. One more week. Just training Lisa this week. This is Lisa.

Lisa, Jonathan. He's a 'regular' too." It was about the fifth customer she had monotonously given the label to.

"You'll get to know me. I'm in here every day." Jonathan barely made eye contact with her, quickly returning his focus back to the placement of the balls in his rack.

"Nice to meet you."

Placing the 15 ball in the last spot, he announced, "They should give me a job here organizing the racks of balls."

Lisa could only stare.

Tawnya ended the uncomfortable silence. "Lisa just moved to Seattle. So make her feel welcome. You want Table 19?" Tawnya asked and turned to Lisa. "That's his..." she airquoted "...table."

Jonathan chuckled with his chin tucked to his chest. "Yeah, cool," he replied, lifting his head and thumbing his glasses back up to their secure place.

Lisa watched the peculiarities of this guy with the instructions from one of her college professors echoing in her ears, *Always look for characters for your stories in your day-to-day encounters.*

"Okay, you're set." Tawnya punched in the sequence of numbers and quickly sent Jonathan on his way by shoving the ball rack just a bit closer to his side of the counter. To Lisa she continued, "We need to refill all the match containers. Come on, I'll show you where the extra boxes are kept." She grabbed a string of keys from a post just inside the back room and headed out from behind the counter. Lisa followed.

Tawnya talked nonstop, offering bits of information about every co-worker and every regular that came through. For Jonathan, it was, "He's nice enough. Just real lonely and he'll want to stand around and talk to you as long as you let him. I heard he was even thinking about asking me out a few days ago. Talk about desperate." She laughed.

Lisa didn't understand. "I wouldn't think desperate. I'd think, more like, out-of-his-league." Lisa thought Tawnya was very pretty.

Tawnya handed her a couple boxes of matches and led her back toward the front desk. She turned her head half way to make sure

Lisa was following and said over her shoulder, "Yeah, I'd say out-of-his-league. Or rather, not-even-playing-the-same-game." She answered Lisa's confused look immediately. "Lisa. I'm gay."

What?!? Lisa hoped she didn't spurt that out loud the way it went off in her head. Tawnya's anticipated glance as she returned behind the counter assured her she didn't and she mumbled meekly, "Oh. I didn't know."

"It's no big deal."

To you, maybe. But Lisa tried to think if she had ever met a real live lesbian before. Cathy had educated her a few weeks back when they went to Capitol Hill and Lisa had wanted to buy a really cool bumper sticker because she liked the color of the hot pink triangle. Cathy saw her grab it from the rack and told her to put it back. Lisa argued with her she wanted it. "Little cousin," she had said. "You buy that and put it on your bumper and you may get attention you're not ready for." At Lisa's confusion, she explained, "That sticker symbolizes that you are gay. And not gay as in happy." Cathy needed to explain one step further. "You are into women." Lisa had quietly replaced the sticker and realized she had a lot of things to learn about this big city thing.

CHAPTER 13

As soon as Jonathan reached his table, he pulled his pen out of his coat pocket and scribbled on the cardboard coaster that was on the table:

Melissa

Is it you?

By the time Keith joined him, Jonathan's heart had stopped racing from the initial encounter with the new girl at the front desk. He had calmed himself down by discarding the coincidences—the hair and eye color, height, new to Seattle—and focusing on the fact that her name was Lisa and not Melissa.

He was pretty much recovered when Keith greeted him. "Hey, Jonathan. Did you see the new girl? She's cute."

"She's okay." Jonathan could still feel the cardboard coaster shoved in his shirt pocket that had the words 'Melissa, Is it you?' scribbled on it. He felt his heart race again.

"Okay. Okay? Dude, what are your standards?" Keith asked as he assembled his cue stick. "Whatever. I hope you're going to be very happy in your solo life," he teased.

"I know. I know. It's just...I'm just. Well, it's complicated." Jonathan had told no one outside his family about Melissa. He grabbed the cue ball and headed to the far end of the table for the break.

"Yeah, you can break." Keith answered an unasked question with a smirk.

Jonathan sent the cue ball smashing into the tightly racked triangle.

"It's all complicated," Keith said. "But, hey, whatever. I finished your galley." He retrieved the book from his backpack and set it on a side table.

"Cool, I'm next." Greg approached and picked up the soft blue unmarked book.

"I didn't even know you could read," Keith said.

"Oh, ha, ha, little funny Asian man. What time is it you go to the dentist again? Tooth hurty?"

"Well, what'd you think?" Keith and Greg looked over as Jonathan broke in to their banter.

Keith didn't answer right away and Jonathan felt his stomach tighten. Keith was the first one outside of family or someone making money on the book to read it.

"Yeah, is it worth my time to read this crap?" Greg elbowed Jonathan in the ribs. Jonathan was still waiting for Keith's response.

"Yeah, yeah. It's solid. I mean, I'm not an expert or anything. But it was a solid story."

"Did it read well?" Jonathan repeated a phrase he had heard his editor use.

"I think so." Keith's answer seemed unsure. "It's not my usual genre. You know, suspense, murder, mystery, John Saul, Dean Koontz. So it was a little different. But okay. I mean, I liked it."

"Okay, good." Jonathan tried to sound like Keith's review was positive, but deep down he was afraid his book may not reach the potential he wanted for it. Still, he had a book being published. That was something.

"I'll be glad to offer my two cents worth as soon as I'm finished." Greg held the galley up and turned to leave, calling over his shoulder, "I'll be right back with your usuals."

Keith scrambled as he chalked his cue. "I didn't mean anything by that. It was good. Just like I said, not my usual cup of tea."

"No, no. I get it. Don't worry. Not everyone is going to love it." But Jonathan had thought everyone *would* love it. For sure his friends.

"Man, though. I think Richard Bach fans are going to be interested in finding out about that part of his life. I really had no idea.

Never even heard he had six kids. So that's a good hook." Keith lined up his shot.

Jonathan knew a huge reader market for his book would include the Richard Bach followers. That really was why he had written it in the first place, right? To tap into that world: to tap into his absent father's world. But it was also *his* story. Jonathan's story. He wanted people to know his story. He wanted people to know he existed. And yet, Keith, his close friend, still only connected with the Richard Bach part of his book.

Keith missed and Jonathan concentrated on the table, making sure to avoid eye contact and positioning himself to walk around the table opposite of Keith. He wasn't mad; he was disappointed. They shot back and forth in silence until Greg returned.

"Dudes, did you see the new girl?"

"Yeah. Jonathan says she's okay," Keith said.

"What? Are you crazy? She thinks I'm hot." Greg set their drinks on the table.

"She told you that?" Jonathan asked.

"She didn't have to tell me. I saw her checking out this fine piece of man." Greg motioned his one free hand from his shoulder down his torso with an end point to his toes.

"Oh, God. Do you think they all think you're hot?" Keith asked.

"Hotter than you, with your Asian persuasion," Greg said.

"Give it a rest. You are so full of yourself," Keith said.

Greg said to Jonathan, "Well, you better move on that before all these Jillian's vultures start hovering at the front desk. You know. Frank. Chris. Keith."

"Don't even lump me with Frank and Chris."

"You're lucky I'm out of the game. You can thank my girlfriend for that," Greg said.

"We'll get right on that," Keith broke in. "Diana, thank you from all the rest of mankind for taking Greg off the market and leaving some girls for the rest of us lesser men," he mocked.

"You know it. You better be nice to her. She's saving you buffoons from a life of loneliness. Now, take advantage."

Jonathan's mood had lightened considerably with Greg's chatter. "Maybe, I'll send her flowers tomorrow," he said.

Greg and Keith looked at him. Greg was blunt. "That's a bit aggressive."

"What?" Jonathan was confused. "No. To Diana. Not the new girl. For a thank you, I meant."

"Oh, geez, good. I was thinking you had no game there for a minute," Greg said. "You guys want the special tonight? Club sandwich, potato salad, beer. Well, Shirley Temple for you, Jonathan. Keith can have your beer."

"Sounds good."

Jonathan and Keith played late into the night. The galley and Keith's reaction to it was long forgotten. Lisa, the new girl, had already left when they checked out. Jonathan felt a twinge of disappointment.

CHAPTER 14

Lisa was into her fourth week at Jillian's. After the Trevor humiliation, she had made the decision to stop going on dates. She was grateful Trevor had not called and had let the awkward situation disappear as if they had never reconnected. She refocused on school and now work. She loved her job at Jillian's and she was meeting new friends and enjoying hanging out with no expectations. Getting up for school on Friday mornings was a challenge. But that was true even before she had the job.

"Hey, Keith. How's it going?" Keith had become one of Lisa's favorite regulars over the past month.

"Good, Lisa. How 'bout yourself?"

"Glad it's Thursday, but wish it were Friday," she said. "It's been a long week. I can't wait to sleep in on Saturday."

"Remember, you have to come to Ivar's with us tonight for Greg's birthday."

"No way. Can't tonight. Five o'clock comes way too early in the morning to hang out with you guys during the week." Lisa had taken the bait a few weeks ago and gone to Ivar's for 'just one.' It had turned into a 'just one more' quickly and before she knew it, it was 2:00 a.m. on a day she had to be up for school at 5:00. That was an unproductive day.

"Just come for a while. It'll be fun."

"No doubt it'll be fun. But why can't it be fun on a Friday night?"

"Because Greg's birthday is tonight. Can't change that."

It did suck having to say no all the time. Lisa liked Greg. He made her laugh. He was always playing little jokes on everyone. Last week when Lisa opened her notebook at school, there was a full page with a huge red heart and the words, "Greg's body is HOT!" spilled across it. He must have written it when her notebook was left abandoned for a moment at the front desk. Lisa smiled thinking about it and said to Keith, "I'll think about it."

"And..." he paused and looked around. "I have somebody I want you to talk to."

"Ah, hell no." Lisa shook her head vehemently. "I think you did your damage trying to set me up with Frank."

"Okay, okay, I know. That was not one of my better moves. But, I think you will hit it off with this guy. You two have a lot in common."

"What? He has boobs and long hair?"

"No. But he's smart. I still can't believe all those Trivial Pursuit questions you knew. He's educated and you'll have a lot to talk about."

Lisa was intrigued. But not totally sold. She was still anxious about the dating thing. "Who is this guy?"

"You already know him. He comes in every day."

"Who?"

"Jonathan."

"Are you kidding me?"

"No. I'm serious. You two have a lot in common. If you'd just talk, you'd realize it."

"But Jonathan? The tie guy? The ball organizer guy?"

"That's the one."

"I don't think so." Lisa was not attracted to Jonathan at all. He certainly wasn't athletic looking and she had noticed he had a big head. As in a physically big head; not ego wise. But she didn't know him enough to know if he had an ego. "Thanks anyway," Lisa added. "Maybe match making is not your forte."

"I still think you should give him a chance. You may be surprised."

"Sorry Keith. Not interested."

"Speak of the devil," Keith muttered.

"Hey Keith, hey Lisa. How goes it?" Jonathan tried a new greeting tonight.

What was Keith thinking? Jonathan was a big man; not quite fat, but close. He hadn't been to a gym lately, if ever. And once again, Lisa noticed the enormity of his head. It was Jay Leno-esque. Maybe it was his chin that was so big. He wore his standard outfit: a dark blue wool coat with beige khaki pants paired with a white shirt and some kind of conversation tie. *Oh, no, no, no, Keith. You have got it all wrong.* Yet she welcomed Jonathan as her job required.

"Hey, Jonathan. You look nice tonight. Cool tie. Is it new?" It was a yellow bus running sideways with stick figures looking out from the windows.

"Got it today. It's in support of cancer research for kids." He turned the tie over to reveal a label reading, Cancer Foundation.

"Neat. You guys sharing a table tonight?"

Jonathan and Keith looked at each other. It wasn't planned but, as in most nights they came in to play, it worked out perfectly.

"Sure," Keith said. "That'll be fine. I need my ego boosted." He jabbed Jonathan with his cue case.

"Good luck. I'm not taking it easy on you tonight. I hope we don't have to call the Waaaaaaaaambulance." He glanced at Lisa.

It's not that clever, Lisa thought, but said aloud, "Good one."

As Lisa handed the rack of balls over, Keith revisited their earlier conversation. "Let me know if you decide to go tonight. We could ride together. I don't want to stay too late either."

"I'll let you know."

As they disappeared up the stairs, Lisa overheard Jonathan say, "What's going on tonight? Where are you going?"

"It's Greg's birthday. We're all going to Ivar's after work. Lisa said she might go," Keith explained. "And if Lisa goes, you have to go." Keith glanced to see his reaction.

"What?"

"Well...I put in a word."

"What do you mean? A word?"

"Just kind of talked to her about you."

"Talked to her about me about what?"

"Told her I thought the two of you would have a lot in common."

"Yeah, I'm sure...a lot in common." Even though at first Jonathan had thought it possible, he had dismissed her from the Melissa radar when he heard she had gone out with the Jillian's gang. He knew what their after-hours' activities were like. "What would we possibly have in common?" Keith usually seemed to be a pretty rational guy, but Jonathan knew he had this one all wrong. Jonathan had been watching and listening about Lisa very closely the last month. Definitely not Melissa. She was a partier and well, she hadn't given him much attention beyond the formal Jillian's greeting. Melissa would be falling over herself to shower him with devotion.

"She doesn't really party," Keith said. "She's social and outgoing, but she doesn't get sloppy drunk or anything. Usually she bows out early because she has school in the morning and has to be up at 5:00."

"Really?" This was not part of the evidence Jonathan had gathered about her.

"She stayed out late once and said she learned her lesson and hasn't done it since."

"What's she going to school for?" Jonathan asked.

"It's court reporting school, like where they type really fast, but not with real words. She's always studying at the front desk."

"I noticed that. Greg said he's always messing with her notebook. I never realized it was for school." Jonathan thought she was doing some official front desk work.

"Jonathan, she's actually really smart. You should talk to her."

"What's your idea of smart? Does she watch Entertainment Tonight? Does she know the whole Nancy Kerrigan-Tanya Harding saga?" He knew too many of those dimwits in college who thought if they could recite the latest Hollywood gossip they should earn their BA.

"The fact you know there's a whole Nancy Kerrigan-Tanya Harding saga makes me question *your* intelligence."

"It's all over the news." Jonathan defended himself.

"I know, I know. I'm just teasing. But really, you should talk to her. Frank and I went to her apartment and played Trivial Pursuit last weekend and she's not dumb. She has a college degree."

"You and Frank went to her apartment?" Now that the idea was there, Jonathan felt jealous.

"It was no big deal. Her friend was up from Tacoma and we invited them to come hang out at Dante's with us. Even tried to lure them with the whole dollar pitcher idea."

"They didn't go for the dollar pitchers?"

"Nope. Lisa suggested her house to play games. It was actually kind of fun. A refreshing change from being at the bar for another drunken Saturday night with UW students."

"Hmmm? Sounds cool. Does she have a thing for Frank?" Jonathan knew Frank was the Don Juan of Jillian's.

"That's the funny part. She made fun of him the whole night."

"Like made fun how?" Jonathan asked.

"Totally called him out for being the player he is."

"Really?"

"Yeah. One time Frank was pouring all his charm on her and telling her something like how beautiful she was or her hair or something like that. She held up her finger and hushed him. Talked to him like a child saying, 'There, there, little Franky, save it for someone who'll fall for it.'"

"Are you serious? What'd Frank do?"

"You should have seen his face. He couldn't believe it. But it didn't stop him from trying."

"He just kept at it?"

"Oh, yeah. Later she got up to get a beer and he's like, 'Wow, you have got some muscular legs. Do you work out?' She said something like, 'Yup, I actually go out and run for exercise, not just running after girls like you.'"

"That's funny."

"It was. It was cool hanging out with girls who just wanted to play games and who weren't falling for his lines. I don't think he liked it so much, but it was fun."

"Sounds like it."

"Oh, oh, oh. The best part was at the end of Trivial Pursuit they did like a face off and each got six questions to answer. Before we played, Frank was all like how he was the 'champ' trivial pursuitist. She kicked his ass. Answered five of hers and even got three of his he missed."

"No way." Jonathan was thinking maybe he should revisit the Melissa thing with her.

"Totally serious. But it gets better. When we left, Frank told me he was going to be going out with her by month's end. She laughs him off every time he asks her out."

"That's good."

"I really think you should talk to her. Maybe tonight. I'll ask her again about going. At least for an hour or so."

"Sounds good. Now, are you going to rack 'em, or not?" As Keith arranged the balls in the rack, a checklist skimmed through Jonathan's head: new to Seattle, outgoing, witty, college educated. Jonathan took a small notebook from his chest pocket and scribbled for the second time regarding Lisa:

Melissa,

Could it be you?

Jonathan

CHAPTER 15

"Are you coming out with us?" Keith was turning in his rack and Lisa glanced at the clock. It was almost ten o'clock; her quitting time on weekdays. "One hour. Then I'll bring you back here. Promise."

"All right. I guess I should buy Greg a birthday shot."

Greg's girlfriend, Diana, approached the front desk and joined the conversation. "Great. You're about the tenth person I've heard say that. He's going to be out of control tonight. But that's cool you're coming. Greg's college buddies are already there. There's some cute ones too. Wink wink."

"What is with everyone trying to hook me up? I'm pretty okay with not having a boyfriend, you know."

"Yeah, but it's fun to match people up and live vicariously through them when you've been in a relationship for three years." Diana was referring to her own long running relationship with Greg. Lisa couldn't figure them out. They stayed together, so it was assumed they liked each other, but they weren't very nice to one another. And when they were apart all they did was complain about their situation. Diana abruptly turned to Keith. "Who're you trying to set her up with?"

Keith quickly averted her question, "No one."

"Who's he trying to set you up with?" Diana accosted Lisa now.

Lisa looked from Keith to her and didn't see the harm. "Jonathan."

"What?!" Diana spat, a little too astonished. "Are you kidding? Jonathan? Our Jonathan? Tie guy, Jonathan?"

"He's a nice guy. What's wrong with that?" Keith defended him.

"Sure, he's a nice guy, but kind of a geek."

Jonathan met his cue again as he walked up. "Who's a geek?"

"Ah, no one." Diana changed the subject. "Are you coming to Ivar's with us for Greg's birthday?"

"I was thinking about it. If it's okay?" Jonathan fished for a direct invite.

"Yeah, everyone's going."

"I'm glad I wore a good tie tonight." Jonathan pulled the end out to showcase his yellow bus again.

"Yeah," Diana appeased him. "Good thing."

They all turned at Frank's, "Hi, beautiful," greeting. Frank was a good-looking man, Lisa would admit that. He had the dark Italian look and the chiseled jaw. His attire was Italian inspired with tight jeans that clinched his ankles. The loafers were leather and the shirt was a long-sleeved gingham print covered by a tight vest that buttoned up the front. His hair had the defined part in the side and the tousled look that took time and gel to perfect. He definitely demanded the attention of women, but when he spoke, Lisa lost complete interest.

An awkward silence followed. Lisa knew he was talking to her but she wasn't about to acknowledge it. "Oh, that's so sweet. Keith, I didn't realize you and Frank had become so comfortable out in public now. That's cool."

Everyone turned to Jonathan as he laughed a little too loud.

"What, uh, I—" Keith stumbled.

And Frank didn't get it. "No. I was talking to you."

"I know, I know. I was just making a dumb joke."

"So whadya say, beautiful, want to ride to Ivar's with me?" Frank kept on.

Diana glanced from Frank to Lisa, then back to Frank. Lisa noticed the eye roll and knew the gossip would start unless she acted quickly. "Ah Frank, what if you get lucky with one of those hot waitresses? That would be awkward if you had to drive me back here while they're caressing that thick curly hair of yours."

Lisa grabbed her bag as Frank stuttered, "What, uh, that's not—"

"Besides," Lisa cut him off and grabbed Keith's arm, "I already have my chariot awaiting. Right, Keith?"

"Yup, let's go. See you guys there."

Lisa was pretty sure she stopped the gossip express when she heard Diana laugh and alert Frank saying, "Ha ha, that's one you'll never get."

"We'll see," Frank mumbled.

"Yeah, good luck," Jonathan added under his breath, skirting past Frank out the door.

At the car, Lisa reminded Keith, "One hour. Then you'll bring me back here, right?"

"Yeah, unles—"

"No. No unless."

"I was going to say, unless you get lured into the charms of Frank and you want him to drive you back."

"Oh ha ha, jackass. Is he for real? Does that shit work on girls?"

"It seems to. For him, anyway."

"Unbelievable."

Keith opened the door to Ivar's for Lisa and a blast of warm air and boisterous voices reached her simultaneously. Ivar's was split in two. To the right, the restaurant area was dark, romantic with low flickering candles on each table. The water-side windows flickered with the lights of the yachts parked at the docks of Lake Union. To the left, the bar area was in stark contrast; light and unromantic. The two rooms were separated by a half wall, so it was hard to believe that the diners could enjoy a quiet, intimate meal. "Here's the deal," Lisa said turning to Keith. "If I get cornered by that guy, I'm counting on you to be my knight in shining armor. As in, save me."

"Absolutely. There's our group." Keith pointed to the bar where shots and bodies were already lined up and cheers were plentiful.

"One hour," Lisa repeated as she waved and greeted everyone.

"Hey, two more shots." The party guy of the group yelled to the bartender. He approached Lisa and held his hand out firm introducing himself, "Nathan. Pleased to meet ya." He reflexively cocked his head quick to the side to jolt his blond floppy bangs out of his left eye, revealing two brown, puppy-dog eyes that were already glimmering with alcohol.

"Lisa," she matched his handshake. "And no. No shot for me." If she had learned anything from college, doing multiple shots was not her thing. Sure she had tried. And then tried again when it didn't go well. And then tried one more time for good measure. But, no, she had learned it was not a good thing.

"Just one. For Greg." Nathan's gangly 6'2" frame moved into Lisa's space and prompted Greg to guilt her.

"Yup, everyone is doing this one. For me. It's my birthdaaaayyy." Greg clutched Lisa within his arms and squeezed her shoulders together.

Lisa twisted out of his grasp. "Okay. One. That's it. I've got yours." Lisa pulled a twenty from her back pocket and a hand stopped her arm at the wrist.

"Put that away, doll. I've got yours." Frank slid uncomfortably close, wedging himself between Lisa and Nathan and she cringed at his proximity.

"That's all right. I can get my own."

Nathan's forearm gently pushed Frank to the side as he handed Lisa the shot. "Too late, sweetheart. I already got it. What do you want to chase it with?" His unfocused eyes danced with the question. "Let me know. Anything you want. I'm buying."

Lisa looked at the clear syrupy liquid in her glass. "What is it?"

"Ouzo. What else?" Greg lifted his shot from the bar.

"Water will be good."

"Water? What? Come on, anything," Nathan prodded.

"I better stick with water. I'm not sure about this." Lisa lifted the glass to her nose and cringed at the smell of black licorice.

"Your call." Nathan stumbled back into his chair. "And a water," he slurred to the bartender as he set a draft of beer in front of himself.

Frank was obviously disgruntled as he sidled up and prodded Nathan. "What about me? Aren't ya gonna buy me a drink, big guy?"

"Chaaa, you're on your own. I only buy drinks for hot, single chicks." Lisa cringed as he actually winked at her as he said it.

Exactly why Lisa hated to have guys buy her a drink. They always think they're *owed* something. It was demeaning. "Thanks," Lisa said, turning to focus on Greg and now Diana, who had appeared next to him. "Hey, happy birthday, old man. What are you? Like twenty-five?" Lisa asked.

"Yup, quarter of a century." Greg lifted his Ouzo to eye level and announced to the group, "To me. Let's drink!" In one motion he threw back his head and emptied the glass bringing it down with an exaggerated slam. Grumbles erupted from the crowd of people around him. "Ah man, you didn't wait for us." "What the heck." "You just did your birthday shot by yourself." "Way to be patient, man."

Greg bellowed to the bartender. "Another shot for me, man. I guess I need one to do with my birthday wishers!" And just like that, Greg was ready to do the group shot with the group.

All the glasses were raised and Frank's start of a toast, "Greg, I think you're a great guy who—" was boldly cut off by Nathan, "Here's to you, here's to me, if ever we should disagree, fuck you, here's to me!" Together, they all toasted their glasses high and then emptied them.

The moment the Ouzo touched her lips, Lisa's mouth began watering and as it streamed down her throat, she could feel the hairs in her nose burn. Echoes of cheers around forced her to keep it down. She squeezed her eyes shut to try and block out the uncomfortable sensation. Her mouth seized into a snarl and she shook her head back and forth violently. This all took just a split second and she opened her eyes and lunged for the water placed in front of Nathan. His laughter almost blocked her from reaching it as he called out, "Amateur!"

CHAPTER 16

Jonathan heard the group before he saw them as he entered Ivar's. And his first vision was of the whole birthday party clan downing shots of alcohol; including Lisa. How could Keith be so off?

He approached the group, knowing he wouldn't stay long now. He hated the pressure of drinkers trying to get him to drink with them. Jonathan knew him not drinking blatantly revealed to others the fact they might have a problem. He found it made people uncomfortable. It didn't bother him they drank. He had done his fair share in college and he had only quit recently since connecting with his dad. When his dad asked him the question, "Why do you drink?" he couldn't come up with an intelligent enough answer he felt would warrant his dad's approval, so he stopped. Jonathan didn't see this as changing to make his dad accept him. He saw it as evolving into the intellectual he knew his fans would expect from him once he became a famous author like his dad.

Keith's command broke him from his thoughts. "Hey, Jonathan, over here!"

Keith was at the far end of the bar sitting to the right of Nathan who was trying to incoherently persuade Lisa into something. Jonathan tried not to stare at them directly as he caught the tail end of the request. "Just one more, for me."

"Hey, man, you just missed the big group birthday shot for Greg." Keith welcomed Jonathan and pulled out the empty stool that was between Nathan and himself.

"Sorry to hear *that*," Jonathan said. "I did see Lisa throw one back though." Jonathan wanted to make sure Keith knew that he had definitely pegged it wrong. He didn't want to be with a partier; he wanted Melissa.

"Geez, buddy. Lighten up. She did one to celebrate with Greg. Look at Nathan trying to get her to do another one. It won't happen. You sure have high standards for someone so desperate to meet someone."

"That's not it. I have specifics."

"Don't we all." There was exasperation in Keith's voice. "And if a girl doesn't meet every single one of your 'specifics' you rule her out without even a chance?"

Jonathan thought about how to answer this. "I didn't say that. I just know who I'm looking for and I'm pretty sure when I meet her, that she is going to act a certain way and do and not do specific things."

"Wow. So what? You have like a list written up and as soon as a girl does something contrary to that list then what? Nothing?"

Jonathan didn't want to reveal to Keith how close his idea was. "Who knows how it's supposed to work?" He turned toward the bartender who looked torn between Nathan persisting on another shot and Lisa repeatedly saying no. Jonathan interrupted, "What do I need to do to get a Shirley Temple around here?"

"Nice subject change," Keith said. "Hey, Larry, can our impossible-to-please Casanova get a Shirley Temple?"

To his left, Jonathan could now hear Frank circling in. "Hey, Lisa, what do you want to drink? I'm buying."

Nathan, still marking his territory, answered for her. "She already said she doesn't want anything. And if she changes her mind, I'm here for her." His cheesy line sounded even worse slurred from the effect of the alcohol.

Jonathan wondered if Lisa would fall for his crap. He turned in time to see Nathan move to drape his arm around her shoulders. She saw it coming too and smoothly moved to her left sliding off the barstool. This caused Nathan to lose his balance and he tumbled off his stool and grabbed the bar for support. "See that," he slurred. "You already got me falling for you."

"What a slimeball," Jonathan muttered to Keith.

"Makes you wonder how he gets any girl he wants."

"Because he's good looking and in shape." Jonathan didn't hide his jealousy about this fact to Keith.

"That probably helps. Maybe we should get in shape? Whaddya think?"

"Like go to the gym or something," Jonathan cringed. He didn't actually want to work too hard at this.

"Why not? You want to be in shape when you go on tour and start meeting thousands of women, don't you?"

Jonathan could see the benefit of this; but still, the gym? He wasn't sure. "I'll think about it."

"Lisa goes to the gym every day," Keith added.

Mentally, Jonathan tallied from his list. In shape, athletic.

Behind Jonathan, Lisa was ignoring Nathan's cheesy 'falling for you' line. "Smooth, Nathan. Maybe you should have some water, too," Lisa said.

"Nah. Why ruin a good buzz?"

Frank had moved unbearably close to Lisa in the whole Nathan falling mishap. She maneuvered away and excused herself to the bathroom. As she walked away, Frank hissed, "Back off, Nathan. You're drunk."

"Whatever, loser. Fair game."

Diana cornered Lisa in the bathroom. "So, what do you think of Nathan? He told Greg he liked you."

"Unbelievable," Lisa said. "He doesn't even know me. And he's drunk off his ass."

"He's harmless. Greg's known him forever. They were frat brothers."

"I never would have guessed."

"Seriously, give him a chance," Diana pleaded. "We could set up a double date or something so you could get to know him when it's not so rowdy. He's a pretty cool guy."

Lisa stared at her with an are-you-kidding-me glance and Diana seemed to let it drop. But then she added, "And what's with Frank? He's got it bad for you. You know he's a player, right?"

Lisa didn't know if she was supposed to respond. This seemed so obvious, it didn't need to be acknowledged out loud. But Diana kept going. "And I see Keith's little match-make Jonathan made it, too. Wow, what's a girl to do?" She winked at Lisa in the reflection of the mirror as they washed their hands.

"Guess it's time for a girl to go home."

"I was teasing. Stay awhile longer. The rest of the gang is coming over from Jillian's. I have a feeling it's going to get crazy."

"Yeah, but I—"

"I know. I know. You have school." She zipped her purse closed as she finished touching up her makeup. "But you can stay awhile. See you out there." She pushed her way through the door.

Lisa was done. She looked at her watch. 10:35. Twenty-five more minutes to reach the hour mark. She wondered if she could negotiate with Keith to leave early. Outside the bathroom, she looked to where Keith had been. Good news and bad news. Good news; he was still in the same spot. Bad news; to get to him, she had to pass Frank, then Nathan, then Jonathan. She thought about sneaking out and walking back to her car. One glance out the window showed rain and wind. No thanks.

Lisa tried to unnoticeably make her way to Keith. Almost, but not quite. Nathan slurred as he nudged Frank away from her seat. "Sweetheart, you're back. Just in time for another shot."

"No, thanks. I gotta go." Lisa dipped and squeezed sideways to edge toward Keith. This put her behind Jonathan, but close enough to tap Keith's shoulder so he turned. "Hey, I'm ready when you are."

Keith pulled his wrist from his drink and turned it toward him. "What? You said an hour. It's only been thirty-five minutes."

"I'm just letting you know I'm ready. I'll hang out if you still want to stay." *A deal's a deal.*

"A little while longer. There's someone I want to chat with for a few minutes." He glanced behind her shoulder. Lisa followed to his target; an older forty-something-year-old with a group of other forty-something-year-olds.

"Really?" Lisa turned back toward him, and repeated, "Really?" She hadn't given much thought to what Keith's 'type' was.

"What's wrong with that?" he defended himself.

"Nothing. Nothing. You surprised me, that's all. You think twenty minutes will do it or should I walk?"

"No, I won't be long. Here, take my seat." He slid around in his stool and held out the front for her to slide on. She looked at Jonathan's back and back at Keith and rolled her eyes at him. Keith left her no other choice. "Just sit down. I'll be back in a minute."

Lisa was stuck. To say no to the open seat in the corner next to Jonathan meant backing into the pressures of Frank and Nathan. Already behind her she could hear Frank. "Lisa, are you sure I can't get you a drink?" She stepped forward and secured the stool from Keith and slid on. "Hurry up," she hissed.

"Ha," he whispered. "Now we're even for the Keith-and-Frank-out-in-the-open joke."

"Not even close to even," she said to his retreating back. Lisa turned the stool toward the bar, blocking out Frank and placing her left arm on the bar to create a barrier between herself and Jonathan.

Jonathan realized Keith's plan to get them together had transpired as he glanced sideways to see Lisa slide on the stool. He wasn't sure if he should talk to her or what he would even say. Maybe, he thought, I should offer her a drink. The fact she put her arm up between them on the bar was probably some kind of warning for him to keep his distance. But he didn't know.

Jonathan decided to copy her and do the same. He brought his right arm up to form his own barrier. As he lifted it over the bar's ledge, his coat sleeve caught a little and he pulled to release it. His hand shot forward and toppled his Shirley Temple toward the back ledge of the bar.

Immediately, Lisa reacted to the glass slamming. There were cocktail napkins on her right and she pulled a stack to throw over the racing liquid to keep it from reaching the ledge and spilling over. She repeated the action, covering as much of the spill as she could.

Jonathan was working just as frantically and stammering, "Oh man, oh gosh, crud."

Nathan piped in from his chair. "Nice goin', man."

Greg, a few chairs down, yelled, "Party foul. Drink!"

And still another anonymous voice announced, "Alcohol abuse." Lisa guessed he didn't know it was a Shirley Temple.

The bartender had already reached their corner with the bar towel soaking up what the napkins couldn't. He calmly asked Jonathan, "Another?"

"Um, yeah, sure. Sorry about that."

"Anything for you, hon?" the bartender asked Lisa.

"I'll take a water, thanks."

"Just water?" Jonathan abruptly looked toward Lisa.

"Yeah, just water. I've seen what those Shirley Temples can do." Lisa continued to dry the bar.

"How embarrassing. I was just putting my arm on the bar an—" He let the sentence drop along with his head.

"No biggie. It's happened to all of us."

"Thanks. Um, yeah, thanks for helping and all, too."

"No problem. Quick reflexes from working in a bar in college. Although usually it was a beer and the college morons were more worried if they were going to get a free refill rather than if it was going to get cleaned up."

"You worked in a bar? That had to be tough."

"Not really. You get immune to this stuff." Lisa waved her hand at Greg's group hollering for another round. "And it was good money for a college student." She turned back toward the bar as her water was delivered.

Jonathan pulled an unused napkin toward him and proceeded to shred it into tiny confetti. After a few minutes of silence, he tried Nathan's approach. "Can I buy you a drink?"

"I already have a drink." Lisa raised her water glass.

"You know what I mean. A real drink?"

"Nope. I'm good, thanks. I'm waiting for Keith to finish up then I'm heading home."

Jonathan could feel Nathan leaning in on him just a moment before he smelled him. "Dude, give it up."

Lisa expertly deflected him. "Nathan. Come on. Give the guy some room. He's recovering from a traumatic Shirley Temple loss." Jonathan caught her quick wink as she reached across him and nudged Nathan softly from his space.

Nathan moved back with a surprised look that quickly changed when he noticed his fresh shot placed in front of him. "Okay, okay. But seriously dude, save your breath, she doesn't want a drink."

Jonathan was impressed; attention deployed and with no hint of frustration or anger from Nathan.

Lisa moved into her own seat and shrugged. "See. Professional." She threw in, "Dude," with a smile to emphasize Nathan's term of endearment toward Jonathan.

Jonathan shook his head with a chuckle and murmured, "Hmm." His mind was swirling with Melissa data; not drinking a lot, friendly, waitressed while going to college. He struggled to start a conversation, but came up with nothing. This was it. He may have his Melissa right here and he was blowing his chance.

Lisa twisted her straw in an effort to keep active. She spun her bar stool around to scan the room. She spotted Keith and he was still involved. Her watch confirmed he had fifteen more minutes.

Nathan and Frank had moved on to new pursuits, Greg and Diana had each drank enough to be affectionate to one another. The others were still ordering shots and drinks to capitalize on their night out. Lisa was way past the time of being ready to go home.

"So, where'd you go to college?" Jonathan's abrupt question sounded among the buzz of activity.

Lisa took her time turning her stool back to face the bar counter. In the bar back mirror, she could see Jonathan looking in her direction. She turned to face him, but still did not answer right away. Returning her attention to her mutilated straw, she decided having a conversation with him was not going to hurt anything at this point. But Keith *so* owed her. She answered, "Idaho State University."

"In Moscow?"

"No. Pocatello." Moscow was always the immediate response.

"I knew that. It's University of Idaho that's in Moscow."

Lisa still wasn't sure about talking to this guy that Keith thought she might have something in common with. He was not typically her type, but he was being nice. She decided to correct him. "Actually. Yes. U of I is in Moscow. But it's Moscow, like Coe, like rhymes with Idaho. Not Moscow, like cow, that's Russia."

"Oh." Jonathan lowered his head again. His fingers fumbled over the ledge of his drink trying to grab the cherry that kept dipping under the ice cubes each time he nudged it. The concentration he showed made Lisa feel bad. He only wanted to talk.

"Pocatello is down in the southeast corner of Idaho," she said.

He finally got hold of the cherry's stem and pulled it from the glass. Ignoring Lisa's explanation, he proclaimed, "I can tie this stem with my tongue."

From watching his lack of finesse, Lisa knew that there was no possible way he was capable of that feat. She called him on it. "I bet I can tie one faster than you."

"You're on." Jonathan plopped the cherry on his napkin and the stem disappeared into his mouth.

"Wait. Wait. Wait." Lisa tried to stop him. "I need a stem."

He mumbled through the struggle of the stem, "Not my problem."

"I see how it is." Lisa tried frantically to get the attention of the bartender who was at the other end of the bar. She looked around. Nothing. The drink condiments were half way down the bar. Jonathan's eyes were mischievous and that spurred her on more.

Lisa hopped from her chair and nudged past Nathan who was still insistent on getting her a drink. "Come on, sweetie, just one."

Lisa was downright rude now that she was on a quest. "Back off, Nathan. Stop. I need to get to—"

Then Frank, noticing she had left the safety of her chair, turned from his blond, and grabbed her elbow. She pulled a little too hard which landed her fist in Nathan's gut. He just laughed, "Ah, feisty too. I like it."

"Guys, come on. I just need...to...get..." She pushed through while she pleaded. "A cherry." Lisa's last lunge proved successful and she quickly headed back with cherry stem already in her mouth.

At their corner, Jonathan sat triumphant with a tied cherry stem in his upright hand.

Even before getting to her chair, Lisa contested the bet. "No way. Not fair. How do I even know you did it with your tongue?"

Jonathan crowed. "Fair's fair. You made the bet. Your own fault you didn't have the materials needed to compete."

"What? That's crap. Rematch. Let's go." Now she was ready.

But Jonathan wasn't giving in. "Nope. I want to maintain my championship for just awhile."

Lisa did think it was a pretty clever move. He looked so proud of himself. She still tried to guilt him into another chance. "Fine. I guess if your life is so pathetic that you have to relish in a cherry-stem-tying championship against one other person who didn't even have a cherry stem, then I guess that's what you have to do."

He didn't bite. She noticed his eyes danced with his laugh. "Yup, I will take that moment." He raised his arms in a victory move and on the way up his left hand cuffed his drink and sent it sprawling across the bar top again.

"That's what you get." Lisa reached for the newly replaced stack of napkins.

"Dang it." Jonathan's victory was short lived.

Lisa starting sopping up the second drink he had dumped in ten minutes. They both frantically cleaned the mess, and then the awkward silence settled in. A quick glance at Keith told Lisa he was going to take full advantage of every minute he had left; which in her calculations was down to five.

Jonathan looked uncomfortable in the silence.

Lisa decided she might as well pass the time. "So, did you go to college?" She wanted to add, 'or are you one of these trust-fund babies whose mommy and daddy are paying for you to party in Seattle until you decide to grow up?' but she didn't.

"Yup." Jonathan's answer was indifferent.

Are you kidding me? Is he playing hard to get? Give me a break. Lisa wasn't going to beg for information from him. She twirled her straw some more and looked at the birthday group throwing back yet another group shot. She did not feel like chatting anymore.

But she got bored. "Where'd you go?"

"Huh?" Jonathan looked at her blankly.

"To college. Where'd you go to college?" Lisa didn't even try to hide the irritation in her voice.

"Oh. Maine University."

"Really?" She blurted. "Is it beautiful there?" Lisa had seen pictures from a trip her mom and dad had taken and it was a place she had always wanted to visit.

"Oh, yeah. Very cool. Especially in the fall."

"I bet. Ever see Stephen King's house?"

Jonathan looked at her oddly. "As a matter of fact I have. That's a weird question."

"Is it as ominous as one would think?"

"Yes. Yes it is."

"He is crazy morbid. I read somewhere he told someone he had the heart of a young boy...on his desk. That is so gross, yet... intriguing."

Jonathan turned his chair slightly to face Lisa. She was animated when she talked. He wanted to hear more. And even though he had dumped two drinks in ten minutes, she didn't treat him like a loser. Their conversation took on the nervous back-and-forth energy of the 'getting to know someone' stage as they realized maybe they did have some things in common.

"Do you read a lot?" *Not a chance*, Jonathan smugly thought to himself. This will take her right off the Melissa scan.

"Yeah. But only recently I've been able to read more for pleasure."

"Pleasure?" Jonathan raised his eyebrows.

"Being an English major in college didn't leave a lot of time to read things that I *wanted* to. Too many mandatory things for class."

"You were an English major?" Jonathan quickly scanned his mental list; some kind of art major. Ha. Not even close. He began to relax realizing she wasn't Melissa.

"Yeah."

"What? With a teaching degree?"

"Just English," Lisa answered after a slight hesitation.

"What are you planning to do with that?" Jonathan heard the condescending tone in his own voice.

Jonathan watched her organize her thoughts before carefully explaining, "I started out in Architecture. After two years, decided I wanted to go to court reporting school. My dad wanted me to stay and finish my degree. I chose the classes that I enjoyed most, which was English, and finished my degree in three and a half years. Now I'm going to court reporting school."

Jonathan's head whirled with this new data. Started as art major, then switched. Likes to read. Continuing education. New to Seattle. Sweat beaded on his forehead.

"Hey, are you okay?" Lisa asked. Jonathan had turned away from her as she chatted on and on. He now sat staring at the mirror behind the bar and his look registered slight terror. He heard her mumble something about talking too much about herself and her voice was floating in a bubble circling his head. When it popped, he heard, "What did you major in?" However, the receptors in his brain did not recognize it as a question until she asked it again. "What was your major?"

Jonathan did not turn to look at her. He took a slow sip of his third Shirley Temple. He ignored Lisa's question and slowly resumed his own inquiry. "English major, huh? Who's your favorite author?"

"So, you're not going to answer questions about yourself?" Lisa questioned.

"Not yet. Who's your favorite author?"

She hesitated a moment, then answered, "Don't laugh. This may show my nerdiness, but I'm on an Ernst Hemingway kick right now."

Jonathan was really sweating now. He couldn't believe it. Not Danielle Steele, or Judy Collins, or who was the other romance novelist right now? Nora Roberts?

Ernst Hemingway? *Is she for real*?

"Why would I laugh at that? He's a classic." Jonathan's voice was dazed.

"I know. Just, I guess, not a real popular author for our generation." Lisa lifted her chin toward Nathan, and Jonathan followed the direction.

"Bet he can't name one novel he wrote," Jonathan said.

"My point exactly." Lisa decided to test. "Can you?"

"*A Farewell to Arms Death in the Afternoon The Old Man and the Sea*—not my favorite—*For Whom the Bell Tolls* you want short stories *A Clean Well-Lighted Place Hills Like White Elephants Get a Seeing Eye Dog Black Ass at the Crossroads*—never published but great title—" Jonathan paused just slightly to catch his breath, "*Nobody Ever—*"

"Okay, okay. I get it." Lisa held her hands up, but was impressed.

"What is it you like about him?"

"My senior paper was researching how his personal life carried over into his writing. You know he committed suicide?"

"What? I didn't know that. That's weird I wouldn't know that. I guess I really never heard about his personal life."

"Then when you start reading his short stories, you can see the desperation in some of his subject characters. And he was a drunk."

"That I had heard."

"He actually had a valid point. He wrote once to a friend, 'When you use your head, what else can change your ideas and make them run on a different plane than whiskey?'"

"If that's the case, our friend Nathan here should be a fountain of interesting and stimulating ideas." Jonathan turned on his stool and motioned toward Nathan as he prepared to do a shot that was being lit on fire.

"Oh, good God. That guy has killed way too many brain cells."

"So. Hemingway? Very interesting."

"Yeah. Bullfighting. Affairs. Drinking. Depression. Fishing. Hunting. War. It's all there in his novels and it's all there in his life. I guess that's what people say: 'Write about what you know.'"

Jonathan sat in silence.

"How about you? Do you read much?" Lisa asked.

"Sure I do. When I can."

"And? Favorite authors?"

"Oh. I have a bunch."

"Do you want to share?"

"Let's see. Tom Clancy. Ray Bradbury has always been a favorite. Robert Fulgham. Richard Bach."

"Lots of modern writers."

"I guess you could say that. But I do like the oldies too. Hemingway I wouldn't say was up there as a favorite, but I can see your point."

"It was just kind of fun. Personally, his writing gets a little too descriptive for me and drags at some points. I mean, get the damn fish already," Lisa said. "I like dialogue and characters interacting with other characters." She continued fiddling with her straw as she talked. "Richard Bach? He sounds familiar. What's he written?"

Jonathan smiled. "Some flying novels and a couple of love stories."

"Love stories? You don't strike me as a trashy romance guy."

"That's funny. I thought that's exactly what you were going to start talking about when I asked about your favorite authors."

Lisa punched him lightly on the arm. "Thanks. Talk about stereotyping."

"Well, it's not often you meet a girl in the bar that lists Hemingway as a favorite author. It's actually kind of nerdy," Jonathan teased.

"Nerdy? Okay, Shirley Temple guy with a school bus tie on."

Jonathan threw his hands up. "Okay, you got me. I'm a nerd, and, shhh don't tell anyone, but sometimes I'm a klutz."

This made Lisa laugh and Jonathan relaxed a little too.

"So anyway," Lisa pushed for more. "Richard Bach? Trashy romance author. Probably Fabio on the covers. What's he written?"

"Not a trashy romance. Sort of a modern day soul mate romance."

Lisa paused for a moment. She mumbled several thoughts that were circling, "Bach. Soul mate. Modern day love story." Then she turned to Jonathan and blurted, "Oh my God. I think I have a book by him." She struggled with the title. "*Bridge of Love*? *Across the Bridge*? Something like that."

"*Bridge Across Forever*." Jonathan gave her the answer.

"That's it," she exclaimed. "I have that book."

"Did you like it?"

"Haven't read it." She looked down.

"You haven't. How come? It's pretty good."

"It was given to me by someone."

"Someone?" Jonathan urged.

"A someone who I guess liked me."

"You guess liked you? Like you guess these guys like you?" Jonathan glanced behind him where Nathan and Frank were still noticeably close.

"Yeah, not funny. They're just intrigued with the hunt; not the prize. But anyway, yeah, he gave me the book when I left for Seattle and said it was like the love story of the decade and to read it and see if it meant anything. Needless to say, I haven't read it yet."

"Why not?"

"I don't know. He seemed kind of pushy, needy. Plus, I don't know if I believe in his 'soul mate' idea. I guess I'll read it someday."

Jonathan thought about this for a moment. He never really considered whether Melissa would believe in soul mates. Was it important that she believed? Or was it sufficient that only he was searching for a soul mate? He would have to talk this over with James. He said to Lisa, "You should read it. It's pretty good. Not a corny love story, but definitely something to think about."

Their conversation moved on to Jonathan's obsession with Ray Bradbury, his recent meeting with Robert Fulgham, Lisa's favorite professor in college who shared a name with Dante, which prompted her to take a course of study in Dante Aligherri which she didn't understand. She finished her anecdote. "But I still took classes from Professor Dante because I had a bit of a crush on him. You know, the aging grey-haired professor look was in a few years back."

"Hey you two. How's it going?" Their chatting was interrupted by Keith.

"Good, good," they overlapped.

"So I see. Lisa, are you ready to go?"

She looked at her watch. "Holy crap, Keith. It's one o'clock!"

"I know. I came by earlier and you two didn't even notice me standing here, so I figured you were okay."

"Oh my gosh. I have to get up in four hours."

Jonathan piped in, "Sometimes in college when I realized I wasn't going to get a full night's sleep, I just decided to make it an all-nighter."

"And just what time do you have to get up for work, mister?" Lisa demanded to know how little sleep Jonathan was going to get.

"Oh, playboy here doesn't have to get up for work," Keith said.

There it is. The catch. The thing Lisa had waited for while Jonathan and she had been hitting it off so well the last, well, she looked at her watch again, two and a half hours. He had no job. Lisa's sarcasm returned. "Ah to be the recipient of a fatty trust fund and live the life of leisure."

"That's not quite how it is. I'm just self-employed."

Self-employed? That sounded important, but not quite logical. Lisa realized she never did ask what he did for a living.

"I'm starving. You guys game for going to Denny's for a quick bite?" Keith asked.

Immediately, Lisa's logic jumped in. "Not me. I need to get to bed. Can you drop me off?"

Jonathan reacted opposite. "Sure man. I'm not tired anyway. Kind of wound up."

"Come on, just a quick bite," Keith persisted. "If you're really tired, I'll drop you off first."

Jonathan looked right at Lisa. "It'd be really cool if you came."

Lisa teetered between heading home to bed and getting a few hours sleep and just pulling an all-nighter like Jonathan suggested. She was wound up also. Her time with Jonathan had flown by and she didn't really want the conversation to end. "All right," she agreed. She turned to tell everyone goodbye. "Where'd everyone go?" Lisa looked at Keith accusingly.

He shook his head and laughed. "Moved on to the next bar about a half hour ago. They all tried to get your attention to say goodbye, but you two were deep in conversation."

Jonathan and Lisa looked at one another and she felt her face heat as she watched his flush.

Keith grabbed her elbow and led her out. "We'll see you there man," he said to Jonathan.

CHAPTER 17

"Keith, he's really nice." Lisa slid into the passenger seat as Keith held the door open.

"Who? Dorky tie guy that you thought you would have nothing in common with?" He shut her door and headed around to his side.

"Okay. You might have been right," she admitted as he got in. "It was so much fun actually having a conversation with someone about something other than beer kegs and body shots."

"I told you."

"I know. We talked about literature and authors and writing styles," Lisa said. She was gushing. "But one question."

"Uh, oh. What?"

"What exactly does self-employed mean?" Lisa watched closely for Keith's reaction as they pulled into the Denny's parking lot.

"He didn't tell you what he does for a living?"

"No. We didn't get that far."

"I'm sure it will come up sooner or later."

"How about sooner? And how about from you? Now. Spill it. Is it legal?"

"Oh my gosh. You're paranoid. Yes, it's legal. Did he tell you his last name?

"His last name—" Lisa thought for a second. "Actually, no, I didn't get that. Why? What is it?"

"Bach."

Bach. Bach? He had told me that. No, wait. That was one of his favorite authors. Bach. Richard Bach. Not Jonathan. Lisa was confused. "Bach? He mentioned a Richard Bach; some author."

"Yeah, some author. Some author that is his dad." Keith hopped out of the car. Lisa followed.

"What? His dad?" Keith was a step ahead of her and Jonathan was waiting on the sidewalk.

As soon as they joined him, Lisa said, "So Richard Bach's your favorite author, huh?"

She caught the exchange between Keith and Jonathan.

"I told her. You know, your dad," Keith mumbled.

"Yeah. I guess I always gotta kinda include him in my favorite author list." Jonathan looked pleased with himself.

"And so exactly what does your self-employed job title mean?" Lisa drilled him.

"That's what I do. I write books. Self-employed."

"Write books? Like an author? Like you're an author?" Lisa knew she sounded like an idiot.

"Yes, an author. Well, not quite yet. Not published, but on its way." Lisa followed slightly behind them to the door that Keith held open.

Keith continued Jonathan's explanation. "He's got his galley copies. You know, to have friends and colleagues read and edit before going to print."

No, Lisa didn't know. Lisa didn't know the whole book publishing process, so she just replied, "Oh."

"You should let her read one," Keith said to Jonathan. "She'll probably rip it apart as an English major."

"That's what I'm afraid of. I watched her rip Nathan and Frank apart all night and they didn't even realize she was doing it. I don't think I could handle her criticism," he teased.

"What's the book about?" Lisa opened up the conversation for them to continue through the meal. She was intrigued. It sounded worth a read. And most appealing was being able to read a book and actually know the person, or not know, but have just met the person that wrote it. That would be cool. She was beginning to look at Jonathan in a whole different way. He didn't seem *completely* unattractive to her anymore. Sure he was a dork, but maybe it was time to explore something a bit different than her typical 'type.'

Lisa was full of questions and Jonathan and Keith bounced answers and ideas back and forth. Between them both, they filled her in on all the details of his growing up estranged from his famous father and the process of writing his book. They finished eating long before they finished the conversation and banter.

Keith stood up and announced, "Okay. 3:30. I'm out of here."

His abrupt announcement caught Lisa off guard. As she started to scoot around the booth, Jonathan spoke up. "Lisa, really, if you want to do the all-night thing, I will stay up with you and we can keep chatting."

"You'd really only get about an hour's sleep anyway," Keith added.

"I know. I'm going to be hating life tomorrow. Well, today really." Lisa did want to stay and continue talking. "And you'll give me a ride to my car?" She asked Jonathan.

"Of course. If I'm lucky, someone at Jillian's will see us and the rumors will start."

"Maybe you'll run into Frank dropping off his evening catch. That would really get him on fire, thinking you two spent the night together." Keith and Jonathan both laughed.

"Hey, hello, still here." Lisa didn't like their school-boy plotting with her as the bait.

"Just kidding."

"Yes. I will drop you off," Jonathan said seriously.

"Okay. I'll stay. But we need to watch the time. I need to be out of here by 5:00."

"I'll make sure. Watch synchronized." Jonathan made a mocking twist of his watch.

Keith grabbed his keys from the table. "All right, then. I'm out of here. Catch you tomorrow. Today. Have fun at school, Lisa. I'll get an extra hour of sleep for you."

"I'll be thanking you when I have to be at work tonight, and don't even think about asking me to go out again."

"I won't. But I can't promise Jonathan won't. He looks pretty smitten."

Jonathan's eyes darted to his ice water, he was clearly embarrassed.

"Again…still here." She was embarrassed, too.

CHAPTER 18

Keith left and the silence returned, but it wasn't awkward. Jonathan had a handful of napkins in front of him on which he had jotted down ideas and pictures since arriving. He was methodically running through checklists in his head. Keith had asked Lisa a lot of the questions that got him to check off: youngest of four siblings, athletic, played sports in high school, had a boyfriend through most of college. "So, do you still talk to your boyfriend from college?"

Jonathan caught Lisa in her own whirl of thoughts. She was amazed they had so much to talk about and how fast the time was passing while they were together. Even thinking it, it sounded silly and cliché. But it was nice it was happening.

"Yes, we still talk," Lisa answered.

"Like a lot?"

"We did, but I'm not sure we will keep in touch much anymore."

"Why's that?"

"I just got a letter from him and it kind of threw me for a loop."

"What do you mean?"

Lisa tried to explain. "His letter was a lot about how we never had a chance because we did not have God in our lives. Which is weird because I thought we did."

"Are you religious?" Jonathan thought about the Melissa list; spiritual, but not religious.

"I'm Catholic. I was raised Catholic. I guess I'm Catholic. And he was too. I sponsored him being confirmed and we went to church every Sunday and all."

"And he accused you of not having God in your lives?" Jonathan was shocked. He didn't know anyone in college that went to church.

"Yeah. We even lived together our last year of college and abstained from sex in a way to have a deeper relationship with God." Even saying it was awkward for Lisa and she felt maybe it was too much.

"I don't get it. So how did he say God was not in your life?" Jonathan remained matter of fact.

"I don't know. That's what threw me for a loop." Lisa was still trying to figure it out herself.

"So are you religious now?" *Please answer no.* Jonathan was willing her to be Melissa.

"I don't know."

Yes! "What do you mean, you don't know?"

"I still go to church, but it's become different for me. It's not so much believing in the Catholic thing or the unified church thing, but more a meditational time to reflect on what just happened the past week and think about what's to come. Or what I want to come." Lisa shrugged as she answered. "It's all very confusing on what to believe."

It didn't seem to bother Jonathan, who continued to doodle and churn thoughts. "Yeah, who's to know what's right or wrong. Maybe we are all just living parallel planes of ourselves anyways. And the one right next to you is devoutly Catholic. Is she having a better life than you?"

"Interesting thought. But one I'm too tired to think of now," Lisa replied. "I need to go to the restroom. All this water," she exited the booth. Looking at her watch, she realized it was five o'clock. "We should head out when I get back."

Jonathan just smiled at her and nodded as he thought; spiritual, but not religious.

While Lisa was in the bathroom, Jonathan block-lettered MELISSA in the middle of his napkin. He was continually calculating. Lisa: not quite Melissa. He scribbled out the ME, which just left LISSA.

Lisa returned to the table and reluctantly told Jonathan, "I really need to go. I have just enough time to shower and get on the road to make it to school."

"Okay. Just have a seat and I'll get the check."

She looked over at his scribbles. His napkin had doodles and frayed, torn edges. In the middle he had written one word: LISSA. Lisa reached over and grabbed his pen from his hand. She placed an X over one of the esses. "Just one S," she said and handed his pen back.

Jonathan did not reach for the pen, staring at the mark Lisa had just made.

Lisa glanced over at him and he remained focused on the napkin. "What's wrong? I just meant that there's only one S in my name."

Jonathan finally looked away from the napkin and met Lisa's eyes. There was a slight flicker of disappointment in them. "You must have known a Lisa with two esses before. It's not a big deal."

"No, it's not." But Jonathan was obsessing. With one swoop, she had grabbed Jonathan's pen and crossed out an S. Lisa. He stared at the edited napkin. This was a farther stretch from Melissa. Melissa. Melisa. *But,* he argued with himself, *just one letter really—after deleting the ME. Could it work?*

Jonathan needed time to process this. His mind was tired and overwhelmed and even though he had so many more questions he wanted to ask her, he couldn't help but think about crawling into bed and sleeping for hours. He was grateful it was Lisa that had to go to school after this marathon and not him. As the waitress set the check down, he came back from his contemplations and reached for his wallet.

"One more question and then I'll get you to your car," Jonathan said.

"But your questions tend to lead to long answers."

"This is an easy one. One word."

"Okay. Shoot."

"What's your middle name?"

She hesitated. "I hate this question."

"Maybe it will be more than a one-word answer, then," Jonathan said. "What's wrong?"

"I was teased relentlessly while growing up about my middle name. Sometimes I even just lied about it."

"Are you going to lie to me?" Jonathan asked.

"I'm guessing I better not, since you'll probably find out eventually," she smiled. "Mayme." She glanced away.

Jonathan repeated slowly, "Mayne?"

"No. Mayme. With an 'm.'" Still, she did not make eye contact.

"Oh. Mayme." Jonathan processed. "That's cool. Is there a story?"

"No story, really. It's my grandma's middle name. I never understood it. My parents had three girls before me, but I'm the one that got Mayme."

Jonathan broke out in laughter.

Lisa's face flushed. "It's not that funny. It sucked growing up."

"No, no, no. I'm not laughing at that. I'm laughing because I got stuck too. I got Stuart. After my grandpa. Third boy and I get grandpa's name. My brothers both got normal middle names and me? I got Stuart. I hate it."

"I can top that." Now Lisa was laughing. "I just found out a few months ago, Mayme wasn't even my grandma's *real* name."

"What?"

"Turns out, it was her *nickname*."

"No way."

"Yup. My mom even was surprised to see on my dad's birth certificate, Mary Jane. She's only ever known her as Mayme."

"Okay. You win." Jonathan smiled and reached on to the table and covered Lisa's hand with his own. Lisa was shocked by Jonathan's bold move. This she had not expected, but realized he was probably just being friendly.

After a moment, Jonathan said, "I like the name Mayme." And he mentally checked off another item; middle name same as grandmother's. "Let's get you to your car."

Lisa pulled her hand back and rose to leave the restaurant. Outside, the morning was now being lit by the awakening sunshine.

The ride back to her car was not long enough to awake the heater in Jonathan's car and she shivered the whole way. She was already anticipating how good the hot shower was going to feel as soon as she got home.

"Do you want to read my galley?" Jonathan asked as they parked behind her car.

Lisa replied, "Of course."

He caught her shoulder with his left hand as he awkwardly stretched to the back seat and handed her a powder blue, soft covered book with no identifying marks except in thick black type: ABOVE THE CLOUDS. And centered below that: JONATHAN BACH.

"Here you go. Feel free to write ideas or suggestions on it. But be kind. I know you English majors get into this kind of stuff."

Do we ever.

"Maybe we could go to dinner when you finish and you can enlighten me to how bad it is," Jonathan said.

Lisa could sense confidence under his words. He did not think it was bad at all. But she was excited. She had never read a book and then actually been able to sit down with the author to discuss it. All the open-ended conversations in college had left her aggravated more than once. Who *really* knows if Twain meant for Huckleberry Finn to be a novel full of racial implications? The guy's dead for heaven's sake; you can't ask him.

"That sounds good," she answered. "I'm not sure when I will get time to finish, but I will try to get to it in between school work and stuff. Should I call you?"

"I'm sure I'll see you at Jillian's," he said. "But, uh, yeah, um you can call me."

"Okay. I'll do that."

"Sounds good," Jonathan said. "Okay, then. I guess I'll talk to you when you call."

"It'd probably make it easier if you gave me your number."

"Oh, yeah, duh." He opened his middle console and grabbed an old, only slightly used Burger King napkin. He scribbled his number on it and handed it over. "Here you go."

Lisa looked at the napkin. “Do you always go by Jonathan? Anybody ever call you Jon?”

“No. Always Jonathan. Like the seagull.”

Like the seagull? Lisa didn’t know what to say to that. She didn’t know there was a seagull named Jonathan. “Okay, then, Jonathan. I guess I’ll call you. Thanks for breakfast and the ride and all that.”

“No problem. Catchya later.”

As soon as Jonathan got home and entered his apartment, he dialed James’ number. The machine answered.

“I met a girl. She may be Melissa. I’m going to bed after an all-nighter talking with her. I’ll call you later when I wake up. This is cool, man. This is really cool.”

CHAPTER 19

Three days later, Lisa dialed the number scribbled on the napkin. She mentally calculated as the phone rang. 5:30. Did he go to Jillian's on Sundays also? But she wasn't working tonight. So she wouldn't see him anyway.

"Hi. This is Jonathan Bach. Leave a message at the beep."

Again, the full name. For some reason that made Lisa uncomfortable; it was so formal.

"Um, yeah, Jonathan, this is Lisa. Lisa from Jillian's." Did she need to clarify further? "We went to Denny's the other night."

"But anyway, I finished your book and, I don't know. I thought I'd call to let you know I finished it. And, well, you said maybe we could go out and chat about it. So yeah, that's what I'm doing, letting you know I'm done. So okay, I guess call me back. Bye. Again, this is Lisa."

Lisa hung up.

"Oh my God. You are so lame." Cathy said.

"I know. I hate talking on those machines. I'm such an idiot."

"You got that right. Does he even have your number?"

"What?"

"Does he have your number to call? You said for him to call you back."

"I did?"

"Yeah. Does he have your number?"

Lisa thought about their exchange. And no, it wasn't an exchange. He only gave her his number. "Ah, crap. Now what do I do?"

"Call him back."

"No way."

"Well, how's he going to call you, Einstein?"

Lisa thought this through. She wasn't listed. Jillian's wouldn't give him her number for security reasons. Jonathan wouldn't bother asking Frank. "Keith," she said. "If he really wants it, he can get it from Keith."

"Whatever. Why don't you just call him back? What if Keith has left on a month long vacation and Jonathan doesn't see him?"

"Good point." But she was making Lisa suspicious. "Why do you all of a sudden care about me contacting a boy?"

"Cause I've watched you the past two days devour that book. And last night when you were crying and laughing all within a matter of half an hour, I just assumed it's something you are dying to talk about."

Cathy was right. Lisa was anxious for some answers. There was something about the intimacy of reading about someone's life that you just met. It was surreal being able to picture Jonathan as she made her way through the book and wondering how close to the truth it all was. "I just don't know if it's all true. His sister died."

"Really?"

"Well, I don't know really. That's when I was crying. But I don't know if it really happened. Can you make up things like that when you are writing a story about yourself?"

"I don't know."

"Do authors add things for the sensationalism factor? I think I would be so pissed if it wasn't true. But, then, I'm sad if it is."

"Good God. Call him back and leave your number. Maybe he'll call tonight and you'll be able to find out."

Lisa's curiosity stifled her uneasiness. She dialed again.

"Hi, this is Jonathan Bach."

She waited for the beep.

"Hello?"

"Oh, uh, hello?" Lisa stammered.

"Yes, hello. This is Jonathan Bach. Can I help you?"

"Oh, geez, I thought it was your machine."

"Nope. It's me. Who's this?"

"Oh, sorry. It's Lisa."

"Hey."

"From Jillian's."

"I know."

"I had just left you a message."

"You did? I just walked in. Yeah, it's blinking. Funny, how that always makes me feel special. A blinking beacon on my little black machine."

"I finished your book."

"You did? That was fast."

"Then, well, I forgot to leave my number so I was calling back to leave it."

Jonathan was silent a moment. "Do you want me to hang up and you can call back and leave it on the machine?"

"Why would I do that? I'm talking to you now."

"I was trying to be funny."

"Oh."

"What'd you think? Five words or less."

"Five words or less? Boy, that's tough."

"I wish I could have told my editor that after her first read."

"Was she rough on it?"

"You can say that. It took a year and a half from her first read to get it into the galley you read."

"Really?" Lisa never thought about how much time went in to getting a book published.

"So now your challenge is five words or less."

Lisa thought for a few seconds before asking, "Did your sister really die?"

"Right to the meat."

"It's five words. Did she?"

"What if I said you had to have dinner with me to find out the answer to that?"

"I'd say how soon can you be ready and where should I meet you?"

"I'd tell you I'll be ready in fifteen and tell me where you live and I'll pick you up."

"I can meet you somewhere," Lisa replied.

"Are you afraid of me?"

"No. That's not it." Cathy's warning of 'always have your car for an emergency exit' sifted through her mind. "It would just be more convenient."

"I think it would be more convenient if I came to pick you up." Softer, he added, "Is that okay?"

"Okay. Okay. I'm at 41 Dravus. Do you know where Dravus is?"

"Can't say that I do."

"It's down the street from Jillian's." Lisa gave him directions.

"Okay, it's 5:30. I'll be there at 6:00. Any particular place you want to go to dinner?"

"Anyplace but Denny's."

"Deal."

Lisa hung up and Cathy started in. "See, aren't you glad I made you call him back?"

"You didn't *make* me."

"Oh, okay. Aren't you glad I led you down the path of enlightenment in order to get yourself a date tonight?"

"It's not a date."

"What do you call getting picked up by a boy to go out to dinner?"

"I offered to meet him somewhere and he wanted to come pick me up."

"Exactly. A date. He wanted this to count as a date."

"No. He didn't. We are just going out to talk about his book. Probably to McDonalds or something. Not a date." Even if it was a date, Lisa wasn't anxious about it. Jonathan did not seem like the one-night-stand kinda guy. She knew she didn't have to worry about him asking her back to his place at the end of the night. She was pretty sure he wouldn't even try to kiss her.

"Oh, naïve, little cousin, when are you going to get it?"

"Shut up and help me decide what I'm going to wear on my *non*-date."

"See. Worried about what you're going to wear. Totally a date. A date, a date, a date." Cathy danced to the bedroom. "Little cousin's got a date."

"Just something casual," Lisa said to her back.

She pulled a top from her closet. "Here."

"Shocker. Black. Why does it always have to be black?"

"Because that's what Seattle wears."

"But it's already so dreary all the time. Why not bright colors?"

"Because we don't want to throw off the chemical balance of the city."

Lisa stared at her.

"I'm kidding. Pick out whatever you want."

Lisa looked at Cathy's side of the closet. Black, gray, dark blue, lighter black, darker gray. "I'll just pick something of my own."

Lisa pulled on a green pair of jeans and a clingy flowered shirt. She could feel every pound she had gained in the past few months sausaging around her bra straps. "We have got to stop eating late night. No more French fry runs."

"Oh, little cousin. That's the joy of life. Midnight food runs and French fries at Nickerson Street Bar. We can not deprive ourselves of these wondrous things." Cathy bounced up and down on her bed.

"Even when our thighs reach redwood proportions?" Lisa pulled the tight shirt off over her head struggling to suck in her folds.

"Especially when. Boys don't like skinny girls."

"Where'd you hear that? Donuts-R-Us?"

"There's nothing wrong with some meat on your bones."

"Yeah, but when you feel like a beached whale, it's time to change a few things." Lisa chose a loose-fitting cotton shirt that matched close enough.

"There, that's cute. Not black and not tight. This could almost pass as a non-date." Cathy followed Lisa to the bathroom. "Uh, oh, but if you're curling your hair, it crosses back into date territory."

Lisa switched the curling iron back to off. "See, not a date."

"Are you putting makeup on?"

"Nope."

"You should put a little on."

"What?"

"Just a little. Here, I'll help." She grabbed her tools and started to make Lisa's face.

"Not too much. I don't want too much."

"It'll be fine. Relax."

"Seriously, Cathy. Just a little."

She finished quickly and Lisa had to admit it was a good job. "Thank you."

"What time is he picking you up?"

"6:00."

"Oops. Strike 1. It's 6:05."

"Maybe he's lost."

"Yeah, maybe."

They went in the living room. Cathy put on her Sade CD.

"Oh, please."

"This is no ordinary love," she sang and twirled with her arms spread wide. "No ordinary love."

"Stop. Stop. Stop. Please. Stop.".

Which only prompted Cathy to sing louder. "I gave you all the love, my God, I gave you all that I could give, gave you love. You took my love." The music from the player could no longer be heard behind Cathy's animated rendition.

Cathy ducked as Lisa flung the closest pillow towards her. She recovered and glanced at her watch."6:09."

"God, stop. You're making me nervous. He probably missed the sign. You know how the street sign is hidden coming from the south."

"Yep. Probably it." She turned Sade down, but immediately broke into, "When the moon hits your eye like a big pizza pie, that's amore!"

"Great. Entertainment while I wait. Wonders never cease at the Queen Cathy abode."

"Come on sing it with me. When the moon hits your eye like a big pizza pie—"

"—that's amore!" Lisa did join in.

"6:14," Cathy chimed.

"Well, good thing it's not a date or he would only have one more minute before I was done waiting."

"About that rule. Why fifteen minutes?"

"What do you mean?"

"Why the magic number fifteen? If the guy's one minute late, isn't he late?"

"Yeah, but I think fifteen minutes is a fair enough amount of time to wait until writing them off. Don't you?"

"I don't know. What if they have a good excuse?"

"Like what? And is there any excuse why they can't call if they're going to be late?"

"Well, last week when that one guy was late, what was his excuse?"

"Who? Brad?"

"Yeah, the construction worker guy that took you to see Jurassic Park. He was like twenty minutes late. So what was his excuse?"

"He didn't need one. He had fine abs." Lisa laughed.

"God, and you say I'm the pig. 6:16."

"Well, it was kind of a quick plan to go to dinner. Maybe it took him longer to get ready than he thought. Had to pick just the right tie."

"He wears ties?"

"Every day."

"What a dork."

"Yeah, he is." Lisa didn't think he was as big a dork as she once did. Not after getting to talk with him on the all-nighter. And certainly not after reading his book. She was hoping that tonight would further show her a side of him that would erase all her first impressions, but she also knew the possibilities of that might be slim. Still, she was excited.

"And you're going out with him why?"

"We are not going *out*. We're just going out."

"Semantics."

"Really. We're not going out. It's cool to read his book and be able to talk about it. He's actually not that bad. It was nice having an intellectual conversation with a guy in a bar. You know, it's usually...what are you drinking? Wanna do a shot? Bet I can shoot a beer in ten seconds or less. Exhausting. And we actually had a nice chat the other night."

"For six hours."

"I know. That's the craziest part. It didn't even seem like that long."

"Eighteen minutes late." Cathy restarted her singing, "This is no ordinary love."

The doorbell chimed.

"Saved by the bell. Not a minute too soon. It's your knight in shining armor." Cathy bowed with a double twisting flair of her arm.

"Any other clichés you can get out before I answer it."

"Better late than never. This looks like the beginning of a beautiful—"

"Shut up." Lisa pushed the intercom. "Hello."

"Hey, Lisa. It's Jonathan."

"Come on up. Apartment 25 on the second floor. Stairs are right in front of you."

"What? No chastising for being late?" Cathy was right on her shoulder.

"We'll get to that. Are you going to hang out right here and hover?"

"Of course. Why would I miss this?"

"Yes, of course. Why would you?"

A soft knock interrupted their banter.

"Ooh, big manly knock," Cathy mocked.

"Behave." Lisa opened the door. "Hi."

"Hey. Sorry I'm late. I ended up on the wrong side of Queen Anne and I was on West Dravus."

"That's all right, maybe just a call would have been nice." Lisa knew Cathy was listening around the corner and wanted her to see that she did address it.

"Well, normally I would have called, but remember...I don't have your number. You never left it for me."

The fact that he had actually thought of calling impressed Lisa. "Then I guess you're forgiven. Come on in while I get my jacket."

Jonathan followed her into the living room where, of course, Cathy had perched. "Don't mind her." Lisa pointed as a way of introduction. "That's my cousin, Cathy."

"Hi, Cathy. Jonathan." He moved forward to shake her hand.

"You're late, Jonathan.".

"Yeah, I already heard that from Lisa."

"She doesn't like late."

"I will remember that for future dates."

"Ha. See, Lisa. It is a *date*." Cathy called loud enough so Lisa heard her in the bedroom. She tried to ignore the heat tingling through her face.

Lisa returned to the living room, trying to give Cathy her sternest glare, but Cathy raised her eyebrows to match the smirk on her face. Pulling on her coat, Lisa said to Jonathan, "You ready?"

Jonathan looked relieved. "Yup."

"Okay, let's go. Bye Cathy."

"Bye bye, little chickadees. I won't wait up." She winked at Lisa.

Again the heat arose, but Jonathan acted like he didn't hear. "Nice meeting you, Cathy."

"Oh, you don't have to make nice with her. She's actually an evil cousin that we keep locked up."

"Little cousin, you know you love me. Come here and give me a hug."

"Nooo." Lisa pushed Jonathan roughly toward the door. "Go, go."

They made it in the hall and Lisa slammed the door in Cathy's face. They could still hear her. "I'll get you my little precious. I'll get you when you get home," she cackled.

Lisa saw the panicked look in Jonathan's face. "Don't worry. She's, um, she's just weird. She's not on medication or anything. She just has a, uh, unique look on life."

"That must make for an interesting roommate."

"It does. Never a dull moment."

"When I think about some of my roommates from college, I would have taken weird over psycho any day."

"You got stuck with the dysfunctional ones too?"

"Boy, did I. Let me tell you."

Their conversation lasted nonstop until they got to the restaurant. Jonathan told Lisa about his roommates that left pizza rotting under their beds and snuck girls in for late night romps and she told him of hers that left piles of dirty dishes for weeks at a time in the sink and dried their hair in the living room shedding all over.

They pulled into a garage and Jonathan asked, "Have you ever been to Cutters?"

"No, I haven't. I've been down here at Pike's Place, but never to Cutters."

"Good. You'll like it. It's one of the first restaurants that has banned smoking." He paused, "You don't smoke do you?"

"Just quit last week." Lisa saw his puzzled look. "No. I don't smoke. I was kidding."

"I guess I'll have to get used to your sarcasm."

"It takes a lot of getting used to. I'm not sure you want that challenge." Lisa got out of the car before he could reply. She wasn't sure where this relationship was going and was surprised by Jonathan's assumption that he would be getting used to her sarcasm. Getting used to her anything. It caused her to figuratively take a step back. "Which way?"

"Over here." Jonathan led her to the elevators. When they got to the lobby of the restaurant he went straight to the hostess to announce their arrival. The restaurant was dimly lit and most tables were occupied by couples dressed in classy evening wear, enjoying flutes of sparkling wine. Outside the expansive windows, the green knoll of a water-view park twinkled with lights that illuminated couples protecting each other from the Seattle evening chill. The ambiance inside and out was one of muted romance. Lisa realized Jonathan wasn't just interested in hashing out his book. At the hostess stand, she heard Jonathan mumble that they were running a bit late. He had made reservations. Cathy was right; this was definitely a date.

Returning, he said, "We'll just be a couple minutes."

"Okay."

"Do you want to wait in the bar?"

"No. It's okay here."

"All right."

Lisa watched Jonathan fumble with his tie. If it was an attempt to straighten it, it wasn't successful. Now it was off-center to the left an inch. It was another of what he called 'signature ties': an old red schoolhouse with stick figure children playing outside. He wore it over a long sleeved dark blue oxford and khaki colored Dockers with a brown belt. Brown shoes and a dark blue sports coat completed his look. If only having his book to go by, Lisa would never have quite pictured Jonathan like this. She smiled with the thought that authors really could portray themselves any way they wanted. His book character never prompted her to think 'nerd,' but here in the flesh was a different account.

Jonathan glanced at the host stand with anticipation. The hostess had left. He was trying to figure out the silence since the elevator. Their conversation had gone fine on the way over, then it wavered. After he admitted he would need to 'get used to her sarcasm' remark, she seemed to get distant, fast. *Gotta play it cool, man. Go slow*. He saw Lisa watching him work with his tie. He felt he looked sharp with his sports coat on, but wished he'd had more time to plan his outfit. The Dockers were the cleanest pants he had, and they'd been worn twice.

Lisa looked nice. He wasn't much for fashion and didn't know how to explain her attire, but she did look nice. "You look nice," he said.

"Thanks. You too. Nice tie." She gestured to where he still held tight to the end.

"Thanks. It's one of my signature ties."

"Yeah, I figured."

Jonathan knew he had already explained the ties to Lisa but it didn't stop him. "I got all these ties from the Cancer Research Center and it's little kids that actually do the artwork and they get proceeds."

"I know. It's cool."

The hostess called, "Bach."

"That's us."

They followed the hostess to their table and not soon enough. Lisa had heard that story about the ties at least three times now. She was beginning to rethink this 'date' or 'non-date.' She enjoyed his intellect and it was appealing to be sitting with the author of a book she read; but he was so socially awkward. She decided the best way to approach this was like a job interview. Formal. Detached. There was nothing date-like about it.

"Here you go." Jonathan held out her chair at the table. A cozy little table tucked away in a darkly windowed corner facing the glittering lights of West Seattle. Nothing like a job interview.

"I wonder if they have anything lighter. You know, if we're going to be going over your book and stuff," Lisa suggested.

"Ah, yeah, sure." Jonathan asked the hostess, "Do you?"

"But, sir, I thought you said—"

"I know, I know. But maybe lighted would be better."

They were seated at the new table and Lisa noted that Jonathan had *asked* for the cozy, romantic table. "This is a lot better."

"Perfect." Jonathan said.

They ordered an appetizer of crab stuffed mushrooms and Jonathan ordered his Shirley Temple. "Do you want anything to drink?"

"No, I'll just have water."

"You can have something to drink if you want."

"I know."

"I mean just because I don't drink I don't expect you not to."

"Okay."

"So, do you want a drink?"

"No, thanks."

Lisa lifted the menu to get a better look at the items. Actually, she lifted it to create a barrier. The thought of excusing herself to the bathroom and walking right out the front door tempted her for a moment. But then she remembered she had not driven. Cathy's voice sounded in her head, 'Told ya so.' Something needed to change, quickly. Using her peripheral, she witnessed Jonathan bump his glass and barely catch it before water spilled across the table. She couldn't help but laugh.

"Oh, sure, make fun of the klutz," Jonathan said, wiping the few drops that had escaped.

"It just doesn't seem possible that you can spill and bump into things that much," she said.

"I know. I used to tell myself that in some way I threw off the balance of the earth. You know kind of like a chemical reaction that my bodily fluids had with the energy of the world. And so everything kind of teeters on the edge near me anyway. When my energy gets close to contacting a solid object, it sends it toppling over before my body even touches it. So really me grabbing it, is just a reaction to something that happened before I even had an effect on it."

"What?" Lisa stared at him.

"I had to come up with something to explain it. Saying I was a klutz just got too boring," he said with a smile.

She was relieved that he was just joking. "So you don't really believe that, right?"

"It's just fun to look at things in a different way sometimes."

"Seems like a logically thought out excuse. But you'd think knowing that, you could still prevent the glasses from toppling by keeping your energy at a prescribed distance. So I'm sticking with the fact that you're a klutz," she said.

"Think what you like, but you may be sitting here with the first human with a chemical makeup that has the power to throw the earth off its axis."

Thankfully, their banter had returned and they eased back into light conversation as they ate dinner. Finishing her last bite, Lisa jumped right in. "Did your sister really die?"

"It's a non-fiction book."

"I know. But did she really die?" Lisa didn't know if a non-fiction story had to be all true.

"Yes. She really died."

"Ah, God. I'm so sorry."

"It was a long time ago."

"And was it in a car crash like you wrote about."

Jonathan gave a small laugh. "Yes, Lisa. It's a true story."

"It's just so bizarre. I mean, I didn't know if you made that up to make the story more exciting. I'm sorry, I didn't mean that was exciting or anything. I mean, I actually cried when I read it." Lisa felt bad.

"You cried?" Jonathan asked.

"Of course. Cathy even made fun of me. I was bawling."

"That makes me feel good."

"What?" Now Lisa thought *he* sounded unfeeling.

"No, not because...well, yeah, this is weird. Not good because my sister died, but good that it evoked emotion in a reader."

"It was so sad. Then I didn't know if it was true or not. And I thought how mad I'd be if it wasn't. Because I would have felt duped. But then I felt guilty because I really didn't want that to have happened to you."

"It happened. This is weird because you're the first person who has read it that didn't know about the accident. I didn't realize that incident would have such a strong impact on readers."

"Reading up to it, I kept thinking, no way, no way, all his foreshadowing—the unbuckled seatbelt, the icy roads, the running late—was *not* going to lead up to an accident."

"So that worked, huh?"

"Totally. Then even when you were talking about looking over at your sister and she had the blood dripping out of her mouth and I knew that meant she wasn't going to make it but still I was hoping it wasn't true."

The waitress approached and dropped them into silence. She cleared the plates and asked, "Would you like to see a dessert menu?"

"I think some dessert would be good. How about you, Mel—" Jonathan stumbled and retracted. "Lisa?"

But Lisa caught it. She knew he almost called her by another name, but she ignored it. It didn't really matter anyway. "Sure. I'll take a menu." Lisa was sure he didn't want her to ask about the slip he made.

And sure enough, Jonathan quickly jumped back into the conversation. "So, anything else besides the accident that aroused your curiosity?"

"Of course. Where do you want me to start? Should I bring out my notes?"

"That's funny."

"No, really. Do you want to see them?" Lisa reached down for her purse.

"Are you serious?"

"I told you I was an English major. You're not getting away with anything." Lisa pulled the galley up to the table.

"Oh boy. You are serious." Jonathan saw she wasn't kidding with Post-Its marking several pages and three pages of notes folded inside the front cover. "Okay. Shoot."

Lisa worked through her notes and questions as they both worked through turtle pie and apple crumble. At one point, Jonathan took out a tiny notepad and wrote something down. Lisa peered over. "What are you writing?"

"Nothing."

"Come on, what?"

"I just wrote down what you said about the analogy of flying in the plane 'above the clouds' and being 'above the clouds' of understanding."

"I was curious if that's what you meant when you wrote it."

"No. No. It's good. I didn't think about that as I wrote it. But I will sure sound profound if I explain it that way on Larry King."

"What? Isn't that plagiarism if you use my idea?"

"Not if you didn't write it down."

"But I did write it down. It's right here." Lisa handed a page of notes to him. "And don't you think you should have meant it that way if you're going to lay claim to it?"

"Who will ever know?" Jonathan teased. He crumbled her paper and pretended to toss it over his shoulder.

Lisa laughed and shook her head. "It's so weird. All these years of reading and analyzing what authors meant in particular passages. It's all a bunch of crap, isn't it?"

"What do you mean?"

"I mean just now when I really thought I'd gotten into the mind of the author and then I ask you about it and you're like, 'Hmm, interesting, I think I'll use that.' It wasn't what you meant at all."

Jonathan paused. "Well, maybe it was what I meant. When I was writing, I was just writing. Getting the story down. All that literature stuff, you know, metaphors and personification and allusion, I didn't really think about that stuff when I was trying to get my story out. I was just trying to get a story out."

"Exactly," Lisa exclaimed. "So like I said, that analysis stuff is a bunch of crap."

"I wouldn't call it exactly crap. But you do need to have an open mind. I found my professors were always like: It is *this* way and *this* is what they meant and there is *no other* way to decipher it. I don't think it should be that way."

"I know. But so many of my English teachers were so uppity and God forbid you suggested something different than what they had already pointed out."

"Like what?" Jonathan prodded.

"One time I wrote a paper on DH Lawrence's *The Rocking Horse Winner*."

"Yeah, I read that."

"So my thesis was that it was all about masturbation."

"What? The story where the little boy rode the rocking horse to envision winning picks for his grandpa, or uncle, or someone?" Jonathan asked.

"Yeah, except when he rides the horse, he rocks back and forth and back and forth and harder and harder and—"

"No, you didn't. You wrote *that* was about masturbation?"

"Of course." Lisa smiled. "Didn't the little boy go blind?" she asked with her eyebrows raised.

"Well, he dies, right?"

"And if you're dead, you're blind," Lisa stated.

"Did you really think that?"

"Who knows?" Lisa said. "But it was more fun than writing on the thesis that ninety percent of the class wrote about. You know, the obsession of wealth leading to a tragedy. Boring."

"That would be a unique way of looking at it," Jonathan conceded. "What grade did you get?"

"I didn't get a grade. I got the paper back with the professor's writing across the top: 'Please redo, choosing one of the themes we discusssed in class,'" Lisa mimicked.

"What a jerk."

"Yes. She was the typical English elitist."

"Did you redo the paper?"

"Of course. The standard five-paragraph essay discussing the theme of a family's desperate attempt to keep up with the Joneses."

"And your grade?"

"An A with a mark down to a B because she counted it late," Lisa said. "But anyway, now I know nobody knows what an author's actual intent is and even if you *think* you know you're probably just coming up with some good idea that an author will use in his interviews if he's lucky enough to meet you before he goes on tour." Lisa teased Jonathan.

"That's for sure. Got any other golden nuggets over there in that mess of notes?" Jonathan tried to grab for her pile.

Lisa lightly slapped his hand away. "Any more nuggets are gonna cost you."

They moved on to coffee and then to hot chocolate before realizing they were the only ones left in the restaurant. The waitress was across the room filling salt and pepper shakers and she came over when Jonathan waved to her.

"Sorry. We didn't realize you were closing up."

"No problem. I have to finish my side duties anyway. Are you ready for your check?"

"I think so. Lisa, do you want anything else?"

Again, Jonathan had started her name with the Meh— but it was so quick that she couldn't tell if it was really the start of a name or more of a Mmmm. Lisa replied, "No. I'm done. What time is it?"

Jonathan clipped the table as he lifted his watch to check. "One o'clock."

"What?"

The waitress chimed in. "Yup. One o'clock. We just locked the front door. But you can hang out for a few minutes while I finish."

"No. No. We're ready," Lisa said. The waitress left and Lisa playfully accosted Jonathan. "Again. With you. I know you are—what did you call it—self-employed, and don't have to get up. But me? I can't stay out this late."

"Hey. You're the one with all the questions. You can't blame this on me."

"You're right, but I really need to get home and get some sleep. Mondays are my worst days, full day of school, and gym and right to Jillian's until about eleven. I'm going to be wiped out tomorrow."

"Yeah, but you'll get to see me at Jillian's. At least you'll have something to look forward to."

She wasn't sure yet if she would be looking forward to that or if it was another thing on her list for the day. For a moment she believed she was looking forward to it. But she didn't want to let him know that yet. She smiled and nodded. The waitress came with the check and Lisa reached down for her purse.

Jonathan grabbed the black pocket that held the check. "No, no, no. I've got this."

"That's okay. Let's split it."

Jonathan persisted. "It's okay. I get to write it off because we talked about the book."

"Really?" Lisa wasn't sure what that meant. But it sounded good; sounded important.

"Yup. Any business to do with the book, I get to write off on my taxes. I just got a new computer and printer and fax. All a write off. And dinners where I talk about the book. Write off."

"Sounds good. What if we go to Europe and talk about the book? Write off?"

"I don't know about that. But I should look into it. Would you go to Europe with me?"

An unanswerable question. Lisa ignored it as she pushed back her chair. "I think I'll go to the bathroom before we head out."

"I'll take care of this and meet you at the front," Jonathan said.

He silently chastised himself again. He knew he had pushed too far. Asking her to go to Europe with him. What was he thinking? Slow down. But she seemed so...well, so Melissa. Or he wanted her to be Melissa so bad. So far, she was matching up pretty well.

Only she was not as charmed by him as he thought Melissa would be. She seemed open and carefree some of the time, but he could feel her pull back whenever it got too serious. *Geez Jonathan, you invited her to go to Europe with you. What do you expect?* And on the first date. That wasn't really a date. She just finished the book and wanted to talk. *But I did pick her up, and we did have dinner, and I did pay. It's technically a date. I'm counting it as a date.*

Jonathan began to sweat. How does this end? *Do I try to kiss her goodnight? Do I ask to see her again? What pretense do I use to get her to see me again?* She went through all her questions on the book. It seems pretty well wrapped up. *Unless she likes me. Does she like me?*

Jonathan signed the credit slip and headed toward the front

lobby. What's not to like? *People like me. I dress sharp. I tip well. And I'm going to be a famous author. Of course, she likes me.*

Lisa was already waiting at the front of the restaurant. As Jonathan approached, Lisa smiled. His napkin had stuck in the waistband of his belt and hung to the side of his hip. She was beginning to consider it cute, rather than dorky. She grabbed at the napkin and he reflexively turned sideways leaving her hand to awkwardly graze the front of his pants.

"Oh, God," she said, laughing. "That's embarrassing."

Jonathan looked down and realized that she was grabbing to pull the napkin that clung to him.

"I'm so sorry. I was just—" Lisa stammered.

"I know. It's okay." He pulled the napkin from his belt and laid it on the hostess desk. "I guess you should know that along with that whole earth's axis thing I was telling you about, I also have this uncanny knack to attract objects to me."

"Oh, really."

"Yes, like a magnet. Is it working on you?"

She stared blankly at Jonathan. Was he looking for an answer? This night was so weird. There were points when she was starting to like this guy. He was intelligent and he was a published author, or almost anyways. But then a second later he would do something so cheesy or say something so ridiculous that she couldn't even believe she was here with him. She felt this now. And she didn't answer. She turned toward the door.

"Hey, I was only kidding. It was a joke." Jonathan followed her out.

"I know. I'm just tired. I'm sorry. I'm ready to go."

"Okay."

They walked without a word to the car and most of the way home. About a block from Lisa's house, she started her goodbye. "Thanks so much for dinner and the conversation. I had a good time." She didn't know how she wanted this to end. Was he going to try and kiss her? Did she want him to? She didn't know yet. It wasn't really a date so she didn't think he would try. But he might. She was, however, grateful that he hadn't put her in an awkward position and invited her back to his place. She hadn't thought he would, but she also thought that of some of the other dates she'd been on.

"I had a really good time, too," Jonathan said.

He parked at the curb and Lisa didn't catch him before he turned his car off. "You don't have to walk me up. It's late." She looked at her watch. "Holy crap, it's two already." She opened her door and he opened his.

"It's not a bother. Besides remember I don't have to get up in the morning." He came around to her side of the car.

"Great. That makes me feel so much better. I'll think about you when my alarm goes off at 5:30." She stepped out on the curb and Jonathan reached past her to shut her door.

"I hope you'll think of me before that." He made an attempt to grab for her hand, but she quickly stepped away.

"I guess I'll see you tomorrow. Thanks again." Lisa hurried toward the door and waved to him as she let herself in.

Jonathan watched her retreat through the opened door. He was sorry it ended so abruptly. But he wasn't desolate for long.

He flew home hardly able to contain the knowledge of what he knew was true. The moment he got home, he grabbed a sheet of computer paper and scribbled out.

February 21, 1993
Dear Melissa,

It's you. You're here.

Love,
Jonathan

CHAPTER 20

The next day at school was impossible. Lisa kept replaying every moment. In the middle of a timed test, she heard Jonathan laugh. In the middle of a steno exercise, she thought about things he'd said. In the middle of a practice drill, she smiled at the image of his napkin hanging from his belt. During typing drills, Lisa recalled the awkward fumble to grab her hand. She finally gave up trying to concentrate and put in a clean piece of paper.

Jonathan,

It's useless trying to concentrate on school today. I keep thinking about you. So I thought I'd write you a letter...to practice my typing, of course.

You are different than any guy I've ever met. It's a weird connection though. A mental one. You're very intelligent and I enjoyed our evening together last night. I don't know how to explain it. I have always been drawn to athletic types. Throwing a football or shooting hoops on dates. You don't seem athletic. Are you? But I've never had such long talks and so many things to talk about with anyone either. It is refreshing, yet different.

Do we have anything in common? I haven't even had the chance to ask. Do you play racquetball? Or run? Or rollerblade? I could teach you how to play racquetball. Would you even be interested in that? I enjoy the mental stimulation, but would you be interested in anything physical? Sports, I mean.

Well, class is almost over and I don't even know if I'll give this to you. I must admit, I am feeling somewhat excited thinking about seeing you at Jillian's tonight. Talk to you later.

Lisa

Lisa pulled the paper from the typewriter and folded it into her notebook. Emily, her classmate, interrupted her thoughts. "You must have aced that timed write."

"What do you mean?"

"You're smiling from ear to ear. Did you do good?"

"I think so." Lisa wasn't ready to share any thoughts yet. She didn't have them clear herself.

"Dude, do you think it's really her?" James asked.

Jonathan had just spent the last hour recapping his date with Lisa to his brother. "Man, bro, it's close."

"That's so cool. Take it slow, though. You want to make sure."

"Haven't I taken it slow enough? I've waited for her for four years. I've already invested so much time into this relationship."

"But she doesn't know that. It's brand new for her. Have you thought if you're going to tell her about all that?" James asked.

"All what?'

"You know, the whole Melissa-exercise thing?"

"I don't know. What do you think? She did mention she wasn't sure she believed in the whole idea of soul mates," Jonathan explained.

"That's tough. She may freak out. She may not understand. Man, I don't know—"

"I don't think she'll freak out. She's pretty cool. She might even think it was a neat idea."

"But if she doesn't, she may think you're a psycho, especially if she doesn't have any grasp of a soul mate or believe in serendipity. That's a tough call, bro."

James had a point. Jonathan wasn't sure if he was going to tell her anyway. "I did accidentally call her Melissa once, and another time started to."

"What'd she say?"

"She didn't say anything, but she did look up at me so I know she caught it."

"You better be careful. That'll blow it for sure."

"I know. Well, gotta go. She's working tonight and I need to iron my pants."

"Man," James said. "You got it bad."

"What do you mean? I always iron."

"Yeah, right, whatever, bro. Catch ya later."

"Catch ya later." Jonathan liked that saying. He would use it tonight.

"Are you smitten?" Cathy had been following Lisa around since she got home from school.

"Smitten? What does that even mean?"

"You know, smitten. Smitten as a kitten." She sang, "Ah, little cousin is smitten as a kitten who has lost her mitten, la, la, la."

"Again. What is smitten?"

"You know, got it bad? In love? On cloud nine? Bitten by the luuuuuv bug?"

"How do I know? I don't even know him that well." Lisa tried to keep her face hidden from Cathy. She was sure the smile she had just thinking about Jonathan would set Cathy off on a barrage of questions. The questions came anyway.

"Oh, you know. Have you thought about him all day? Do you have butterflies in your tummy? Wrote any love letters?"

Heat crept across her cheeks. *How did she know I wrote a letter?*

"You did write a letter. Let me see, let me see," Cathy pleaded.

"You don't even know what you're talking about."

"Oh no? Let me see it. Your face is red as a beet. Don't lie to me. You know you wrote one. Let me see it."

"Don't you have like anything to do?"

"Nope. Left my whole afternoon open to harass you."

"Someone should give you a raise, cause you're good at it."

"I know. Now, give me the letter."

"It's not that big of a deal. Besides, I don't know if I'm giving it to him. I wrote it real quick in class."

"Enough. Give it to me, give it to me, my pretty." Cathy twisted her hands and hunched over like the wicked witch.

"Do you ever just act normal?" Lisa handed over the letter from her bag.

"Normal. That's no fun. Now let's see the budding writer that you are." Cathy perused through the letter and tossed it quickly back. "That's no fun."

"What? What do you mean, no fun?"

"Where's the part where you want to ravish his body and do naughty things to him?" Cathy asked.

"You're so bad." Lisa shook her head.

"I know. Now where's that part?"

"I'm not writing that."

"Come on. Let him know. I have an Anaïs NIn book in my drawer if you want some ideas on what to write."

"Anaïs Nin?"

"The erotica writer. What? She was never on your reading list in college?"

"Can't say I've ever heard that one."

"They say you have to read her books with one hand." Cathy threw her head back and laughed at her own little inside joke.

"You know, things aren't all that funny when no one understands what you're talking about," Lisa said. "Now, what are you talking about?"

"I'm talking about writing a real love letter. Not one about racquetball and how intellectual he is. How boring." She drew out the final word.

"I don't even know how I feel yet. I'm not writing that."

"Do you like him? You've spent quite a bit of time with him already. You have to have some idea."

"Yeah, I like him—"

"Then write some juicy stuff."

"—but, I don't know how I like him yet." Lisa could see the potential of a relationship, but there were some things that were so awkward about Jonathan. Thinking about it, she realized maybe not 'awkard' but just 'different' from any previous relationship she had. Was that a bad thing? Or a good thing? Past relationships had ended for one reason or another. Perhaps leaning toward 'different' was the recipe for a lasting partnership.

"Why do you have to be so analytical all the time? Just go with the feeling and let it out. Maybe it will get you laid for once," she said.

"God, you're so bad. That's not what I'm trying for."

"You should try for it once. Maybe you'll like it."

"You're going to hell, you know that, right?"

"At least I'll have fun on my way."

"That's for sure. Now, leave me alone. Some of us have to go to work."

"Oh, yes, work, work, work. You have fun with that, little cousin. I'm going to The Pink Door to see Fi Fi La Ray perform a monologue on the intricacies of life in Grand Paree." Cathy tossed a fake boa around her shoulders and glided to her bedroom.

"You are so weird."

Left alone for a minute, Lisa's thoughts returned to Jonathan. She had butterflies, she admitted, applying a bit more makeup than usual. She wondered, would he like this shirt or should she wear a skirt instead of pants? She'd go shopping this weekend for some cute tops. *Oh, this is ridiculous. I barely know the guy. He could be a psycho, for heaven's sake.*

Jonathan gave himself a pep talk as he opened the door to Jillian's. *Be smooth, be funny, you're looking good today, good tie, clean shirt, ironed pants, don't be overly eager, don't say anything dorky.*

"Hey Lisa, Lisa, Bo Bisa." Jonathan couldn't believe what came out of his mouth.

For Lisa, the thought came quick and clear; *dork*. But her stomach clenched in an unusual knot that thrust a bubble up through her throat as she answered in an uncomfortably high pitch, "Hey Jonathan, Jonathan, Bo Bonathan."

They both laughed awkwardly as Greg, who had walked up to the front desk, said, "Oh my God. I'm gonna be sick. Is this what I think it is?" He spread his arms to include them both.

"What?" Lisa asked.

"Are you two a...thing?"

"What? No," Lisa answered.

Jonathan said nothing.

Greg looked quick to him. "Well?"

"Huh? What are you talking about?" Jonathan stammered.

"Oh my God. Diana told me Keith was setting you two up. Spill it."

They both stared blankly and said nothing.

Greg pushed, "What's the deal?"

Lisa was interrupted by a customer. "Hi. Welcome to Jillian's. Did you want a table?"

Greg pulled Jonathan around the corner and up the stairs, but Lisa heard him say, "Come on, you're in my section today, buddy. I'll come back down and get your ball rack."

Upstairs, Greg wasted no time. "What's going on? Did you guys go out?"

Jonathan was excited to talk to someone about it. Someone

besides his brother and dad that always made the connections to Melissa with him. It would be good to get a perspective just on Lisa and the present without the history he knew.

"Yeah, we went out last night."

"And—"

"And what?"

"How'd it go?" Greg posted himself on the stool by Jonathan's table.

Jonathan wanted to blurt out his reply, but he was also enjoying Greg's interest in his life. "Don't you have customers to wait on?"

"Nah, man. You're my first one."

"Then I'll take the usual."

"Come on. Did you guys...you know?"

"You know, what? What? No. Not that."

"Why not? She's hot man," Greg said.

"I know that. But, no. It wasn't like that. How about that Shirley Temple?" Jonathan was stalling for time. He wasn't sure what to tell Greg about this. He wasn't sure what 'this' was.

"All right. All right. But when I come back, I want details."

Greg wasn't gone long and when he returned, Keith was approaching the table with a rack of balls.

"Hey, Jonathan. Lisa said you were up here but didn't get a table. What's going on?"

"What's going on is he was so nervous he couldn't even ask her for his rack of balls. Girls have that effect on guys." Greg laughed alone at his double entendre.

"What? Wait. I'm lost. Fill me in," Keith said.

"I'm still waiting for him to fill me in. They went out last night."

"And?" Keith set the rack of balls on the table.

"And nothing. He says he got nothing." Greg caught Keith up.

"I didn't say I got nothing. I said we didn't...well, you know... what you said." Jonathan felt embarrassed, not because he didn't have anything juicy to share, but because he wasn't sure they would understand the connection he felt with Lisa. The connection without sex.

"Well then, you got nothing." Greg was already losing interest. "You want anything to eat?"

"I'll take a salad."

"A salad? What's this? No burger with extra mayo and fries? Man, you really got it."

"Got what? I feel like a salad today," Jonathan said.

"Yeah, right. Trying to watch the waistline? Can you believe this, Keith? He's getting a salad."

"I'll take a salad too. Nothing wrong with eating healthy every once in a while." Keith half-smiled and lifted his head in quick understanding toward Jonathan.

Jonathan had already moved to the table and unloaded the balls carefully. He felt Keith watching him as he placed the ball carrier on the floor and reached for the rack above the table. He methodically clicked the balls into place. Keith brought his cue case to the table and continued looking at Jonathan as he unlatched it.

Finally Keith spoke, "I can wait all day, man."

Jonathan's smile spread as he placed his cue on the table and began its assembly. The light side of the cue slipped from his hand and snapped loudly as it landed. Jonathan recovered and connected it to the thick end. Then he looked at Keith. "Oh, man. She's great." He felt the emotion pour from his mouth as he said, "We've had such a good time."

"I told you." Keith finished assembling his cue and placed the case on the floor. "Does she feel the same way?" he asked returning to the level of the table.

"I don't know. Did she say anything about me when you checked in?" Jonathan held his breath.

"She just told me that you were up here and forgot to get a rack. I said 'that's weird' and she said Greg was harassing you. I didn't think that was any different than normal."

"Did she say why Greg was harassing us?" Jonathan deflated slightly. He was hoping for any clue.

"No. But she was checking in two other people, so we didn't really talk. Why? What was he harassing you about?"

"What was who harassing who about?" Greg appeared with Keith's drink.

"Just asking Jonathan what you were harassing him about at the front desk?" Keith said.

"You should have seen them all goo-goo eyes and acting like dumbshits in front of each other down there."

"We were not." Jonathan defended himself.

"Yeah, hey, Lisa, Lisa, Bo Bisa," Greg mocked in a sing-song. "You really need some help on your pick up lines."

"It wasn't a pick up line and besides she returned the greeting."

"Cause she's got it bad too. She's acting like a dufus."

"Really?" This inflated Jonathan.

"I'm not doing this." He mimicked like a high school girl, "What'd she say about me? Does she like me? Blah, blah, blah. I'm outta here."

As Greg retreated Keith asked, "So are you going to ask her out again?"

"Absolutely."

Lisa's shift seemed to last forever. She performed her duties amid constant stomach flutters, thinking of Jonathan upstairs. After a few hours, the anticipation rose because she knew he would probably be checking out soon. Still, he caught her off guard.

"Hey, how's it goin?" *Cool, Jonathan, be cool.*

"Oh, you know, keeping everyone at Jillian's happy."

"We're ready to check out. Keith's on his way down with the balls."

"Okay." Lisa fumbled in her pants pocket to pull out the folded up typewritten note. "I, uh, well I didn't know if we'd get a chance to talk much today, so I wrote you a letter."

"Cool. Thanks." *This is good, this is really good.*

Lisa thought he'd be a little more excited. She immediately

regretted giving it to him. "It's not that big a deal. I jotted down some thoughts I had. You don't have to write back or anything."

"Okay." Jonathan paused. "I was wondering—"

"Hey, Lisa, here's our rack," Keith interrupted. "I hope you stopped our time when Jonathan came down. Hate getting charged when we're not really playing."

"Stopped it as soon as he came down. Saved you the extra twenty-seven cents."

"Right on. Thanks," Keith said. "Jonathan, I'll walk out with you."

"Sounds good." Jonathan shoved the note in his coat pocket. "Guess I'll catch ya later." He was pleased with the cool way it sounded.

"Okay. Bye. Bye Keith."

Lisa wished she could take the letter back. He acted so aloof. Now she battled with her thoughts. Did he even like her? Was she assuming too much thinking he'd want to spend any more time with her? Why didn't he spend more time talking with her? Great. Now he'd read the letter and be uncomfortable and have to come and tell her he wasn't really interested and thanks, but no thanks. Lisa finished her evening in complete confusion.

CHAPTER 21

Jonathan raced home to rip open the letter. He first perused it, catching words here and there--mental, intelligent, anything in common. But then he slowed down, and took it in word for word. It was Melissa. He could feel it. Exact phrases that she wrote him over the past four years caressed his eyes. 'I keep thinking about you.' 'I could teach you how to—in this letter—play racquetball.' 'I am feeling somewhat excited about seeing you tonight.'

Jonathan didn't know if he should call James first or reply to the letter. He decided on James and as soon as he answered the phone, Jonathan said, "It's her. Man, I know it's her. Listen to this." He explained the letter and made the connections for James. "What do you think?"

"It sounds like you're on your way. But take it easy, bro. Slow."

"What do you mean? Why are you the cynic all of a sudden? This whole crazy scheme was your idea."

"I know. I know. Just make sure."

"How can you deny the letter? I didn't even ask her to write it. And I never mentioned anything to her about teaching me new things. You can't argue with that."

"I'm not saying it's not her. I'm just saying keep running her through tests."

"All right. All right. I gotta go, man. I'll call ya tomorrow." Jonathan didn't want his mood depleted further. Hanging up the phone, he rested her letter to the side of his keyboard and fired up his computer. He started his reply:

Dear Melis... Delete, delete, delete, delete, delete.

Dear Lisa,

I am so excited you are feeling the same way. I have loved my time with you so far. And yes, I want to learn how to play racquetball. I wanted to ask you out again and started to, but then Keith came up. I hope to get another chance to ask you soon. I would like to show you some things. Things I love about this city. I know you are fairly new to Seattle. Have you been to the Space Needle yet? If not, I'd like to take you. You would love the view. Let me know when you are free, because I can go any time. Hope to see you soon,

Jonathan

Jonathan read and reread what he'd written. It sounded familiar. He had written to Melissa many times about showing her the city. Was it enough? He really wanted her to know that he liked her, but also didn't want to seem too desperate. He would not lose Melissa now that he'd found her. He decided it was just right after a few changes and printed it out.

He went to bed excited. This letter was not going into a shoebox. It was going to Melissa!

CHAPTER 22

It was three days before Lisa saw Jonathan again at Jillian's. For three days, she chastised herself for giving him the letter. And for three days, she could not stop thinking about him. She even passed on a movie date the night before because she was sure Jonathan was going to call. He never did. Her heart jumped when she first saw him, taking in his now familiar attire.

"Lucy, I'm home." Jonathan tried the Ricky Ricardo accent and failed miserably.

"Hey." Lisa cringed as he confirmed, once again, his social awkwardness.

"How's it goin?"

"Good." Lisa was confused about how to act. Was she supposed to be excited to see him? Or was he just a 'regular' at Jillian's. Plus, she was upset he hadn't even called.

Jonathan was stumped. She wasn't being cold, but she wasn't as friendly as usual and she *had* written the letter. Didn't she remember? He had a reply for her in his coat pocket. It took all his willpower—and much prodding from James—not to call her these last three days and pressure too fast. But now she didn't seem to want to talk to him at all.

"I guess I'll take table 19 if it's open."

"Keith's up there. You want to join him?"

"That'll work." He struggled with what to do now and the idea of Melissa won as he reached in his pocket and pulled out the folded note. "Here. I wrote you back."

Lisa's heart raced and she grabbed the neatly folded sheet of paper. "Thanks."

As soon as Jonathan disappeared upstairs and Lisa checked that no one was coming toward the desk, she unfolded the letter. She felt the tension of excitement through her whole body as she read the letter through three times. He did want to spend more time with her. He wanted to show her Seattle. That was good, right? Why wouldn't he call then the last three days? Boys were so difficult to figure out sometimes. But, right now she didn't care. He did want to see her.

Upstairs, Keith pocketed a three-bumper bank shot as Jonathan reached his table. "Nice shot, man."

"Yeah, basically I've just beat myself three times in a row."

"Nice. Maybe I should get my own table today."

"Nah, I'm ready to play a real person. How's it goin'? You're in a better mood today."

"What do you mean?" Jonathan asked.

"Don't try and act like you haven't been moping the last few days." Keith circled the table gathering the balls for the rack.

"For sure. I thought we were going to have to serve you a box of tissues with these damn Shirley Temples." Greg joined in as he set down Jonathan's usual drink.

"I don't know what you guys are talking about." Jonathan assembled his cue.

"I know exactly why he was moping," Greg said.

"Please impart us with your keen insight, oh wise one," Keith prompted.

Greg went into his high school girl mimic again. "Cause Lisa, Lisa, Bo Bisa wasn't working."

"Come on. I wasn't moping."

"Please." Greg rolled his eyes before heading off to another table. "I'll be back to get your order."

"Well, you called her, didn't you?" Keith asked.

"No." Jonathan avoided Keith's stare.

"No? Why not?" he demanded.

"I don't know. My brother thought it would be better to play it cool."

"I don't know your brother, but he's an idiot."

"No, he's not." Jonathan was quick to defend James. "He's got a point. I don't want to seem too desperate."

Keith shook his head as he arranged the balls for the break. "But you like her, right? And she gave you a letter, right?"

"Yeah—" Jonathan paused.

"So she gave you a letter on Monday and now it's what, three, four days later. And you never got in contact with her?"

"When you put it like that—"

"When I put it like that? Any way you put it, that's an ass move."

"Geez, don't sugar coat it." Jonathan chalked his cue and went to the far end from Keith.

"Hey, man. I'm not trying to be a jerk. But, that's not cool. How'd she act when you saw her?" Keith asked.

"I don't know. She wasn't overly friendly. But seemed okay."

"I bet she's pissed. I'd be pissed if I were her," Keith said.

"She didn't seem pissed. I don't know." Now Jonathan was thoroughly confused. He shouldn't have listened to James. He lifted his head quickly. "I did give her a letter though."

"You did? What'd she say?"

"Just 'thanks.'"

"And what'd you put in the letter?" Keith asked.

"Asked if she wanted to hang out again, maybe go to the Space Needle."

"Good God. Are we back in Junior High, writing letters back and forth?" Greg returned offering his opinion. "Did you put little hearts by her name?"

"He didn't even call her these last three days," Keith reported.

"Why not, man? Ass move. I thought you liked her," Greg added.

"Damn. Where was this advice the last few days?" Jonathan realized he made a big mistake.

"I just figured you were moping cause things didn't work out. I didn't know you were being an ass and not calling. Next time ask for the big man's advice." Greg pointed heartily to his chest. "I woulda told you to call her. Idiot."

"Yup, me too," Keith conceded.

"Great. Wonderful insight on the 20/20 hindsight." Jonathan broke the rack harder than normal shattering four balls into pockets. "At least I got that going for me."

A few hours later, Jonathan finished playing pool and approached the front desk. "Saturday," Lisa said.

"What?"

"Saturday. I'm free all day Saturday until I have to work at 5:00 if you want to show me Seattle. And no, I haven't been up in the Space Needle."

"Oh. Oh. Cool. You read the letter?"

"Yup."

"Then Saturday it is. Consider me your official tour guide." Jonathan glanced nervously down as he slid his rack of balls toward her. "I'll pick you up at 9:00."

"Don't be late," Lisa said.

"I won't. Cathy warned me that you don't like late."

CHAPTER 23

Saturday morning, Jonathan showed up at 9:00 and Lisa raced down the stairs to the front door of the building so they didn't have to endure a 'Cathy' encounter. Their first stop was breakfast on the south side of Queen Anne at his favorite restaurant, Café Minnie's. There was a line out the front, but Jonathan assured her it was worth the wait. Inside, the café waitstaff swarmed from table to table. It was a cheery place with sunshine pouring through windows that made up two sides of the room. A third wall was covered with old black and whites complete with the classics: Monroe, Sinatra, Elvis, Martin, and others. The fourth wall shielded the restaurant from the sight of the busy kitchen, but did nothing to cover the sounds of clanking pots and stressed-out kitchen workers scrambling to keep up with the never-ending stream of orders.

"This is so cute," Lisa said.

"I come here a lot late at night. It's the only other 24-hour place besides Denny's around. Well, not counting 13 Coins, but that's down by the airport, too far."

"You stay out late a lot, don't you?"

"I do my best writing then. You know, fewer people around."

"That makes sense. Are you working on another book?"

"Number two." This wasn't exactly true. Writing a book was a lot of work.

"What's this one about?"

"I can't reveal all my secrets." Jonathan made a clumsy wink.

"I'm curious—" Lisa started.

"Uh oh. This sounds ominous."

"Curious why you didn't call me at all after I gave you the letter." Lisa was blunt.

Jonathan looked down to his lap where his fingers nervously tore at his napkin. He decided to go with honesty. "I took advice from someone I shouldn't have."

"Someone told you not to call me?"

"Yeah. Said I'd seem too desperate." Jonathan gauged Lisa's reaction.

"Well, I'm sure the someone wasn't Keith. And Greg, well Greg maybe, cause he's such a—I don't know—gangsta of love." Lisa pointed at him with a trigger finger and made an exaggerated wink.

"No, it wasn't them," Jonathan said. "It was my brother."

"Oh? Does he know about me or was this general advice he's given you?"

"No. About you."

"Well, I'll let you in on a little of my own advice. Ass move." Lisa delivered her opinion with a smile.

"Point definitely taken. That's exactly what both Keith and Greg said."

"Good to know. Those two are smarter than they seem."

After breakfast, they visited Green Lake. Jonathan knew from Keith that Lisa liked to work out, so he figured taking her on a walk would show her that he also enjoyed exercise. It would be his first time walking around the whole lake.

"This is really cool. I didn't even know this was here." Lisa was impressed with the small lake surrounded by a walking path and park. The Seattle sunshine had brought crowds of people to enjoy the paradise situated among the dense urban neighborhood. Picnics were spread both on tables and blankets covering grassy hills where children ran about playing and squealing in delight. An intense volleyball game commenced on a well-maintained sand court and Lisa knew she would be back here to join in a game sometime soon. Colorful kayaks carried adventurers back and forth across the calm waters of the lake. Jonathan and Lisa reached the walking path and joined several others in their journey to circle the lake.

"People roller blade around and run and bike. I think it's about two and half miles all the way," Jonathan said.

"That's not too far. Do you ever run it?" Lisa asked.

"Nah. Just mostly bike." He had biked it once. "I have played tennis over at those courts though." He had done that once also.

"We should play."

"Do you play a lot?"

"Nope. Only played a few times. More a racquetball player."

"Maybe I can teach you tennis and you can teach me racquetball."

"You're on." Lisa was surprised yet excited that he was interested in physical activities. He was nowhere near the athletes that she had dated in the past, but at least he was willing to try. Jonathan reached out to grab her hand and she responded. They proceeded around the lake taking in the bustle of activity.

Stopping for lemonade, Jonathan took notice when Lisa placed a straw in each drink and handed him one. Selfish Celeste would never have done that. Melissa would have. Lisa did.

She laughed when she went to take a sip and the straw slammed into the side of her lip, "God, you're rubbing off on me."

"I told you it's out of my control. The chemical aura must be including you in it."

From Green Lake, they drove south on the 99, across the Aurora Bridge that spanned high over Lake Union, and into Seattle Center where the Space Needle took center stage. Reaching the top, Lisa was not disappointed. Jonathan watched her enjoy all the same things he did about it. The view of the Olympic Mountains and Puget Sound to the west included two Bainbridge ferries passing one another midpoint. Jonathan pointed past them. "That's West Seattle, or Alki, over there. Have you been yet?"

"No, but Cathy has told me there's an incredible fish and chips place over there."

"Sure is. Alki Spud Fish and Chips. We'll have to go there for lunch one day." Jonathan was excited to already be planning a future outing. Circling to the south side, a majestic Mount Rainier glowed in the distance while the sunlight shimmered off its snowy face.

"It's massive," Lisa exclaimed.

"Wait till you see it from a plane window. Most flights in and out fly right over it," Jonathan explained.

"Gorgeous, I bet."

As they made their way west, Jonathan singled out first Capitol Hill, then the tallest building on First Hill. "I lived in the penthouse of that building when I first moved here."

"What?"

"My dad's city place. They were rarely there, so he let me stay."

"Pretty lucky. What were those views like?" Lisa asked.

"Absolutely amazing. I lived next door to John Saul too."

"Impressive."

"And that's the University of Washington." Jonathan continued toward the north side.

"What's that body of water beyond?"

"Lake Washington. Lake Union, the closest one, connects with it. They are both fresh water but Lake Union connects with the Sound."

"How does that work? Doesn't the salt get into the lake?'

Jonathan laughed. It was the same thing that had perplexed him when he heard it. "Nope. There's locks. The Ballard Locks. It's how boats pass into the lake. Salt water is heavier so it settles to the bottom and drains through a pipe." Jonathan repeated what he had learned from the tour guide.

"No way."

"Yeah. We can go there someday, too." This was getting better and better. He had so many places to show her. "There are fish ladders so you can see the salmon when they come up to spawn."

"That would be amazing," Lisa said.

Before moving all the way to the north side of the Needle, Lisa noticed almost straight below them her place of work. "Look. There's Jillian's."

"It looks so small from up here."

"It's so neat to see all this from a different perspective. You can follow along Westlake Avenue all the way to my apartment," she said.

"And that's my apartment building over there." They had

completed their circle and were back again on the north side, looking right at Queen Anne. Jonathan pointed to the western side of Queen Anne hill.

"You must have a great view."

"Not as great as the First Hill view, but it's pretty spectacular. Especially at night."

"I bet."

"We could run by there on the way to your house and you can check it out."

"Okay." It came out before Lisa even had a chance to analyze the situation.

"Great. We better get going now if we're going to have time," Jonathan said.

Jonathan had not planned on bringing Lisa back to his apartment at the end of this day. But it worked out perfectly. Riding up the elevator to the eighth floor of his Gem Way apartment building, he realized they had about fifteen minutes. But still he sweated. He wanted to take his coat off, but knew the mess that would be under his arms by now, so he didn't dare.

Stepping off the elevator and onto the balcony, the Space Needle was already in view. "We were just up there," she gazed toward the Needle. "I could look out at this forever."

"I know. It's intoxicating. I love making up stories of what's going on in everyone's life down there as I sit up here."

"There's a real separation." Lisa took in the view of downtown Seattle sprawled out in front of her. The Space Needle held court with only the tall black Columbia building sharing attention in the background. Closer to them, just over the winter tree tips, the Seattle Center Coliseum was indicative of a historical fair. Further away, the white peaks of Mount Rainier were faintly outlined on the horizon, blending cloud and snow evenly.

"Here. This is my pad." Jonathan opened the door to Apartment 806 and the entire place was visible in one sweep except the bedroom, which was hidden behind the one wall. "It's really small. But the view makes it worth it."

"Definitely," Lisa agreed.

Jonathan stepped across the living room and pushed the button on his answering machine. "Hey, I got a blinking red light." He knew it wouldn't be a girl, so he didn't even think twice about listening to it.

"Hey bro. How'd things go with Melissa? Call me as soon—" Jonathan pushed Stop.

Lisa retreated to the balcony right after hearing the male's voice mention Melissa. She thought it had gone well the other night. And today, too. But obviously Jonathan was involved with another girl. Which was fine, she guessed. She was dating other people too. Well, she hadn't dated anyone since their first night at Denny's. But still, she was open to date other people. It's not like they were even dating. Just hanging out. She liked the idea of being in a relationship and had started thinking lately maybe it was heading that way with Jonathan. But now she realized maybe they were just heading toward friendship, especially if he had a girlfriend.

Jonathan joined her on the balcony, pulling the door closed behind him. "Just my brother, checking in."

Lisa crossed her arms and pursed her lips in answer.

"You ready to head out?" Jonathan asked.

She started toward the elevator a step ahead of him. *You can't be mad at him. You're not dating. He just took you around Seattle for the day.* These thoughts calmed her as he drove her home. Even though she was disappointed, she was still polite. "Thanks so much for showing me around today."

"No problem. I had fun."

"So did I." She wondered if he had brought Melissa on the same tour recently.

"We'll have to do the tennis thing soon."

"Sure," she answered as they pulled up to her apartment and she got out of the car. She held the door open. "You don't have to get out. I'm running late anyway. I'll see you at Jillian's later. Thanks, again." She closed the door and hurried to her building before he could answer.

Damn. She heard. Why hadn't he just waited to play his messages? Now what was he supposed to do? She probably thought he was seeing someone. And he didn't want her to think that. He definitely didn't want her to think that.

He headed home and called James. "Dude, she heard your message."

"You had her at your apartment?"

Jonathan knew this was the part that would shock James—having her at the apartment. "She heard you ask how it went with Melissa. Not how it went with *Lisa*, but how it went with Melissa."

"Are you sure?"

"Not positive. But it had been going great until that point and then she got real distant."

"She heard."

"Now what do I do?"

"Tell her."

"Tell her what, the whole thing?" Jonathan wished there was someone, anyone, who he could consult about this besides James. James had been the one to tell him not to call her and that had turned out to be a mistake.

"Why not?"

"Because I don't know if it's her."

"What do you mean? Didn't you say it was going great?"

"Yeah. But there are still some things I'm not sure of."

"Like what, dude?"

"Most blatant, the name. Her name's *not* Melissa," Jonathan pouted.

"Wow, Jonathan. How much closer can you get? Lisa, Melissa. You could even tell her that I messed the name up on your answering machine and thought you had said Melissa and not Lisa."

"I guess that could work. Just so she knows there isn't another girl."

"Or you could even—if you do end up dating—call her My Lisa. Like she's Your Lisa. My Lisa. Melissa. So close."

Pondering this a moment, Jonathan agreed with James. "You're right. That's even kind of cool. My Lisa. Mylissa. Melissa. Man, that's it. That's really close."

"Or, even, like it's *you* and Lisa. But when you say it, it's *me* and Lisa. Me and Lisa. Melissa." James was talking fast now.

"That's even better." Jonathan liked this. The whole idea was coming together.

"Are you seeing her tonight at Jillian's?"

"Just changing and heading there now."

"You need to clear up the whole answering machine thing as soon as you can. You know women, thoughts start going off in their head and before you know it, she's broken up with you before you even started dating."

"Good call. I'll write her out a little something before I go, in case I don't get a chance to talk to her."

"Good luck. Call me in the morning."

Jonathan quickly scribbled:

Melissa,

I had a really great time today. I hope you did too. I'm not sure if you even heard, but when my brother left his message he asked if I had a good time with Melissa. He meant you. I had told him about you and he thought your name was Melissa not Lisa. Just wanted to make sure you didn't think I was seeing someone. Maybe we can shoot pool when you get off tonight. Let me know.

Jonathan

He folded it into his pocket and headed to Jillian's. When he saw the crowd at the front desk, he was happy he had the letter to give Lisa. They had no chance to talk and he slid it quickly across the counter to her with his ID.

A few hours later, Lisa had a moment to open the letter. It was difficult for her to swallow past the very first word: Melissa. Reading further, she was even more confused. All the explanations. But yet he addressed the letter to Melissa. The letter cleared up nothing and when Jonathan approached she was still guarded.

"Hey, Lisa. Did you read my letter?"

"Yeah. A few minutes ago."

"So are we cool?"

Are we cool? What does that mean? She couldn't guess. "Sure, no problem."

"Do you want to shoot some pool when you get off?"

"I don't know when I get off tonight. It may be awhile."

"Keith and I are planning to play late."

"You'll both be playing?" Lisa felt comfort in that. "I'll think about it."

Jonathan didn't get it. He thought he had explained to her about what happened but she was still being distant. He needed to get this cleared up. "Are you sure you read the letter?"

"I'm sure. Why?"

"Just wondering if you understand that my brother just got the names mixed up? He was talking about you"

"I got that. Just confused if *you* have the name right."

Jonathan was stumped. "What?"

"You didn't address that letter to me."

"What?"

"You didn't address it to me. It's addressed to Melissa."

"No." Jonathan struggled to remember what he had written. Lisa could see panic wash over him. He choked. "Did I really?"

"Yup, to Melissa." Lisa pushed the letter toward him, keeping her finger on it and watched Jonathan twist his tie as he looked down at the letter. He was clearly uncomfortable and at a loss for what to say. She waited.

"I must have been thinking about that name when I was writing the explanation out to you," he said.

Lisa still waited.

"And put it by accident."

She watched him, awkward and nervous, and a thought struck her. She didn't think he was smooth enough to outright lie so she asked, "Are you dating someone?"

"No. No."

Lisa felt relief. He didn't hesitate or stammer. It somehow must be a misunderstanding. A customer approached. "I gotta get back to work."

"Pool later then?"

"Maybe. We'll see." She didn't want to let him off the hook too easily.

Jonathan was elated when Lisa appeared after her shift. "Okay. Wannabes. Cutthroat. I'll rack." She grabbed the triangular rack and started around the table to roll the balls toward it.

"What? Wait. We weren't done with our game yet," Keith protested.

"Oh good God. Game number six thousand four hundred and eighty five will go unfinished. You must be devastated. You wanna play cutthroat, or not?" Lisa demanded.

"Man, you're feisty." Keith gave in and helped roll the ball nearest him toward her.

Jonathan liked it. Melissa was feisty.

"Time for me to see if you *regulars* even know how to play this game."

"It's on. I break since I was winning that last game." Keith took the cue ball and no one protested. "Lisa, you be six through ten and Jonathan you're last, and big ones."

Lisa retrieved a cue from the wall. "And I'll even use one of these fine Jillian's custom cues while you use your personalized pro status pearl inlayed mahogany wood pieces of crap." She grabbed the chalk to ready the tip. "Do you have your own special chalk and hand softener that you have to use too?"

"Actually, I have to use the beige colored one on my tip. But I keep it over here on this end of the table." Jonathan was serious.

Lisa rolled her eyes. "Oh, brother. I was kidding."

"I'm not as high maintenance as him. I use the common blue chalk." Keith readied his cue to break.

"I'm not high maintenance," Jonathan insisted. "A softer chalk doesn't ruin my tip."

"Yup. High maintenance along with klutzy." Lisa teased as she pointed to an obvious food stain that had found its way to his shirt.

He glanced down. "That was totally Keith's fault. He backed into me."

"I don't know what you're talking about, man." Keith looked up from his shot.

"Oh, thanks."

"You'll have to come up with some kind of cosmic explanation as to why you always spill food on yourself," Lisa said.

"I do not."

"Yes, you do," Keith said, missing his shot. "Everyday you have some food stain somewhere."

"I'll have to agree with Keith on that." Lisa headed for the cue ball. "I've seen evidence on more than one occasion."

"What is this? Bash on Jonathan? In fact, I do have a theory as to why that happens."

"No, no. We're just kidding." Both Keith and Lisa held up their hands.

They played pool for three hours with banter among them. Jonathan continuously checked things off in his head: outgoing, sarcastic, funny, feisty, 5'7", brown hair, can shoot pool, doesn't smoke, doesn't wear a lot of make up, drives a red Renault Alliance. And he reasoned away the unmatched items. Melissa—but James had helped him with that by pointing out how close it was. From

Iowa—but that starts with an I, just like Idaho. There were only a few more things he wanted to know about her to be certain she was the one. Did she write for her high school newspaper? Were her original parents still together? Did she have dogs or cats growing up? He decided to push for one of the answers right now. "Have you seen Keith's dog yet?"

"No," she said, turning from collecting her ball out of the pocket. "What kind of dog is it?"

"Cocker Spaniel."

"They're so cute. We had a Cocker growing up."

Check.

Lisa definitely felt more comfortable than when she had shown up for work that night. The more she hung out with Jonathan, the more she believed he was not dating anyone. He would have brought the other woman around Jillian's, for one. And two, she couldn't picture him with a girl. He was most certainly not a ladies' man, but for some reason she wanted to get to know him better and hang out again.

"It's 2:30. Last game. I'm wiped," Keith announced.

"Okay. I've won five games and you each have four. So either one of you pool studs tie me and the other loses. Or I win two more than either of you. I like my odds." Lisa had used a few distractive measures to win most of her games. Like pitting them against one another, so they would not shoot at her balls or doing a little dance or waving her arms in line of their shooting vision. But she took her wins as she could.

Jonathan seemed happy shooting pool, but Keith was a bit more competitive. "Let's make a wager. If there's a tie for a winner, the loser buys breakfast for everyone and if you beat us both, we each owe you a breakfast."

"Sounds like I win either way. I like it. But trust me, you'll each owe me a breakfast after this."

"Save it. Jonathan, you good with that?" Keith asked.

"Yup. Your rack, since you lost the last game."

"I know." Keith started the rack and tried to justify it. "I like going last anyway. Lets me size up my competition."

At the end of her victory, Lisa shook Keith's hand. "Good thing you did that sizing-up-the-competition thing. It really worked for you."

"I would have won if Jonathan hadn't played the chivalrous card and shot my ball when he clearly had a better shot at yours."

"Hey, wait. I always take the bank shot over the straight shot."

"Oh right, buddy. You so let her stay in the game. She should have been out three turns ago. But I get it." Keith winked at Jonathan and they both smiled.

"That's crap. How about giving me credit for my win? He didn't *let* me win," Lisa insisted.

"Uh huh, yeah, right. Next time it's just me against you and no mercy." Keith was busy untwisting his cue.

"Maybe there is no next time. I'll just forever revel in my win and take my two breakfasts and always tell the story of me beating you two in pool," Lisa said.

"Ha. Never happen. But I bet you could get Jonathan to pay up his portion of the bet right now."

"What?" Jonathan was snapped out of whatever daydream he was in.

"I said, you could take her to breakfast and pay up your part of the bet now. I'm going home. I got family stuff tomorrow."

"I could do that." Jonathan turned to Lisa. "You want to go to Denny's."

"No." Lisa waited. Jonathan looked down uncomfortably like she knew he would. "Not after you've introduced me to Café Minnie's. That's where I want my bet paid off."

Looking back up at her, he said, "You're on. I'd pick there over Denny's too."

Jonathan bumped the table and teetered the drinks sitting on top of it. "That darn universe thing again," Lisa said.

But driving to Café Minnie's, Jonathan knew this had nothing to do with the universe. This time it was sheer excitement, mixed with a bit of anxiety, at being able to spend more time with her. His stomach fluttered knowing he would be able to check off—or at least find out about—the last few things on his list.

As they entered Minnie's, the waitress called out, "Hey, Jonathan."

"Hey, Julie." Jonathan felt important that he was recognized and he hoped it left a favorable impression on Lisa.

"Everyone knows you in this city," Lisa teased.

"Julie usually waits on me when I'm here in the wee hours."

"The usual?" Julie was already setting down his Shirley Temple.

"For me? Yeah. I'm not sure what Lisa will get. The Marilyn Monroe is real good."

"That does look good. I'll have that."

As Julie retreated, Jonathan jumped right in. "Did you do any writing for your school newspaper in high school?"

"That's a random question."

"Just wondering. Since you were an English major. Thought maybe you got interested in it earlier than college."

"No. We didn't even have a newspaper at our high school."

Damn.

"Or maybe I probably would have."

That was enough to dull his disappointment. "Did you like to write?"

"Definitely. I had this awesome English teacher in high school. Mr. Hanson. Man, he gave a lot of homework. Other teachers would actually get upset because all the students would always complain about 'Hanson homework.' I secretly kind of liked it."

"I know what you mean. I always liked a good writing assignment."

"He would do these really obscure things with our assignments and everyone would groan and I loved the challenge.'"

"Like what?" Jonathan liked watching her excitement build as she explained how her obsession with writing started.

"One time, we had written these stories we had to piece together with three other people. Like we only had the gist of the plot line and we all had a section to write, then had to compare and get them to work. You know, like coordinating points of view and similar character traits."

"Sounds interesting."

"It gets better. I had had knee surgery and I was going to the doctor to get my cast off one day and he asked me what I was going to do with the cast."

"Why?"

"That's what I asked. He said he wanted it and asked me to bring it in the next day if I could."

"And did you?"

"Uh huh. It was nasty, smelly. It had been on for six weeks."

"What'd he do with it?"

"He put it on display in front of the classroom and said since I had so graciously offered it up as a sacrifice to the class that each section of the stories we wrote had to somehow incorporate it."

"No way."

"Yeah. My classmates were pissed. I mean it changed all the stories having to mention this random object."

"You would have been a good reporter then. Situations are always changing as more facts come in."

"I probably would have loved it."

Jonathan quietly decided that was good enough.

Check.

Lisa barely noticed Jonathan's quirks anymore. He dripped jam on his shirt and she accepted it, not even looking for an explanation.

They worked through breakfast talking about everything from writing to Seattle to sports and then to family.

"I know pretty much all about your brothers and sisters. But do you still have a relationship with your mom?" Lisa asked.

"Of course, I do. Why?"

"I don't know. It seems the way she was portrayed in your book, she might have some bitterness toward you."

"That's interesting you picked that up." Jonathan was careful in his answer.

"Has she read the book?"

"Yeah, she read it."

"And?"

"And, we had a couple go-arounds with the lawyers getting her to sign off that she wouldn't sue me."

"Really?"

"Yeah. She wanted to be depicted in a more admirable light."

"I can understand that."

"But I also have to write the truth; or my version of the truth."

"It wasn't that bad about her. It's just sad she kept so many facts from you and didn't let you form your own opinions about your dad."

"And that's the point I wanted to get across."

"What about your dad? I mean, did he have to sign anything? There were some pretty searing things about him being a son-of-a-bitch deadbeat dad. He must have been upset."

"He's always been supportive of my decision to write it, but I secretly don't think he wants the book to publish. But I'm safe on him not suing me. Some legal loophole about public figures being fair game to write about as long as it's not libelous. And he's considered a public figure. The lawyers at William Morrow figure all that out."

"So if it's based on a truth and you are just sharing your thoughts about it, you're okay?"

"I think that's how it goes."

"What if his memory of truth differs from yours?"

"Then he should write his own book."

"Good point."

"But you know all about my family. What about you? You said you had three sisters." Jonathan wanted to segue into the history of her parents.

"Yes. All older."

"Ah, youngest child. Me too. Or since my sister died, I have been."

"Most of my life, I've felt like an only child," Lisa said. "My parents retired when I was twelve and we moved to Idaho. All my sisters were already out of the house by then, so no one came with us."

"They're much older?"

"Next one to me is nine years older; then they're all two years apart."

"Are you close with any of them?"

"Not really. I mean, I've never had a relationship with any of them. We all get along and spend most holidays together, but we don't have much in common."

"I know what you mean. Seems we've all taken different routes, and when our paths cross, we know we're family but we don't really *know* each other."

"Exactly."

"I feel closest to James even though we took two entirely different routes; me, the rule-abiding, school-guided path and him, the self-taught, rule-breaking path."

"I'm the only one that went to college; they're all married," Lisa said.

"All married?"

"Yes, and in their family-raising mode. Way different points in our lives."

"Have they been married long?" Jonathan felt they were getting closer to the real question he had.

"I think it's twelve years, ten years and five years. Right about there."

"No divorces?"

"Not in my family. My parents have been married forty years."

Bingo! Original parents still together. Check.

"That's impressive," Jonathan said.

"Yes, it is."

"Everyone in my family's been divorced."

"Everyone?"

"I guess not everyone. One of my sisters has been married three years. And I've never been married. But other than that, yup, starting with my mom and dad and then two brothers and other sister, they've all had their practice," Jonathan held up air quotes, "marriages."

Lisa shifted uncomfortably in her seat when Jonathan relayed his idea of a 'practice' marriage. "People in my family marry for good," she clarified. "There's no practice." After a second's pause, she added, "Does it bother you they've all been divorced?"

"Oh, no. They are all with much better mates now."

"But why'd they get married if they weren't sure about the first?"

"Just getting their feet wet, I guess."

"Do you think you'll have a practice marriage before your real one?"

"I hope not. I hope I've learned from them." Jonathan could see Lisa relax.

"I've never thought of marriage as a stepping stone to another marriage."

"Not a stepping stone. It's just if things don't work out—" Jonathan could see Lisa's face fall.

"You work them out," she said flatly.

"Of course you do. But what if you're unhappy. Should you stay when you are unhappy?"

"You should try and work it out."

"But if someone is really truly unhappy, should they stick it out for the duration of their life? Their one life?"

"I don't know. I guess I've not seen an unhappy marriage. My parents always get along and my sisters, even though I don't see them often, seem happy."

"My brother was miserable in his marriage. And so was his wife. Rather than stay miserable, they got divorced. Now they are both remarried and living the happily ever after," Jonathan explained.

"I guess that's good. But I just want to do it once," Lisa said.

"Me too. I think everyone wants that. Everyone wants the forty years, like your parents. Just sometimes it doesn't work out that way," Jonathan said. "And my family is proof of that."

"That's too bad. Maybe you can change that."

"I hope so."

They finished breakfast and Jonathan was more sure than ever this was Melissa. As they departed in the early morning sunrise, they made plans to go see the movie 'Groundhog Day' later that afternoon.

The movie set off a whole batch of new topics to explore as they went up to his favorite park on Queen Anne to talk against the backdrop of the Seattle skyline.

They shared ideas and thoughts of how they would spend their last day, then if they had a month, or if they had a year. They worked over the characters and discussed ideas of how the movie could have been better. Lisa loved analyzing a movie like this. It was energizing. All her friends in college quit going to movies with her because she was constantly ripping apart the plot and characters and they couldn't stand that she couldn't just enjoy the movie; flaws and all.

"If you had to change one pivotal decision you've made in your life, what would it be and how would your life be different now?" Jonathan challenged Lisa.

Lisa knew the one major decision she had made so far in her life and that was to break up and move away from Jason. She wondered often if she had made a mistake. It had been so much easier being in a relationship and not having to do this awkward dating thing. "I would probably change the decision to break up with Jason, my college boyfriend."

This startled Jonathan. He didn't want Melissa to be pining for an old boyfriend. "Do you think you'll get back together?"

Lisa thought for a moment. "No." As she said it she knew it was the truth, but the fact she had just acknowledged it out loud took her breath away. She gazed out at the view of downtown Seattle and tried to slow her heart rate.

Then she explained both for Jonathan's benefit and her own. "I don't think it will work. He wants to be in a small town and I've seen what our lives would be if we stayed together; because it's his parents. Living in the same town their whole life. And his dad is the high school football coach and their lives revolve around that."

"And not that that's bad," Lisa continued. "They're great people. And I would be happy. But I also think I would always have this nagging in the back of my head, 'What if?' What if there was something else out there...outside this small town? I want to see this world and have bigger experiences than football and drinking every Friday night. Does that make sense?"

"Of course it does."

"I don't want to be with someone and then at forty years old realize I haven't even lived. That I haven't had any life experiences. You see these women, or men, in their forties all of a sudden not wanting the life they chose at twenty and they tear a family apart—kids and all—to now pursue their life." Lisa was babbling.

"Yeah, at least there were no kids involved in my brothers' and sisters' practices. They were out early enough before that started," Jonathan said.

"Anyway," Lisa continued. "Jason never talked about anything beyond football and becoming a teacher and a coach and I think at the end of it all, I would feel I missed something."

She stopped for a moment and then more confidently answered his original question. "So, no. We will never get back together."

Jonathan hated to be happy, because he could feel she was sad about the realization she only just now came to. He reached around her shoulder and pulled her into him. "You can be together with someone *and* share bigger life experiences."

Lisa turned toward Jonathan and saw his desire to kiss her. The hesitation lasted a bit too long and it got uncomfortable. She pulled back and said, "What one decision would you change?"

Jonathan cursed himself. *What a coward*. Why didn't he just lean in and kiss her right there? It was the moment and he let it slip away. He looked down awkwardly in his lap. "I'd change my decision a moment ago and would have gone for it."

"Gone for what?" Lisa asked, knowing exactly what he meant. She turned toward him again and simultaneously he lifted his chin and leaned in.

It was a slow, soft kiss. Jonathan made sure it was by repeating to himself as his heart raced; *be cool, man, slow, it, down, don't seem too anxious, soft, like this happens all the time*.

Lisa's thoughts raced also; *kiss me, really kiss me*. Why is he just setting his lips there, doing nothing, really, is he doing this because he thinks he has to, he doesn't seem that into it, and the last thought that forced her to pull away, is this his first kiss?

Jonathan moved to pull his arm from behind her back and his watch clutched a strand of hair.

"Ouch."

"Oh, gosh, sorry. I—"

"It's okay. Hang on." Lisa unwound her hair and as it freed, Jonathan took her hand in both of his.

"I really like spending time with you, Mel—" shit, "Lisa."

She caught it, but knew he had explained before and didn't want to hash out the same conversation. "Me too. But it's getting late. I need to get home. School tomorrow." The late nights were getting to her and she was exhausted.

"Can I see you again? I mean, can we make plans to go out together again?"

"How about playing racquetball on Tuesday?" Lisa asked.

"Sounds good."

Tuesday they met at the gym where Jonathan signed up for a membership telling Lisa he was planning on joining one anyway, so it might as well be now. Jonathan knew Keith had wanted him to sign up at his gym, but Lisa was better motivation. She handily beat him five games but it was fun and he felt victorious about getting in a good sweat. Until Lisa told him, "Forty-five minutes on the Stairmaster now."

He thought for sure she was kidding, up to the point when she actually climbed on the Stairmaster and starting punching in numbers. She was well on her way when he climbed on the one next to her. "How does this work?"

"Just follow the prompts. It will ask for time, weight, level. Just do fifteen minutes if it's your first time."

How about five? Jonathan thought. It took him three minutes to get all the information input correctly and by then he was out of breath and his legs felt like lead. Still, he climbed on.

At five minutes, he was done. He pushed the stop button and the machine slowed.

"Harder than it looks, huh?" Lisa laughed.

"Nah, I just want to go lift some weights for a bit."

"Okay. I'll be here." Lisa didn't think he'd last long at the weights either, but she thought it was cool he was trying things and making an effort to do things to be with her. And the fact he bought a membership meant he might make a habit of it.

After their workout, they tried to make plans to do something again. Lisa said, "I'll be here Thursday 3:30 to 4:30 before going to work. But I want to do treadmill for forty-five minutes. So I could play racquetball for about fifteen." She didn't want to give up her workout time.

Jonathan readily agreed. "That would be perfect. Greg wants to play racquetball too. So we can come early and I'll practice a bit, then maybe I could give you a game."

And so they began a racquetball regime and hanging out here and there after work and going to dinners and movies on nights when she had time and spending weekend days exploring Seattle and Green Lake and playing tennis and rollerblading. They also started an exchange of letters they would trade when they saw one another at Jillian's. The relationship was developing perfectly for Lisa. He wasn't pressuring her physically and she wasn't getting rejected. She was happy not to be in the dating scene anymore, dealing with all the anxieties of confusing expectations. He was definitely different, but she felt for the first time she was falling for someone mentally.

CHAPTER 24

After about three weeks of this, Lisa got pressure from Cathy. "You're getting serious about this guy." Cathy accosted Lisa one Sunday after she turned down her offer to go to dinner. She had plans with Jonathan.

"We get along really well."

"And what are you doing tonight? Going to play volleyball, or run, or skate? Poor guy. He's probably never worked out so much in his life."

"I don't think he has. He joined my gym and it's the first time he's ever belonged to a gym."

"He must have it bad."

"I think he's enjoying it though. He gets so excited when he actually sweats."

"I'm sure he's loving it. You know he's just doing it for you, little cousin. That's what men do to get what they want. Appease you until the honeymoon stage is over and then all that stops."

"I don't know. I think he really likes it."

"We'll see," Cathy said. "So what are you doing tonight that's more exciting than going out with me?"

"We're going to Greg's mom's house for dinner and cards. I guess it's something they do every Sunday night. She cooks for everyone and then they play games."

"And then what?"

"What do you mean, and then what?"

"Then what are you two doing?"

"He'll probably bring me home."

"Home here or home to his place?"

"Home here. Why?"

"Has he brought you home to his place yet?"

Lisa knew exactly what she was edging toward and she decided to blurt out the answer before Cathy could ask the question. "No, we have not slept together."

"You haven't? Haven't you hung out together everyday for like three weeks?"

"Yeah." Still reeling with embarrassment from her disaster with Trevor, Lisa had avoided being alone with Jonathan at his apartment. She wanted to make sure they were both at the same place in the relationship before risking humiliation.

"Has he kissed you?" Cathy asked.

"Once."

"Once? What the hell? Was it a good kiss at least?"

Lisa hesitated and Cathy pounced. "Oh God, it wasn't even a good kiss. What are you doing?"

"I didn't say it wasn't a good kiss."

"But you hesitated."

"That doesn't mean anything. It was all right."

"All right?"

"Yes. All right. It wasn't a real kiss, really. And I think he was nervous. So it's nothing to judge."

"Is he gay?"

"What? No. What? Why?"

"Well, why won't he make a move?"

"I don't know. He's shy about that."

"Oh my God. He's a virgin. Is he a virgin?"

Lisa thought about her last thought as their first kiss ended, *was it his first time*? "I don't know. I don't think so. He had a girlfriend in college."

"You haven't even asked."

"No. Why would I ask?"

"Well are you thinking about having sex with him?"

Lisa could feel the heat flush up her cheeks. "I don't know."

"You know. Have you?" Cathy pushed.

"Yeah, I guess. Well...yeah, I guess," Lisa said.

"Then you better get 'the talk' out of the way before the moment."

"What talk?"

"Man, you are naïve. You need to find out if he's had partners and if he's been safe with them. You know, safe, condoms."

"I know what safe means," Lisa said.

"If he hasn't, you better make sure he's been tested."

"Tested for what?"

"AIDS, you idiot. Or any other STD."

"How do you bring that up in conversation?"

"You say—repeat after me—have you been tested for AIDS?"

Lisa did not respond.

"Repeat it. Have you been tested for AIDS?" Cathy was stern.

"Have you been tested for AIDS?" Lisa said lamely.

"Yes. That's right."

"I just blurt that out right between bites of my cheesecake?"

"You blurt it out as soon as you can. Just get it out of the way."

"Okay, okay. I'll ask him tonight."

Greg's mom lived in the iconic West Queen Anne School on Galer and 5th Street that was originally an elementary school and had recently been converted to condos. The outside was a massive red-brick, school-looking building. But inside, high windows and warm accents resembled nothing of a classroom. The irony for his mom was she had actually attended first grade in the exact space that was now her condo. She explained where the chalkboard had been and calculated where the teacher's desk had once sat front and center. Then she laughed as she pointed out the corner where she had had her bum swatted with a ruler for talking too much.

Dinner consisted of eight people conducting a pizza challenge with the top three pizza places on Queen Anne. Each pizzeria delivered a large specialty pie and the battle began. Pagliacci's won by a long shot. A heated game of cards followed with the competition being friendly, yet fierce. It was fun and fast and the banter was constant. As they left, Jonathan apologized for it, although with a hint of how much he loved it. "Sorry about that. It gets pretty intense when we get together on Sundays."

"It was great. My family is just as competitive."

"It's cool Greg's mom does this for us each Sunday. Gives us all a place to call home once a week."

"Do you always do the food delivery competition?"

"Nah. That was the first time. She usually makes an incredible meal for all of us. So that was kind of different."

"It was fun."

They had reached Jonathan's car and he opened her door for her. "It's only 10:00. You want to grab some ice cream and go to my place for awhile?"

"Sure," she said, but inside anxiety fingered its way through her body.

"Let's stop at Safeway and get some Ben and Jerry's," Jonathan suggested.

"Sounds good." Cathy's lecture repeated in her head, *Have you been tested for AIDS*? But it would not come out. Lisa felt sick to her stomach and cursed herself for not being able to say it. What's the big deal? This is what adults do, right?

"Do you have a favorite Ben and Jerry's flavor?"

"I've only had it once. It was at an actual Ben and Jerry's parlor in Long Beach. I've never got a carton of it. But it was, I think, had pretzels, and chocolate, and banana or something fruity, or not fruity, it was peanut butter." She was talking fast and incoherently, and couldn't complete a thought. Just ask him about the AIDS thing, she prepped herself more.

"It sounds like my favorite, Chubby Hubby."

How do you blurt out a question about sex when the conversation includes the words Chubby Hubby? "I don't think I could ever enjoy eating anything called Chubby Hubby. Just the name makes me feel the extra pounds I'm carrying."

"Oh, no. You have to try it before you decide not to eat it. It's the best."

"I think what I had was called Chunky Monkey, or something like that." Lisa knew the sex question was getting farther and farther away.

"That's a good one too."

"Do you know all the flavors?"

"Pretty much. But I'm trying to cut back and eat healthier. Maybe I should pick up some fruit while we're here."

"And some condoms." She couldn't take it back now. It was out there.

Jonathan stopped abruptly and turned. He stared at her. He didn't say anything.

Lisa felt the flush rush through her. Was he going to say anything?

"I'm okay," Jonathan whispered.

"Oh God, I can't believe I said that. I don't know how this is supposed to work. My cousin said I'm supposed to ask about AIDS, but I don't know when to ask something like that. And I guess to start would be to know if you are safe, so I just said the condoms. And then...what do you mean, you're okay?" Lisa couldn't shut up. Jonathan stood there. "What do you mean when you say, 'I'm okay'?" Lisa repeated.

"I mean, I'm okay. I've got that covered." Jonathan's face flushed also.

Great, so he's expecting this, Lisa thought.

"Not that I'm expecting anything," Jonathan quickly added.

"So, you're okay, like you already have some?"

"Yeah."

Does he do this all the time, she thought.

"Although I guess I should check the expiration date. It's been awhile," Jonathan explained.

Lisa figured this to be the end of the preparation-for-safe-sex talk, but wasn't sure if she was ready to have sex with Jonathan.

She cleared this up. "I'm not saying we're having sex tonight. I just thought we should be prepared if it does happen anytime."

"Okay." Jonathan reached for a tub of Ben and Jerry's and two tumbled to the bottom of the cooler. Reaching in, he paused in the cool air.

As quickly as it started, Lisa changed the conversation. "So what kind of fruit did you want to get?"

"What?"

"Fruit. Let's get some fruit also."

"Oh, yeah." Jonathan was armed with two tubs of Ben and Jerry's and headed toward the produce. "I wish I had a juicer. My dad has one and it's so good when you juice fruit and then add diet ginger ale."

"What kind of fruit?"

"You've never juiced before?"

"No."

"You can juice anything." Jonathan continued on about what kind of fruit to juice and the vitamin benefits until they checked out.

"Sounds good. Maybe I'll have to get me a juicer." Lisa was glad the conversation was back to normal.

At Jonathan's apartment, they pulled the couch up to the front window and ate their tubs of ice cream watching the city life in the distance. Jonathan made Lisa talk. Really talk. She would tell him of some thing in her life and he would follow up with questions like, 'What do you expect to gain from that?' or 'What would the parallel you be doing right now with a different decision?'

He took an interest in her life. Even though he was a klutz and not much of a smooth operator, Jonathan remembered the things she shared with him. He always remembered her friends' and families' names and the things she told him about them. He was a conscientious listener and when she talked he watched her with caring eyes. She was growing attracted to him. Even his head didn't seem as big as it once was.

Lisa liked he could express his feelings and just sit and talk about life. He seemed genuinely thrilled she was there with him. He made her the top priority. The TV never got turned on. When the phone rang, he never made a move to answer it. After three hours of non-stop conversation, Lisa stifled a yawn and declared, "I should be getting home. School tomorrow."

"You ever take days off?" Jonathan asked, squeezing her hand.

"Not so far."

"Maybe you could take one off tomorrow?"

"No can do. Have a timed test. Besides I'm thinking of taking next Monday off because it's my birthday."

"It's your birthday?"

"Yup. The big twenty-three. Actually I was going to ask if you wanted to come to dinner next Sunday night with my family. Nothing big. It'll be the weird one you already met, Cathy. And her sister and husband."

"Definitely. That sounds cool."

"It's a date then. But right now, you need to take me home, please." Lisa smothered another yawn.

During the week, Jonathan only got to spend one afternoon—really one hour—with Lisa, playing racquetball when he met her at the gym. She had testing all week at school and when he saw her at Jillian's, she looked exhausted. But he still felt good about it, because she had written him two letters—and he returned the gestures. Her letters were like watching Melissa bloom. Ideas and phrases his Melissa had written to him years before now came from an actual person. He started a new shoebox for 'Lisa' alongside the Melissa boxes. He eagerly added any tidbit to fill the box. The need to make this as real as possible consumed him and he found himself on the phone for hours a day hashing and rehashing the events and letters with his brother.

"Dude, you really need to get a life, get a job." James had been trying to get him off the phone for half an hour.

"I have a job. And besides I'll be going on tour next month, so there's nothing really I can do right now," Jonathan defended.

"How about writing another book? You're obsessing so much about this Lisa-Melissa thing. Are you using any of your time to put it together in any kind of a novel?"

"Of course," Jonathan lied. He didn't have time for any of that right now. And writing a novel was so exhausting. He stayed at Jillian's until late so he didn't have to be home alone, and by the time he woke up around 1:00 or 2:00 he had to get ready to go to the gym and maybe play a game with Lisa. Then he'd get home and shower and get his clothes ready—he'd done laundry twice already this week and had ironed his khakis every day—before going to Jillian's.

"Good for you. But I, for one, have a *real job* and I need to get some things done. So ciao for now, brother."

"But you never answered my question: What should I wear for dinner tomorrow night?"

"Really, bro. Do you have that many choices? Um, khaki pants, button-down shirt, tie? What else would you wear?"

"Sports coat, or no?"

"I don't know and I don't care."

"Fine help you are. I guess I'll wear the coat then," Jonathan decided.

"Great. Great. I'm sure that will solidify this relationship perfectly. I'm sure she'll think, 'Oh, he wore a coat tonight. That means we are going to be together and live happily ever after. Good thing he wore the coat,'" James mimicked.

"Okay, okay. I get it. Thanks for nothin'. Talk to ya later."

"Yeah, later. Oh, and Jonathan?"

"Yeah?"

"Maybe you shouldn't wear the coat," James laughter could be heard as he hung up.

"Damn him."

Lisa chose the Bahn Thai on Queen Anne for her birthday. It was a quaint house on Roy Street that had been converted into a restaurant and had the best Thai food in all of Seattle. They all met at 6:00. Jonathan showed up in his khaki pants, blue sports coat, and a signature tie Lisa had not seen before.

She greeted him with an awkward hug and started the introductions. "You've met Cathy. This is her sister, Tammy. Her husband couldn't make it. This is Jonathan." They shared polite handshakes and then Lisa and Jonathan took their seats.

"Nice tie." Lisa tried to make Jonathan comfortable.

"Thanks. I just bought it today. It will be my new special occasion tie." He held the tie out, thinking they could see it better. It had a little boy at the bottom being lifted off his tiptoes by a huge, colorful bouquet of balloons that he clung to. He explained the signature tie thing to Lisa's cousins. "It's kinda my thing. The signature tie." Lisa kicked Cathy under the table as a signal to keep her mouth shut. Cathy's eyes rolled.

Jonathan had never had Thai food before and they had fun introducing him to too much of the tofu, phad thai noodles, swimming rama, and iced coffee. They all ate more than was comfortable and Cathy still ordered the coconut ice cream.

After dinner, Lisa opened up gifts and cards. Jonathan leaned over to whisper, "I got you a present, but it was too big to bring in."

"Too big? What is it?"

"I can't tell you. You'll have to wait and see."

"Okay."

"Do you want to come over to my place for a little while?"

"I drove with Cathy." Lisa knew sex was the next stage if she went home with him tonight. She even had the feeling he would make the first move, saving her from possibly getting rejected. She had already decided she wouldn't reject him if it got to that point.

"That's okay. I'll bring you home later," Jonathan said.

"Remember, I have school in the morning."

"I thought you were taking it off for your birthday?"

"I don't think they've declared it a national holiday yet," Lisa said.

After goodbyes, and a Don't-do-anything-I-wouldn't-do caveat from Cathy, Lisa left with Jonathan. On the passenger seat of his car was a large wrapped package. "What is it?" Lisa held it on her lap and shook it slightly. "A toothbrush?"

"A little big for a toothbrush."

"I know. I was kidding." Lisa's humor was often lost on Jonathan.

Entering Jonathan's apartment, Lisa was greeted by a large bouquet of a dozen red roses. "They're gorgeous."

Jonathan quickly tried to explain. "I didn't know what color to get. I know red is love and we haven't known each other that long, but I didn't think that yellow for friendship was a strong enough sentiment, and the white, well, I'm still a little confused on what white stands for. So," he finished. "I decided on red."

"They're perfect. I've never got a dozen roses before."

"I also got you a cake and ice cream." Jonathan went to the counter and tilted the cake so she could read the *Happy 23 Birthday Lisa* piped in red. The cake was decorated with red roses and trimmed with ribbons.

"That's so sweet."

"Maybe we can have some later. I'm still full from dinner." Jonathan patted his stomach.

"Me, too. Can I open my present now?"

"Yes, yes. I hope you like it." They sat on the couch.

Lisa tore at the paper. "I love presents." The box revealed a juicer. "Nice. Is this what you said your dad uses?"

"Yeah, it's the top of the line. I got some fruit too, so we can try it if you want."

"Definitely'" Lisa continued with opening the box to get the actual juicer out. "Really, this is so great. You made my birthday special."

"Hmmm." Jonathan stood up. "Maybe I can really make it special." He grabbed Lisa's wrist and pulled her to him. He lifted her chin and kissed her.

Really kissed her. Lisa's mind raced, *Oh, thank God. Thank God, he does know how to kiss.* The abruptness of it caught her off guard though and she started to laugh.

"Not exactly the response I was hoping for," Jonathan said.

"No, I just...It's just that—" Lisa continued to laugh uncomfortably. "Just, you know, it was sudden. You caught me off guard."

"Well, then this will really catch you off guard." Jonathan grabbed her hand and led her toward the bedroom.

"What's gotten in to you?"

"It's just time. It's time." Jonathan sat on the bed and pulled her in close.

They spent the next few hours exploring, and talking, and laughing. When it was close to midnight, Lisa mentioned she should get home.

"Just one day. Just take one day off. It's your birthday," Jonathan pleaded.

Lisa was hoping he would ask. She had already made up her mind to stay the night and the rest of the next day together with him if he asked. "Okay."

"What?" Jonathan sat up on the bed. "What? Really?"

Lisa laughed at his excitement. "Yes. Really."

"Like for real? You're not kidding?"

"No. I'm not kidding. You should feel pretty special."

"Oh, I do. You bet I do. I'm going to be your servant for the next twenty-four hours and you're not going to regret this." He leaned over and kissed her again.

"Then as my servant, I have my first order of business for you." Lisa playfully pushed him away.

"Anything. Anything at all. You got it. What would you like, m' lady?"

"I would like a big piece of cake and ice cream served to me right here, right now."

Lisa wrapped the sheet around her and nudged Jonathan out of the bed with her foot.

"You got it! One piece of cake and ice cream coming right up. You sure you don't want me to juice up anything for you."

"No way. Too healthy. I want cake and ice cream. I'll have you juice my breakfast for me tomorrow."

Jonathan was now out of bed and leaned over and grabbed Lisa's face between both his hands. "That sounds nice. Breakfast. I'm really happy you're staying."

"Me too. Now cake. Ice cream. Move it."

Jonathan hummed gathering the desserts. It was too good to be true. Melissa was right here with him. After all these years, she finally showed up. And she liked him too, just like he planned.

Lisa broke his thoughts. "What are you humming?"

"Sting. Fields of Gold."

"Don't think I've heard it."

"What? He's the best. Listen." It took a few minutes for Jonathan to get the CD playing. Just as the first chords played, he brought in two plates filled with cake and ice cream.

"Are you kidding? We can't eat all that," Lisa said

"We can and will." He handed Lisa a plate. "Well, what do you think?"

"I think we should go to the gym."

"Huh? No. What do you think about Sting? And, no, no gym on your birthday. Day off."

"What? I thought you liked the gym? He sounds good."

"I do like it. But some days you just need to take off and tomorrow is one of them. I know, he's great. In fact, he's playing here next week. Do you want to go?"

"What night?"

"I think Friday."

"I work on Fridays."

"Well, maybe you can get it off."

"Skip school. Skip the gym. Skip work. I'm starting to think you're a bad influence on me Mr. Jonathan Bach." Lisa dabbed a bit of frosting on his hand.

"I'm a good influence. And you're going to see just how good." He licked the frosting off and leaned over and kissed her. Both of them set their plates down and let the ice cream melt.

Much of the night was lost to everything but sleep. Lisa woke to the ringing of Jonathan's phone. He looked at the caller ID on the bedside table, "It's my dad. He said he'd call this morning. Is it okay if I get it?"

"Of course," Lisa said. She glanced at the clock. 9:00 a.m. She had not slept in in many months; not that they had really slept.

"I'll put him on speaker. He wants to meet you."

"Are you sure this is the time?" She pulled the sheets up to her chin.

"It's not like he can see you."

"Oh yeah." She rubbed the sleep from her eyes. This was not how she pictured her first meeting with Jonathan's dad.

"Hey, Dad."

"Hey, Jonathan. Do you have a minute?"

"Yeah, of course."

"How did the birthday dinner go with Melissa?"

Lisa's stomach crashed at the mention of the name Melissa again. This was no longer just a coincidence.

"Lisa, Dad. It's Lisa." He glanced sheepishly over at Lisa.

"Oh, yeah," he said. "That's going to be hard to get used to. It's been Melissa for four years. Lisa."

Lisa sat up abruptly. Melissa. Four years? This was not a misunderstanding of a name as Jonathan had told her. Four years? What? What was going on? She moved to get up from the bed. But Jonathan pressed down on her wrist.

"It went great, Dad. And she's here with me right now."

His dad remained silent. Lisa pulled her wrist from Jonathan's grasp and moved to get up again. He let her this time.

Finally, his dad said, "She's there with you? Hello, Lisa."

"Hi," she said. But it wasn't okay anymore. Jonathan had explained Melissa away a few weeks back. And now here she was again, right in Lisa's face. And after she slept with him. She was rejected again anyway, but this time, after the fact. She went to the bathroom.

From the bathroom, she heard Richard say, "Have you told her?"

"No." Jonathan was barely audible.

"I guess now is the time. Sorry about that."

"No worries. But I better go."

"Let me know how it goes. Bye. Oh, wait, Jonathan. Can you do dinner Saturday night? Both of you?"

"I'll get back to you." Jonathan was curt.

As the conversation ended, Lisa ran the cold water and splashed her face. *How could she have fallen for this?* She felt sick to her stomach. She'd gotten involved with this guy when she'd known in her gut there was another girl. She had to get out of here. Now. Her clothes were in the bedroom and she could hear Jonathan out in the living room, so she quietly opened the door.

"Hey." Jonathan was waiting for her.

"I gotta get going. Can you take me home?"

"Come here for a minute." Jonathan patted the couch next to where he was sitting.

"I really need to go." Lisa went into the bedroom and carefully grabbed her things and got dressed.

Walking back into the living room, she saw Jonathan still sitting there. Waiting.

"Are you going to take me home or should I call Cathy?"

"I wish you would come and sit down and talk to me for a minute."

"I'm not sure what you could say. I really just want to go home."

"Lisa, it's not what you think." Jonathan reached out his hand. "Come here."

But Lisa stood her ground. "It's not what I think?" She spoke slowly. "Two or three times you start to call me Melissa, your brother calls me Melissa, you send me a note addressed to Melissa, your dad calls me Melissa. How can it not be what I think, Jonathan? There's someone else. And now I'm sick about what happened here." Lisa hung her head, but then she lifted it and looked him squarely in the eye and whispered, “And you allowed it.” She bit the inside of her cheek so she would not cry.

“Can you just give me a minute? It’s not what you think.”

“You’ve said that. But you haven’t really clarified what you mean by it. So, what? You have a girlfriend back in Maine? You got a lost love you’re pining for? What is it, Jonathan? What don’t I get?”

“If you can come here for a minute, I’ll explain.” Jonathan reached under the couch and pulled out three shoeboxes.

Lisa squinted her eyes to read the covers. Box one was labeled in black Sharpie *Melissa*. Box two was the same. Box three was labeled *Lisa*. Lisa stood still. Anger was now making it hard for her to breathe. Her breath came shallow and her mouth twitched with the struggle to hold back her tears. “Why are you showing me this? I don’t want to know about her. I think you should take me home.”

“Lisa, really, please, sit. She’s not a girlfriend, she’s not a past girlfriend.” He hung his head. “She’s not real.” The silence was heavy waiting for Jonathan to deliver his next line. “She’s you. You’re her. You’re Melissa.”

CHAPTER 25

Jonathan had heard the phrase, 'do or die' but had never fully felt the effect until this moment. He didn't know where to start. He lifted the lid off the box marked *Lisa*. "Look. These are all the letters you've written me over the past few weeks."

Lisa stood quietly, her arms crossed.

"And these," he lifted first one lid marked *Melissa*, then the other, "these are from, well, from Melissa, but—"

Lisa let out an exasperated sigh. "I told you I don't want to know about Melissa." She spat the last word in jealousy.

"Again, she's not real, Lisa. Look." He pulled the very first list he had written out of the box and held it up for Lisa to see. The paper was thin and ratty from being folded and unfolded so many times and it was smudged and dirty from years of use. "It's dated 1988."

"And...so? You must still be hung up on her if that's all your family talks about."

"I guess you could say I'm still hung up on her." Jonathan laughed uncomfortably, but then realized this was a bad time to joke as Lisa grabbed her purse.

"Okay, then. Good luck with that." She headed toward the door. "I'll find a way home."

"Lisa. It's you. Look, Melissa's made up. She's not a real person. I made her up. All of this." He picked up the two boxes. "This is fake." Jonathan's desperation got Lisa to look back. He continued, "Four years ago, my dad and brother challenged me to manifest what it was I wanted in a girlfriend. They told me to make her up, make a list, write letters to her, have her write back. I was so lonely at the time. I thought I'd give it a shot. So I created her in my mind and wrote down things about her and for four years, I—"

Lisa took the few steps back toward the couch and slid into the cushions.

"Lisa, are you okay? You don't look good." Jonathan went to get her a glass of water. He handed it cautiously to her. "Are you okay?"

Lisa stared at the boxes on the floor. "It's all fake?"

Jonathan couldn't tell if her voice registered doubt or disgust. "Well, kinda fake. Here, look at this." He handed her the list. "You tell me if you think it's fake."

Lisa accepted the list from Jonathan. Along the top read: August 1988—The Birth of Melissa. She scanned the contents. The first line read: *Just starting college this month*. Lisa quickly calculated the coincidence and thought, big deal. The second line read: *From Iowa*. She looked at Jonathan who was watching her intently and said to him perhaps a bit too harshly. "This isn't me. I'm not from Iowa."

"Just keep reading," Jonathan pushed.

The rest of the list swirled in her head: majoring in art, honor roll, small high school, long-term relationship in college, waitressed in college, brown hair/eyes, 5'7", dogs, original parents, three older siblings, drives red, older car, continuing education, will teach me sports, can shoot pool, middle name same as grandma's.

Lisa handed the list back to Jonathan.

"Well?" he asked.

"Well," Lisa paused. "Is that why you asked me my middle name that night?"

"Is that all you have to say?" Jonathan smiled.

Lisa said nothing for a full minute. Things began to sink in. She recalled Jonathan asking all these specific questions. As they sat at Denny's that night, she even felt at times that she was being interviewed. Then, at Café Minnie's, the random questions she now realized weren't so random. Every bullet on the list Jonathan had covered with her the last few weeks. "It's weird. You wrote this all four years ago?"

"Yes, but can you see the similarities? Look almost every item matches up and the ones that don't, well, they're close. They're damn close."

"Close." Lisa's thoughts drifted. *Is this cool...or is this creepy?* She picked up the list again and shook her head in confusion.

"But, look, it's not just the list." Jonathan pushed the Melissa boxes toward her. "Come here and sit down."

Lisa slid from the couch to the floor and saw inside the two boxes now. They were crammed with papers, and napkins, and notes, and cards. "Oh, God. I don't know. I don't know about this. What is this?" she stammered.

"Just keep an open mind. Here, read this." Jonathan handed her a letter from the box that had been labeled with her name.

"I don't have to read it. I wrote this," Lisa said.

"I know. But read it and refresh your memory of what you wrote."

Lisa scanned through the letter she had written to him days ago. Then Jonathan reached into a Melissa box and unfolded a typed letter. "Now, read this one."

Lisa took the letter and began to read, *Dear Jonathan*. Halfway through, she looked at the top of the letter: it was dated 1990. Back to the letter, Lisa noticed that phrases were eerily similar to ones she had read from her own letter. *Thank you for showing me the Space Needle and Green Lake. I love sitting and talking with you for hours analyzing the situations around us. Playing pool with you was fun. I look forward to spending more time with you. It's nice to hang out with someone who enjoys reading and writing.*

She handed the letter back to Jonathan.

"Well?" He waited again.

"Pretty generic. And it seems you manipulated many of those things; Space Needle, Green Lake, pool, you know."

"Fair enough. Read this one." He handed her another letter. This one started, *Dear Melissa*. It was dated 1992. Lisa read it through to the end: *You've said you were coming for four years. I've waited. I'm not going to write anymore. I don't want you to write. I just want you to be here. Now.*

"You broke up with her?" Lisa didn't even know what she was asking at this point.

"Yeah, but don't you get it. Right when I broke up with her is right when I met you. Crazy, huh? And you can't say that the similarities aren't there. It's just too coincidental. You're Melissa. You're her." Jonathan's excitement was not rubbing off on Lisa.

"So for four years—these two boxes full—you maintained a fake relationship?" Lisa shook her head.

"It was just done in fun. It's not like I had a real girlfriend and was doing this. I just did it until I met someone."

"And now? Now that you've met someone?"

"That's even the crazier thing. Like I said, I had stopped writing to her right before I met you. And then here you are. And, it's just too perfect."

"Perfect? Perfect for who? For you?" Lisa asked.

"No, for both of us. I mean, you like me, right?"

"Yeah, I did...I do." Obviously, Lisa liked him. The physical intimacy . . . they had just taken a huge step forward in their relationship. "But this is just weird. I don't know about this."

"Really, Melissa, it was done for fun."

"You mean, Lisa, right?"

"Oh God, yeah, Lisa. I'm just so excited to get this off my chest. Here look at some more."

Lisa and Jonathan spent the next two hours looking at all the letters, and lists, and notes. At one point, Lisa compared the experiment to something she had heard. "I just read about this thing. Jim Carrey post-dated a check to himself for 10 million dollars."

"And years later, he was able to cash it," Jonathan added.

"Yes."

"I read about that too."

"It seems as if you've done the same thing," Lisa said.

"What do you mean?"

"Well you've imagined something you wanted in your life and then you got it."

"Yes, yes," Jonathan agreed.

"It's like you post-dated your soul mate."

"Post-dated a soul mate. Yes. I like it. That's good."

"I suppose you'll steal that idea for your book too." Lisa laughed.

"Yes, I suppose I might."

"Just make sure I get a mention in the footnotes."

"You got it."

She continued reading the letters and notes from the boxes. Some of them were quite comical and Lisa lightened up as she realized this was a creative experiment Jonathan had tried with his brother and dad. Albeit, one that hit pretty close to home for her but it was flattering to actually be the one Jonathan had created to come into his life; or close to the one. The idea stuck in her head this was quite possibly the makings of romantic serendipity with a Pygmalion-like twist.

CHAPTER 26

Cathy saw things entirely differently. "Holy crap, little cousin, what a psycho."

Lisa finished explaining the whole scenario after she had had a few days to let it settle herself. "Oh, come on. You've met him. Not quite the psycho persona." She defended him; she'd grown quite fond of the whole Melissa process. The fact he wrote things about her years before ever meeting her was an idea of what fairytales are made of. What a neat story to tell grandkids someday.

"Yeah, but—" Cathy shook her head. "Come on. It's just—" she struggled to explain. "It's just weird."

"It's not weird. I mean, think about it, it's kind of cool." Lisa sat on the couch and curled her feet up under her.

"Cool that a psycho obsessed about a woman for four years that he completely made up. Talk about a Pygmalion effect." Cathy joined her on the couch.

Lisa's eyebrows shot up.

"What? You think I've never read anything?"

"No, it's just—"

"It's just nothing. Jonathan is Pygmalion and you're his sculpture, Galatea. Or this Melissa is his Galatea. And he's fallen in love with Melissa. And now you've walked in to this whole made-up world of his."

"But I'm real. I'm a person he's met. I'm not fake."

"He sees you as a person he's known for four years. What happens when you don't fit into his nice little box—or shoebox, like you said?"

"Come on. You've met him. He's rational. He knows I'm not really Melissa," Lisa said.

"Rational does not write letters for four years to a figment of his imagination," Cathy replied.

"Can you just for a second think of it as something fun. I mean, really. What if there is something to this manifestation thing? You know, thinking about something and wanting it so bad and then it happens? How do you explain that? You wanted those K2 skis so bad and kept talking about them, and eyeing them in the store, and trying to figure out how you were going to get them. Admit it, you were *obsessed* with them. And then a pair shows up on your doorstep."

"A pair didn't just *show up,"* Cathy snarled the last two words. "Your dad sent them to me."

"But he had no idea how obsessed you were over them. To him it was a nice gesture. To you, it was the be-all and end-all of gestures. Those skis coming to you are like me coming to Jonathan. You even sleep with them."

This flipped Cathy's attention. "What? You slept with him? When? How was—"

Lisa held up her hand. "Not doing this."

"Come on. It was on Sunday after dinner, wasn't it? Your birthday gift?" She sang the word birthday. "How cliché. For a writer, he's not very original."

"Oh my gosh. There is no pleasing you," Lisa said.

"Yeah, but did he please you? That's the question."

"Again. Not. Doing. This. I'm going to get ready." Lisa stood from the couch and headed for the bathroom.

"Getting ready for what? Now where are you going?" Cathy was right on her heels.

"We're going out to dinner with his parents tonight," Lisa stated.

"Oh, good God, no. Have I taught you nothing? This shit is getting real." Cathy struck the back of her hand to her forehead and heaved an exasperated sigh. "No, no, no. She's gone. She's gone."

"You're such a drama queen."

"Admit it, you're so so gone," Cathy said.

"I guess I am. We're planning to drive down to California next week for Spring Break, so you might as well get your say out about that now also." Lisa tried to deliver it nonchalantly knowing Cathy would be all over her.

But Cathy just stared. Then dropped her chin to her chest and faked big heaving sobs and bellowed, "No, no, no."

"Just be happy for me," Lisa said.

When Cathy finally looked up she moaned, "Oh, I am. I am Maahhh....lissss.......ahhhhh,"

CHAPTER 27

By the end of the week, Jonathan and Lisa had finalized their decision to drive to California. It was Lisa's school Spring Break and she was able to get her shifts covered at Jillian's. Jonathan was still two weeks out from going on his book tour. They had plans to meet his two brothers—James and Rob—and one of her sisters, Lynn. Both his brothers had commented they were excited to finally meet Melissa. Lisa's sister knew nothing about Melissa.

Starting out, Jonathan encouraged almost immediately, "So tell me about these sisters of yours."

"What do you want to know?"

"I'm meeting Lynn, right?"

"Yes."

"And the other two—" he prompted.

"Lori and LuAnne."

"Yes, Lori and LuAnne. Where are they?"

"They both live in Los Angeles also. But LuAnne and her husband will be out of town this week. I never got a hold of Lori."

"You've said you and Lori aren't close, right?"

"Right. She was out of the house by the time I was six and we've never really had a relationship."

"And LuAnne was the one that was still in the house when you were growing up?" Jonathan asked.

"Yes. She's eight years older, so she was around 14 when the other two moved out."

"Are you close?"

"I guess as close as can be. She's married with a kid now. We do have some connection with the whole court reporting thing. She's been doing it for about six years now."

"Were you close when you were growing up?"

"What is this? Twenty questions?"

"Of course. Maybe one hundred questions. Is that okay?" Jonathan reached across the hand brake and squeezed Lisa's knee.

"Yeah, it's okay. But what about your sisters?"

"Same story. Being the youngest, you tend to be forgotten when they move out," Jonathan said.

"Yeah, but in LuAnne's case, we moved out on her. When my parents retired and moved to Idaho, she was still living at home."

"So the whole time you lived in California, you lived with her?"

"Yes."

"How was your relationship?"

"I always feel she had a bit of resentment toward me because all my classes—piano, tap, softball, ice skating—she was always employed by my parents to be my driver. She'd even have to pick us up from school on alternate days with my friends' mom."

"You were busy."

"Yeah, I can't remember ever not being in some kind of class. I loved it. But I'm sure she didn't imagine getting her driver's license would lead to being her little sister's chauffeur." Lisa reached in the back seat for some snacks. She opened a bag of chips and offered it to Jonathan.

"Barbeque, my favorite."

"I know."

Jonathan paused to look at Lisa. They had only been together a short time, but she knew all about him and paid attention. He was doubtful Celeste could name his favorite chip. His heart swelled. More and more, he knew this was going to work. And even though he had known pretty much all about her before they even met, he still wanted to know more.

"Did LuAnne ever tell you she resented you?"

"Oh, no. It's just something I would imagine she felt. I don't even know if she did. I was a little shit, though," Lisa said.

"Like what?"

"Well, sometimes I would get home before her and she had this soap opera she liked; the one with Luke and Laura."

"General Hospital," Jonathan filled in.

"Oh my gosh, no. Tell me you didn't watch that."

"Of course, I did. All the girls in the dorm, religiously at 2:30 would be in the TV room to watch it. To be where the girls were, I watched it."

"Such a ladies' man. I can picture it. So suave, so smooth," Lisa teased.

"Hey, I knew all the characters and plot lines and if a girl missed an episode I would offer my services to fill her in," Jonathan said.

"Oh, I'm sure you would, Casanova."

"It actually wasn't a bad show," Jonathan continued.

Lisa looked at him sideways and arched her brow. "So, anyway," she continued, shaking her head, "I would be home before LuAnne and if I heard her Volkswagen pull up, I would lock the front door."

"You rat."

"It gets worse. We would race each other to the back door. If I won, she was locked out. If she won, I was in a world of trouble."

"Meaning?"

"She's strong. I mean, freakishly. I think from shoveling all the horse manure all those years."

"Wait. As in figuratively?"

"No, literally. She had a horse growing up and was at the stable more than at home. She would literally shovel pounds and pounds of shit. Her arms were like tanks. To this day, no one in our family—and I have some big, athletic, male cousins—has beaten her at arm wrestling. I'm telling you, freakishly strong. And she's little, like five foot nothing, the shortest in our family."

"What would she do if she caught you?"

"She would get on top of me and pin my arms back with her knees and then pound my chest with her knuckle. I never, ever, broke free. And one time she had this needle and was like, 'Repeat after me. I will never lock my sister out again and if I do I will get this needle put in my eye.'"

"Did you repeat it?"

"Of course."

"Did you ever lock her out again?"

"Of course."

They both laughed. "You were a little shit," Jonathan said.

"I know. But she did her share too."

"Like?"

"As the younger sister, you'd think I would be the tattletale. But she was the worst. And she would set me up."

"I'm sure you would do just fine setting yourself up," Jonathan said.

"Hey, whose side are you on?" Lisa reached across and punched him in the arm.

Jonathan grabbed his arm as if he was really hurt. "Yours. Yours. Of course, yours."

"We had this freezer in the garage and my mom kept it locked."

"Why would she lock it?" Jonathan asked.

"You've seen pictures of me as a kid. It's obvious I loved to eat."

"Yes, it was obvious."

"Again. Whose side are you on?" Lisa asked. "Well, mom would put the good stuff in there. You know, Girl Scout cookies, homemade chocolate chip cookies, Girl Scout Cookies, peanut butter balls, Girl Scout cookies. Girl Scout cookies. The good ones. Thin Mints."

"I get it. Girl Scout Cookies."

"Yes. And LuAnne would always find the key and unlock it and then tell me—slyly—that it was unlocked. Well, that's all it took. The cookies? They never had a chance," Lisa said.

"Would she eat them?"

"Maybe one or two. Me? One or two also. One or two...*boxes*. And then she'd rat me out."

"Like just tell on you?"

"Not straight out. But at the dinner table, when mom would ask, 'Who ate all the Girl Scout cookies?' there was only one answer. And LuAnne would give it. Because ultimately, it was me who ate them all."

"She sounds brilliant."

"Oh, yeah, brilliant. Setting up her little eight-year old sister," Lisa said. "But she was okay. She'd take me to the stables with her. Although one time, her horse swiped its head to get a fly and took out a chunk of my neck in the process."

"What?" Jonathan was surprised.

"It wasn't bad, but it was bleeding. She didn't even take me home. Insisted she had to give Scooter a bath first. So I sat around while the flies swarmed around the gash."

"That's terrible."

"Actually, it turned out okay. She got in so much trouble. My mom was pissed. She got grounded for like a month," Lisa said.

"Sounds like you two had some adventures," Jonathan said.

"We did. Good memories. We get along fine now, just not real close."

"Sounds like me and my sisters." Jonathan changed the subject. "I think we'll stop in Redding. Then we can make San Diego late tomorrow."

"Sounds good," Lisa agreed. "Are we meeting up with your brother—is it, Rob?—tomorrow night?" The trip had been planned so quickly, they hadn't talked about the minute details.

"Not tomorrow night. He said he had something going. But we'll stay overnight and then meet up with him the next morning."

"We're staying overnight at his house? And he's not around?" Lisa questioned.

Jonathan hesitated slightly. He knew it might seem odd to Lisa they would not be staying at his brother's house. Especially since her sister, Lynn, was so adamant in her hospitable invitation. "We're not staying at his house. We'll get a hotel close to his house." He added, "His place is small; he doesn't have room."

"Oh." Lisa sensed there was something Jonathan wasn't telling her. But she thought she'd probably figure it out soon enough.

The next day, they got up early and continued to San Diego. The second day of the trip flew by also as Jonathan and Lisa continued to share childhood stories and make up stories of passengers in passing cars. The trivia cards even made an appearance as Lisa tested his knowledge.

On the morning they had planned to spend with Jonathan's brother Rob, Lisa was surprised to meet Jonathan's polar opposite.

Rob greeted them with, "Hey, man. I can't hang out today. I gotta get some groceries." He stood behind the closed screen door, his arms crossed over his chest, another barrier between them.

"No problem," Jonathan said.

"Just wait there. I'll walk you to your car." Rob closed the door.

Lisa looked at Jonathan. "He does know we just drove over 1200 miles to see him, right?"

"Yeah, I guess I'm not surprised. We're not that close."

"That's not the point. He knew we were coming, right? And he's going to get groceries?" Lisa was mildly irritated and highly unimpressed.

Rob opened the door and stepped out with a box full of bottles. "Hey, bro. Thought you could use some perfume. Now that you got a lady." He winked toward Lisa.

Jonathan grabbed the box that Rob shoved into his chest. "Thanks, man. That's great."

The three of them walked the pathway to the parking lot and approached Jonathan's Subaru. "Looks like you have room to drop me off at the store," Rob said. "That way I don't have to take the bus." He opened the front passenger door and slid in, asking Lisa, "You don't mind sitting in the back, do you?"

Lisa eyed Jonathan over the top of the car and he shrugged his shoulders.

"No, of course not," she said, moving suitcases and bags in order to squeeze in.

At the store, Rob turned to Jonathan with his palm up. "Thirty bucks, man."

"Thirty bucks, what?" Jonathan asked.

"For the perfumes. They're five bucks a bottle and you got six. That's a deal. Usually I charge seven bucks. But you know, family discount, and all."

From the back Lisa said, "You know, Jonathan, I don't really wear perfume, so we don't need it." She felt the look before she turned and saw it. Rob's eyes clearly said, 'Back off.'

Then he turned to Jonathan. "Oh, the ladies all love this stuff. You can save it and give it to your next lady."

Jonathan struggled to get his wallet from his back pocket. As he opened it, Rob eyed it like a vulture. Jonathan handed him two bills. "Here you go, man. Thirty bucks. Good deal."

"You know, I could use some bus money if you have any spare."

Again Lisa interrupted. "That's not a good idea. We need that for gas money to get home. Especially after the hotel cost last night." This time, she eyed Rob with her own look.

Jonathan pushed another twenty at Rob. "Here you go. Have a good one, man. Good seeing you."

Rob got out of the car and Lisa opened the back door to move to the front. When she shut the back, Rob slammed the front door and left them both standing there. He chuckled, stuffed the fifty bucks in his front pocket and retreated.

"What a jerk." Lisa slid in the front seat. She looked to Jonathan, who gripped the steering wheel with both hands and rested his head in the middle.

"Seriously, what a jerk," she repeated.

Jonathan lifted one hand as if to put her on hold and she realized he was crying. "Hey, what's wrong? He's not worth it."

Jonathan looked up at her with red eyes. "You don't understand. He hasn't always been that way. He's had a rough time."

"It doesn't matter how rough a time you have; you don't treat people like crap."

"He's pretty bitter. And I think a bit jealous of me."

"And so that makes it okay?"

"He became a pilot, I think, to get my dad's approval and attention. They used to fly all the time together. Now he sees me close to dad because I wrote a book."

"Why doesn't he just go and fly with your dad?"

"He can't."

"Because he's a jerk?" Lisa laughed, then felt bad because Jonathan looked so beat up, "Sorry."

"No. He can't because he lost his license."

"Lost it, how?"

"He didn't do a proper pre-flight and there was an accident. And, well, the passengers—" Jonathan shook his head. "There was an accident."

"Oh, shit. That sucks."

"I guess that's why I'm a little more patient with his idiosyncrasies. Like I said, he's had a rough time."

"He still doesn't have to be an ass," Lisa mumbled under her breath.

Jonathan started the car and backed out of the spot. They drove north on the I-5 in silence. At the sign for the Mission San Juan Capistrano, Lisa finally spoke. "Why don't we get off here and check out the mission?"

"Thought we'd just head up to your sister's." Jonathan's voice revealed he was still sulking.

"She's not expecting us until later this afternoon, so we have lots of time."

"Fine."

The mission was crowded with busses full of students and tours crisscrossing paths all over the grounds. Jonathan and Lisa walked around in their own thoughts until Lisa finally asked, "Are you mad at me?"

"No."

"Then why are you treating me like crap right now?"

"I don't feel you were very empathetic toward my brother."

"Empathetic? We weren't even there long enough to establish empathy. He basically dismissed us."

"I told you, he's had a rough time."

"Seems to me he's going to continue having a rough time the way that he treats people. I mean, come on Jonathan, right in front of me he tells you that you can give the perfume to your next girlfriend. What's that supposed to mean?"

Jonathan gazed off to the distance and remained quiet. Lisa

continued, "Seems you should be showing empathy to me for having been so disrespected by your brother." When Jonathan still wouldn't engage, she persisted. "I mean, you're going to meet my sister in about four hours and she's had a rough time of it, too. She lost her husband last year and is raising her kid on her own, and yet she will not treat you with one iota of disrespect. And never in my wildest dreams would she ever turn us away at the door." Jonathan faced Lisa. "So, excuse me, if no matter what has happened to your brother, I still think he acted like a complete jerk and was extremely rude to me."

"You're right." Jonathan was barely audible.

"What?"

"I said, you're right. There was no excuse for Rob saying that to you." Jonathan grabbed Lisa's hand. "I'm sorry."

"It's not your fault. You don't have to apologize."

"But I should have said something to him talking about you like that. I feel like I'm walking on eggshells around him. And you're right, he needs to get over it."

Lisa leaned in to Jonathan and let him wrap his arms around her. He kissed the top of her head and whispered, "Did we just have our first fight?"

Lisa pulled away and looked up. "I don't think we really had a fight. Just a mishap." She wrapped her arms around the top of his shoulders and kissed him.

Jonathan pulled away and held her face in both his hands. "I love you, Lisa."

Lisa's heart triggered. *Whoa, this was fast*. She'd known Jonathan for less than two months. But she knew. "I love you, too."

They shared a long embrace as birds fluttered around them and school children screamed in delight at new-found excitements at the Mission. Lisa knew it was corny but in the bright blue sky, she felt as if the birds were singing just for them.

After several minutes, Jonathan pulled away, and kissed her lightly once more. "Let's get going. We'll stop to buy flowers for your sister. I'm excited to meet her and put this behind us." He grabbed Lisa's hand and led her to the car.

CHAPTER 28

Meeting Lisa's sister, Lynn, Jonathan realized—just as Lisa had predicted—how completely different this was going to go than the Rob fiasco.

"Hello, weary Washington travelers." Lynn did not just greet them. She bounded off her front porch and ran first to Lisa's side and hugged her so tight that Jonathan heard an *umph* escape. Then, pulling Lisa with her, Lynn careened to Jonathan's side and grabbed him and squealed, "And this must be Jonathan. Nice to meet you." Her hug was more embracing than any hug Jonathan had ever received from his own sisters. But then, they hadn't grown up surrounded in affection and public displays.

"Hey." Jonathan struggled to talk in the embrace. "It's great to meet you too." Emerging from her hug, Jonathan stared from Lynn to Lisa and then back to Lynn. The same golden, brown hair and brown eyes and face structure caught him off guard. "Wow, you two look so much alike."

"Wait a minute," Lisa protested. "Don't forget to add, 'Except for the ten-year age difference.'"

"Too late," Lynn laughed. "He said it, we look exactly alike."

"He did not say *exactly,*" Lisa said as she hugged her sister again.

"Okay. Okay. Okay." Jonathan put his arms up in mock defense. "I see I'm going to have to be careful with this one. Let's just say you two are definitely sisters."

"That works."

Jonathan dipped back in the car and presented Lynn with a bouquet of sunflowers. "These are for you."

Clearly she was impressed. Jonathan saw her look to Lisa and raise her eyebrows, then back to Jonathan. "Well, well, aren't you sweet—"

Jonathan stood a little straighter, enjoying the praise.

"—or a kiss ass," Lynn finished. She looked to Lisa. "Which is it?"

Lisa glanced at Jonathan, who shrunk a bit.

"Oh, my God, I'm kidding. Obviously he doesn't know our sarcastic trait yet." Lynn playfully nudged Jonathan.

"Well, he knows it, it just sometimes takes him a minute to get it." Lisa curled under his arm. "She's kidding, Jonathan. And by the way," Lisa addressed Lynn. "He's sweet."

"That's all I need to know." She grabbed Jonathan on the other side.

Jonathan finally got a chance to talk. "Oh, boy, now I've got two of you to handle. This could get complicated." But Jonathan already knew he liked Lynn and he squeezed her back. "Come on, grab your bags. We have a busy schedule tonight."

"I told you we didn't have to do anything special. And where's Liana?" Lisa couldn't wait to see her little niece.

"She's at the sitter's for tonight."

"Ah, I wanted to see her." Lisa was disappointed.

"You get her all day tomorrow. She can't wait for SeaWorld. It's all she's talked about the whole week. You're going to have your hands full."

Jonathan piped in. "It'll be a blast. Lisa's told me all about her. And I too, love Shamu."

"Tonight, it's just us," Lynn continued. "It's the first time my baby sister's been here in over two years and the first time I've met her beau. Please. We're going to have some fun. I hope you like country music and I hope you're not afraid of a mechanical bull, Jonathan."

Jonathan whispered to Lisa as Lynn led the way into the house, "I'm hoping that is one of her sarcastic-ha-ha-got-you comments."

"Afraid not. It's her thing."

"I think the visit with Rob is leading at this point," he joked.

"You wish. You're going to love her."

"I can tell."

"Come on, slackers. Get your things in here and go freshen up. We leave in fifteen minutes," Lynn called from within the house.

Jonathan realized Lynn wasn't kidding as they walked into a popular steakhouse in Hermosa Beach. There it was, ominously placed right in the middle of the restaurant atop a padded maroon mat. The dreaded bull. As they took their seats, Jonathan was sure it was for show and ignored it until he heard his name called across the restaurant.

"Jonathan, you're up."

He thought he'd misheard. But looking up from his menu and seeing Lynn smiling and Lisa nudging him from the side, he knew this was for real.

"No way. No way am I doing that." Jonathan just wanted a good steak and to get to know Lisa's family better.

"Oh, yes. You're up. Come on, it'll be fun. I'll tell him to take it easy on you." Lynn was already standing next to the table and pulling on Jonathan's hand.

"Lisa, tell her this isn't my thing," Jonathan begged.

"Um, yeah, Lynn, this really isn't his thing," Lisa said with no effort whatsoever.

"Oh, thanks."

"I've got nothing to do with this. You're on your own. She's definitely not going to listen to me." Lisa said.

Lynn led him around to the gate. He wasn't sure about this at all. But Lynn assured him, "Don't worry. Just squeeze your thighs and hold on tight. I'll tell him to go slow."

"All right, but seriously, tell him really slow." Jonathan almost fell as he tried to balance on the padded flooring. Getting to the bull didn't alleviate his fear; the thing was huge. He didn't even know how to get on it so he jumped and laid his full belly perpendicular across its back. He could hear Lynn, "Take it easy on him, first timer," and the mechanical bull driver's snappy retort, "No, really. I never would have guessed."

Jonathan finally got on; facing the correct way even. He saw

Lisa waving and cheering him from outside the ring. "Hang on," she called. "Just have fun."

Fun? "Okay." He smiled limply.

The bull lurched forward. But it was slow. *This isn't so bad,* he thought. It went into reverse; again, slowly. *Piece of cake.* The back end started to rise up, forcing his body weight forward and he heard Lynn yelling, "Lean back, stay back!" so he reversed his torso to get parallel with the rear. Shit, he was practically professional. Then the driver did something that made the bull punch forward a couple times. Jonathan squeezed hard and leaned back further and managed to stay on. *Challenge me*. The bull punched a few more times and Jonathan laughed out loud as his whole body lurched back and forth. He saw Lisa laughing and clapping. And then the bull punched forward once, twice, three times, and continued until Jonathan yelled through his laughter, "Okay, okay, enough, stop."

The bull stopped and set upright. The whole room started clapping. Breathless, Jonathan released his death grip and waved with one hand. At this point, the bull curled and swirled in slow motion and Jonathan toppled over and landed with a thud on the padded floor. He looked to the driver who mimicked Jonathan's one hand wave and smiled. Jonathan lay back on the mat and laughed. He could hear Lisa and Lynn whooping and cheering, "Jon-a-than, Jon-a-than, Jon-a-than," and soon the whole room joined them. He struggled to stand and hold his balance on the wobbly floor and lifted both arms in a victory pose.

Lynn met him at the gate with a hug. "Nice job, you're not a virgin anymore."

"Guess not. That was actually pretty fun."

Reaching Lisa at the table, Lynn said, "You got a good sport there. I can't believe he did it."

"I know. That's why I love him."

"What?" Lynn said. "Oh boy, we need to talk. Sit down, you two."

Jonathan eased when Lisa assured him, "Don't worry. This is

her big sister questioning phase. You'll do fine." She squeezed his hand and scooted to sit closer to him.

Lynn started in. "So what are your intentions with my sister?" She even tried to maintain a straight face while using her 'adult' voice.

"I guess my intentions—"

"Don't even answer that," Lisa interrupted.

"Shut up, Lisa. Yes, he does have to answer it." Lynn looked to Jonathan, "Shoot."

"Well, my intentions are, I love her, too. She's my soul mate."

"I know all about that. I read your dad's books, you know. I'm *that* era."

"She is," Lisa explained. "She used to have seagulls all over her room; posters, carvings, stuffed birds. I didn't even know it had to do with a book."

"Really? I guess you are of that age," Jonathan said.

"I'm going to ignore the age remark," Lynn stated. "But yes, Richard Bach was on my high school reading list. And yes, I identified with Jonathan the seagull breaking out of the flock and reaching his goals."

"Oh God, Lynn, stop," Lisa chastised her. "You're becoming stalkerish."

"It's kind of cool, you know. I mean the son of Richard Bach just rode the mechanical bull. You couldn't even write this shit," she laughed. "Or, I guess, maybe you could, since you're an author."

Jonathan really liked Lynn. So different than the dysfunction and anger that beleaguered his family. He hoped Lisa wasn't making her own comparisons of their families. Because, no doubt, his was the lesser of the two; even if he had a famous dad. Although, their next stop was to meet James and his wife and of everyone in his family, James was definitely Jonathan's favorite. Even though James had his quirks too, he thought Lisa would like him, especially after Rob.

They returned home and Lynn announced that Lisa would be staying in her room with her. "Girl talk," she said before she hugged

Jonathan good night and whispered in his ear, "If you hurt her, you'll have me to deal with."

Lynn crawled into bed next to Lisa. "Spill," she said.

"Spill what?" Lisa asked.

"Don't give me that. You've known this guy, what? Two months? And already 'love'? What's going on?"

"I don't know. It feels right. Different, but right."

"Different? What do you mean different?"

"I've only ever dated jocks. You know. Our dates were playing basketball, throwing the football, active. And now, it's like so mental. Like we talk; we analyze things. Books, movies. I don't know."

"Okay, okay. I get it," Lynn said.

"I mean, he's publishing a book. It's so weird to get the chance to talk to an actual author."

"Whoa, wait. You're not in love because of stars in your eyes, are you?"

"What do you mean?"

"You know, because of what he's done; what he may do. Potential? Don't fall in love for potential," Lynn preached.

"I don't think that's it. I've never really been a star chaser. In fact, kind of the opposite. They all put their pants on one leg at a time, just like us."

"Now you're just talking in clichés."

"No. It's like you with Richard Bach and your stars talking about him tonight. I mean, we went to dinner with him last week and I didn't even—"

"What? You got to meet Richard Bach?" Lynn practically yelled.

"He is Jonathan's dad, you know."

"But you got to meet him? What's he like?"

"Like I said, they put their pants on one leg at a—"

"Shut up. What was he like?"

"I don't know. He's just a man. He's just the dad of the guy I'm dating." Lisa had actually found him quite curious. She could definitely see why Jonathan had these universe theory ideas. Richard had mentioned a few ideas of his own, one being about 'walk-ins.' Jonathan had brought a photograph he had found of his dad in front of an old crop duster plane. Richard had taken one glance at it and declared, 'Now, that's a walk-in.' After his explanation, the idea that Lisa came away with was that Richard believed lives consist of several souls that inhabit people's bodies throughout their lives. They come in, reside for a while and then move on. Looking at photographs, physically you can identify yourself; however, who you were at the time depended on the 'walk-in' that inhabited your body. Lisa felt most comfortable when she asked Richard if he really believed that and he flipped his hand and laughed, diminishing the idea to 'Who knows? It's just fun to ponder things in different ways.' She did find the idea intriguing, but she didn't know quite how to explain it to Lynn.

"Wait. Did you meet Leslie too?"

"Yeah, Lynn. That's his dad's wife."

"This is unbelievable. Okay. So what happened?"

"Nothing happened. We went to dinner and had a nice time. They're nice."

"Nice. Nice? That's all you have to say. They are the epitome of the love story for this century. Are they like in the book?"

"He does call her Wookie," Lisa offered.

"That's cool. That's what Ron used to call Liana when she was born." The rare reference to Lynn's late husband caught Lisa off guard. But Lynn was continuing, "Are they still in love?"

"I don't know. I didn't ask them."

"But you can tell. Were they?"

"I guess." Lisa hadn't noticed anything special about them. He opened the door for her and she had covered his hand on the table as he talked of their adventures. They spoke of attending the operas and symphonies and ballets often in the city. And they held hands as they departed from the restaurant. But that was normal couple activity.

"So nothing? You're not going to share anything with me?"

"There's nothing to share. We had dinner. They talked a lot about Jonathan's upcoming tour and who they liked as interviewers and who they didn't."

"Who'd they say?"

"They mentioned that Paula Zahn was one of their least favorite interviewers. I don't remember the others."

"You're clueless."

"I'm not clueless. It wasn't important, I guess. I was more aware that I was meeting the parents of the guy I was dating. You know, trying to make a good impression on them; not worrying about their impression on me."

"I guess I can't accuse you of having stars in your eyes, then," Lynn conceded.

Lynn was right. Lisa hadn't approached the evening that way. But it could be because she had never heard of Richard Bach before two months ago. So it wasn't like he was really famous to her. Maybe if it had been Stephen King, she would have been more inclined to ask for an autograph. "Wait. I do remember something that happened."

"What?"

"At dinner. It was so awkward. One of the waitresses came to our table and asked if he was Richard Bach. When he said, 'yes' she basically started crying at the table telling him how he had changed her life and how his book had saved her. It was really creepy."

"No way. What'd he do?"

"He listened and then, I think to shut her up, he offered his autograph. He wrote something on a napkin. And she was bawling and thanking him. It was so uncomfortable."

"Does that happen a lot?"

"I don't think a lot. I mean, he's an author and it's not like his face is everywhere and he's not real recognizable. But they did say they carry guns."

"Really?"

"Yeah, something about a psycho fan they had a scare from in the past."

Lisa knew this was the stuff that Lynn was interested in. But she really wanted to tell her about Melissa. She wasn't sure how she would take it. Cathy had been less than enthusiastic about the whole idea. But, Lynn, being such a Richard Bach fan was sure to find it intriguing. She was about to start the story when Lynn grabbed her tight. "Well, Lisa, I like him. He seems like a nice guy. I'm glad you guys came to visit."

"Yeah, me too."

"Better get some sleep. We have a big day at SeaWorld tomorrow. Liana can be a handful."

"I can't wait to see her. 'Night."

Liana was dropped off early, so by the time Lisa and Jonathan got up she was already at the kitchen table with her mother.

"Come on. You're going to have a big day. You need to eat." Lynn placed another slice of apple on Liana's plate.

The apple was forgotten as Liana slid off her booster and ran to Lisa. "Auntie." She wrapped herself around her legs. "We go see Shamu today?"

Lisa bent down to pick her up and hold her on her side. "Yes, we are. Are you excited?"

"Uh huh. Look at my new shoes." Liana lifted her foot to show off her white and pink Stride Rites complete with matching pink socks.

"Oh my. Aren't those cute. And I love your little OshKosh B'Gosh dress."

"I know. Me too. But mom put the bow in. It's silly." Liana reached up to finger the matching pink bow that was decorating her ponytail.

"I like it."

Liana just snarled and agreed, "Okay."

"Liana, this is Jonathan. Jonathan, Liana."

Liana hid her face in Lisa's shoulder. "Oh my. Are you going to be shy now?" But Liana just hid deeper.

Jonathan lightly grabbed her foot. "I sure like your shoes too. Wish I had a pair like that."

Liana cautiously looked at him grabbing her foot.

"Maybe we could get me a pair to match," Jonathan said.

Liana giggled.

"What? You don't think they'd have my size?"

Liana lifted her head. "Boys don't wear pink, silly."

"I don't know. I think they'd look pretty stylish with my tie." Jonathan held out his dark blue tie that was covered with lighter blue dolphins.

"Hey," Liana grabbed the end. "Dolphins."

"Yup. Special for today. I couldn't find a Shamu tie though. He's my favorite."

"Me too," Liana squealed.

"We have to sit in the front row to be close, but we'll probably get wet," Jonathan explained.

Liana looked curiously from Jonathan to Lisa to her mom. "I don't wanna get wet."

"That's half the fun. I'll cover you so you don't get too wet," Jonathan said.

"Okay," Liana agreed. She turned to her mom. "Can we go now?"

"You haven't eaten your breakfast yet. As soon as you eat, we can go," Lynn said.

"I'm not hungry. And I did eat. I had a 'nana."

"You had a bite of banana." Lynn pointed to her plate.

Liana squirmed out of Lisa's arms and declared, "I'll go get my coat," as she ran from the room.

"Little Miss Independent. Already thinks if she changes the subject, we'll forget," Lynn said. She grabbed Jonathan's tie. "What's with the tie? We're just going to Sea World, not the Ritz."

"He always wears ties," Lisa explained.

"And I thought the dolphins would be perfect for today," Jonathan added.

"Yes, they will," Lynn agreed. "Come get something to eat and we'll head out."

Jonathan and Lisa followed her to the kitchen and made bowls of cereal and prepared toast with peanut butter and jelly. When they got to the table to sit, Liana was still nowhere to be seen. Her plate sat with her untouched toast and the almost whole banana.

"Hey, kiddo," Jonathan called.

Lisa turned to see Liana peaking out from behind the wall. "Come on, Liana. We want to get there early so we get a good seat for Shamu."

"There's lots of shows," Liana informed us.

"What is she? Fifteen?" Lisa asked Lynn.

Jonathan was still trying to coax her out. "Come on. I'll show you my favorite way to eat bananas."

Liana took a step toward the table to see what Jonathan was doing. Jonathan grabbed the banana from her plate and took his knife. He dipped it deep in the peanut butter jar. Liana made it to the edge of the table to watch. Lynn nudged Lisa and smiled. Jonathan made a big show of spreading the peanut butter all along the length of the banana and Liana giggled and smiled. "You have to make sure the whole banana is completely covered in peanut butter," he explained as he covered both tips. "Then if you have honey, it's the best, cause you just dip it in. Do you have honey?" he asked Lynn.

"Sure. But are you going to eat that?" she asked.

"No. It's for Liana." He held the banana out to her. "What do you think?"

Liana threw her head back and laughed.

"It's really good. Try it," he urged.

"Nope." Liana crossed her arms dramatically "'lergic."

"What?"

"Can't. 'lergic to peanuts," Liana said.

"You're allergic to peanuts?" Jonathan looked from Liana to Lynn. Liana was laughing; Lynn was nodding.

"Well, why didn't you say so?"

"Don't have to eat it now," Liana said with a sly smile. "Let's go, Mom." Liana pulled on her mom's sleeve.

"You're gonna be in trouble with that one," Lisa said to Lynn.

"No doubt. How old is she?" Jonathan asked.

"I'm two going on twelve," Liana stated proudly showing her two fingers in a wide V.

"That's what her grandma told her," Lynn explained.

"All righty then. I guess breakfast is over. Let's get this show on the road." Jonathan stood from the table. Then he bent over Liana. "I'm going to get you back for that one, little squirt," he said.

Liana grabbed his hand to lead him down the stairs. "But, we go see Shamu now."

For the rest of the day, Jonathan was Liana's best friend. She would only let him push her in her stroller and at all the shows she would sit on his lap and point out all the things going on. When he bought her a stuffed Shamu, it was all over. She clung to the Shamu with one arm and held tight to his hand with the other.

At lunch, Lynn leaned over to Lisa. "He's really good with kids. Does he want any?"

"Whoa. Slow down there."

"Well, do you think he does?"

"Yeah, I'd think so. He's great with his nephew also. And I guess now—look at him with Liana." Lisa was watching Jonathan swing Liana to his shoulders and carry her across the patio. Liana was laughing and clutching her Shamu and wrapping her free arm around his head. Lisa imagined him as a dad and it made her smile.

When they reached the table, Liana made her voice real deep and greeted them, "Hello, ladies," with a bow of her arm.

"What the—" Lisa laughed.

"Perfectly delivered, m' lady." Jonathan held his hand up and Liana swatted it with a high five.

"Okay, you two. I'm not sure you should be left alone anymore," Lynn said.

"Look. Uncle Jonathan got me." Liana pulled from her pocket a lollipop in the shape of an octopus.

"Great. No breakfast. And more sugar. Are you staying up with her all night, Jonathan?" Lynn asked.

"Sure. But only if we get ice cream." He tugged on Liana's shoe.

"Yes. Yes. Yes," she squealed.

"No. No. No," Lynn replied. She reached for Liana and said, "Come on, let's get to the Shamu show."

They took off a few feet ahead and Lisa pulled Jonathan's arm. "*Uncle* Jonathan?" She raised her eyebrow.

Jonathan smiled and shrugged his shoulders, "She's cute."

That night, Lynn and Lisa fell into bed exhausted. "It was a good day, sis," Lynn said.

"It was."

"Jonathan's nice. He's great with Liana."

"I know," Lisa agreed. Lisa loved watching Jonathan interact with her niece and she fell more in love with him, even picturing the future they could have.

"Tomorrow you're driving to San Jose? You're meeting his brother there?" Lynn could barely keep her eyes open.

"Yeah, and I'm taking him to Huntington Beach first to show him where I grew up and went to school."

"Fun. Take him to the Jack-in-the-Box where we used to hang out at the beach."

"Of course. Love you, sis." Lisa yawned.

"Love you, too. 'Night."

CHAPTER 29

"Here. Pull in here. This is where I went to school." They had already driven through Lisa's old neighborhood where everything looked so small to her. The five-bedroom house where she grew up looked like a dollhouse. And now the church she'd thought was so massive stood like a little shack in front of them.

They pulled into the St. Bonaventure parking lot. Children were clumped in their various activities as it had been eleven years ago when she was here. Hop-scotchers threw trinkets into squares and hopped one-footed through the maze. Jump-ropers double-dutched, their chants echoing through the yard. The volleyball game was boys against girls and a girl was overhead serving, dropping the ball between two boys who glared at each other, insisting it was theirs. Interspersed among the students were teachers and nuns monitoring the activities.

"No way. That can't be Sister Raphael. I can't believe she's still here." Lisa pointed to the nun standing back by the entrance to the school. "Still making sure no one goes in the classroom during recess," she said.

"Want to say hi?" Jonathan asked.

"No. She probably wouldn't know me. I do remember she told my mom they were making the biggest mistake of their lives moving me to Idaho when I was in the eighth grade."

"Why would she say that?"

"I don't know. Traumatic for my age? Too big a change? Or more likely lost tuition for her school," Lisa said with a laugh.

"That's probably it. Did you think your parents made a mistake?"

"Absolutely not. It was the best thing they could have done. I loved Idaho."

They drove around the back of the church where a sports field opened up. "I used to think that was the biggest field in the world. That's where our annual carnival was held. So much fun. Many girls had their first kiss on the top of the Ferris wheel," Lisa said.

"You?"

"I wish. I had the biggest crush on Steve Ross, but he was way out of my league. I wasn't one of the popular girls. Too tall," she said. "I was always lined up in the back row with Irene Wright and Maureen Flannigan. Good for basketball, but not cute and petite like the boys liked."

"Never thought I'd be dating a Catholic girl. You know what they say." Jonathan reached over and squeezed her knee.

"Shut up."

After circling the church, Jonathan asked, "Are you going to show me where you hung out on the beach?"

"We're heading there next. Are you going swimming?"

"Are you kidding? It'll be so cold. I'm not that adventurous."

"That's what I thought. Until I saw you on that bull," Lisa said.

"I still can't believe I did that. Nobody is going to believe I did that."

"I know. I bet you're the first guy in history that ever rode the bull with a Snoopy tie on also." Lisa tugged at the tie he was wearing again today. Even traveling, he dressed in his khakis and signature ties.

"Wish we had a picture of that." Jonathan was at the exit of the parking lot. "Which way to the beach?"

"Left onto Springdale. We'll go to the beach by the Jack-in-the-Box since that is where we always used to go. It's a ways from the pier, but we never went there."

"Cool. I want to see where you used to go. Plus I could go for a cheeseburger. We could have a picnic on the beach."

"Perfect."

They sat at a table outside with cheeseburgers, fries and vanilla shakes. "So this is where you grew up, huh?" Jonathan asked.

"Yup, but I was still young, so I was always here with a parent or friend's parent. It's not like I was a cool kid hanging out on her own."

"What's one of your favorite memories?"

It was the type of question Jonathan always asked and Lisa loved. She reached across the table and wiped the ketchup that had dribbled down his chin. "One day I was here with Leah and Monique, my neighbors. Their mom, Chiyon, brought us. She had taken us to the store before coming and we got candy. Mine was a Chick-o-Stick. I loved Chick-o-Sticks."

"What the heck is a Chick-o-Stick?"

"I don't even know. It was like crunchy outside and had peanut butter, I think, inside."

Jonathan's burger had dripped out the opposite side and spilled down his shirt on his last bite. He was pouring water on his napkin to begin dabbing at the smudge.

"After swimming, we had returned to our towels and Chiyon told me she'd eaten my Chick-o-Stick. I was so mad."

Jonathan laughed as he made the stain worse.

"No. I was like *really* mad. I couldn't believe it. Then Chiyon started laughing and I realized she was kidding. She held my Chick-o-Stick up and it was the most glorious thing I had ever seen."

"Only you would find glory in a Chick-o-Stick."

"You don't understand. I loved these things. So I took my Chick-o-Stick and stomped off in a little tantrum. I could still hear Chiyon laughing when I made it to the water's edge. I turned around to her and when I did a wave hit me and knocked me over."

"No way. You lost the Chick-o-Stick anyway?"

"Nope. That's the funny part. My whole body went down and under but I kept my arm raised high and Chiyon said all you could see was that damn Chick-o-Stick raised above the water. She thought that was so funny. She told that story many times over the years."

"That's hilarious."

"Later it was. But at the time, I was so pissed."

Jonathan gave up on the stain; it was there to stay. He got up from the table and walked around to grab Lisa from behind. "You're great."

"If you would have seen my little outburst over that stupid Chick-o-Stick you probably wouldn't think that."

"I'm sure I'd still think that. Come on. Let's go for a walk to the water." Jonathan gathered the trash to deposit in the bin.

"Okay, but be careful not to get hit by a wave. They can knock you over in a second."

Jonathan took his unfinished vanilla shake from the table and holding it up said, "Well, if I do get knocked over I will hold this high over my head because I am obsessed with vanilla shakes."

"Not funny," Lisa chided.

"A little funny." Jonathan grabbed her hand.

They walked a ways and Lisa told a few other stories of her childhood. Jonathan finished his shake and put the cup in the sand. "Let's sit for a minute."

"Okay," Lisa said. She slid her flats off and wiggled her toes into the sun-heated sand. Digging deeper with her whole foot, it became cool. The waves crashed rhythmically to the shore as she grabbed handfuls of sand, letting it sift softly through her fingers. The sea air swirled and whipped her hair across her face. She missed the beach.

Jonathan took the straw out of his finished shake and was fumbling with it as he kept asking questions of Lisa. "Would your parents ever take you here?"

"No. I don't ever remember them coming to the beach. They both worked a lot."

"But then they got to retire early?"

"Yes, they both retired when I was twelve. It was great. I got to spend a lot of time with them. And summers were the best because we traveled the whole time since they didn't have jobs." Jonathan got up from the sand and pulled Lisa up. They walked only a few steps when he suddenly stopped. "Are you okay?" Lisa asked.

"Yes." Jonathan got down to one knee.

"Are you okay? What's wrong?"

Jonathan grabbed both her hands and looked up. "Nothing's wrong. I've loved seeing where you grew up. And I've loved these last few months. And I love you, Lisa." Jonathan paused. "Will you marry me?"

"What?"

"Will you marry me? I'm asking you to marry me." Jonathan pulled Lisa's left hand out and slipped the straw he had formed in to a makeshift ring on to her finger.

"Are you—? What—? Are you being—"

"I know. I know. It's fast. But I know. You're exactly what I've been looking for. For four years actually. And here you are. And I don't ever want you to leave."

"But we—"

"Lisa, I'm asking you. Will you marry me?"

Lisa stared down at him. She looked at her left hand with a straw ring. She looked back at Jonathan. "Yes. Yes, uh, I will marry you. Oh my gosh. Oh my gosh. What are we doing?" Lisa was laughing and pulling Jonathan up to her.

"Really? We're really doing this?"

"Well how can I say no to this gorgeous ring?" Lisa held out her hand to admire the red and white Jack-in-the-Box straw wrapped around her finger.

"I know. I know. I didn't plan this very well. But just being around you on this trip and seeing where you grew up, I wanted this to happen in a place that was special to you."

"It's perfect." Lisa embraced Jonathan and they both exclaimed, "We're getting married!"

CHAPTER 30

Driving north to San Jose, Lisa told Jonathan she thought it best if they waited a bit before announcing their engagement. Let it sink in. Jonathan understood. It was fast. He hadn't really planned for this to happen. But he was excited about it. He couldn't wait to tell James. They had agreed to tell James, but they would wait until they got back to Seattle to make the calls to her family and the rest of his.

Arriving at James' house was much different from the Rob experience, but still not quite the welcome they received at Lynn's. James and his wife were welcoming and Jonathan would never had thought it was lacking had he not just spent time with Lisa's sister. His brother, who he always looked up to, seemed a bit aloof. A bit arrogant, really. He never noticed it before, but he was now looking at James through Lisa's eyes. She handled it well. Although, she was much more quiet than she had been the rest of the trip.

When they had a minute alone, Jonathan grabbed her hand. "Are you okay?"

"Of course. Why?"

"You just seem so quiet."

"I'm fine. Hard to get a word in."

"I don't know what's up. He must be nervous or something."

"He really likes to talk about himself, doesn't he?"

Jonathan didn't know what to say. This was James. His older brother. His idol. Why couldn't he tone it down and be a little less cocky?

"You can talk whenever you want. Don't be shy," Jonathan prompted.

"As soon as he asks me anything, I'll give some input." Lisa smiled.

"Hey, hey, so Jonathan. I gotta tell you about this new software program I just perfected. It's gonna be big, bro, real big."

"You should have Lisa tell you about the software she uses with her Stenograph machine. It simultaneously translates her Steno language to English," Jonathan tried.

"I've heard about that. Cool. But this, bro, this thing I'm working on is amazing," James boasted.

Jonathan squeezed Lisa's hand hoping she appreciated his effort. Throughout the evening, Jonathan became aware of how James' wife added little to any conversation. She was quiet in a way he hadn't noticed before and James spoke to her with little affection. At one point demanding her to, "Get me a water with lemon." She delivered his every whim with a soft touch on his shoulder and a serene smile. No 'thank you' from James. Was this the relationship model Jonathan was supposed to go by? Why had he not noticed this before?

At last, after about four hours, James addressed Lisa for the first time. "So how does it feel to be Melissa?"

Jonathan could see the question caught Lisa off guard. She stared at James with a deer-in-the-headlights daze. James was not giving Lisa an identity of her own outside of Melissa. Jonathan held her hand tighter knowing she was trying to process things before answering.

After an awkward silence, James repeated, "How was it learning that Jonathan created you before you were even you?" Jonathan felt Lisa stiffen. This was not going well.

"I was actually me before Jonathan created Melissa, so I guess you'll have to figure that one out," Lisa finally replied.

Before James could get out another question, Jonathan blurted, "Bro, we got some news. We got engaged." Jonathan knew the 'bro' sounded awkward and the whole announcement was delivered in a way that made him uncomfortable so he was sure Lisa would be also. But there it was. James' wife quietly said, "Congratulations."

James stood and shook Jonathan's hand a little overzealously. "Nice. We all got to start somewhere. Hell, I was already married to my second wife by your age. Right, honey?" He slapped his wife's ass and she giggled. Giggled. "But maybe you're the one Bach to get it right the first time. Welcome to the family, Melissa." He leaned over to hug her.

"It's Lisa."

"Huh?"

"My name is Lisa. Not Melissa."

"Oh, yeah, right, right. That's going to take a while to get used to. So Jonathan, come here. I want to show you this software idea."

Lisa could not wait to get away from Jonathan's brother.

"Why don't we take off tomorrow and head up the coast by ourselves for a few days?" she suggested as they lay in bed that night.

"I don't know. James is really excited about showing us San Jose tomorrow," Jonathan said.

"Or he's real excited to continue talking about himself." Lisa could not stand him for another full day.

"I know, I know. He can be a bit overwhelming at times."

"He didn't even show interest when you were trying to tell him about your tour," Lisa said.

"He's just excited about his new software thing," Jonathan said.

"And you were excited for him and told him as much. But from him to you; nothing. His little brother is leaving on a book tour next week and he didn't even care enough to ask you how you were feeling about it. So self absorbed."

"I'll always be his little brother. And he'll always feel like he's the wiser one who needs to teach me things."

Lisa could tell Jonathan was disturbed. "Seems you have to defend your brothers an awful lot."

"You don't understand. We're not the Cracker Jack family like you have."

"Cracker Jack family? What's that mean?"

"You know, the caring, nurturing family brought up by your

original parents who have been married for four decades. How like Cracker Jacks are the perfect combination of salt and sweet." Jonathan turned on his side to face her. "There's nothing wrong with it. It's just not the norm."

"It's the norm to treat people with respect and show them kindness and show an interest in getting to know them. Your brothers don't care one lick about your girlfriend. Fiancé."

"But it's enough for them to know I'm happy. And if I've chosen you, you must be okay."

"So, you're saying their stance is they don't have to spend time to get to know me at all?"

"They already do know you. They've been reading about Melissa and reading her letters for years. We've talked about how you match up."

"But that's not me."

"Like it or not, it is you." Jonathan leaned in to kiss her.

Lisa felt defeated. "What was the whole thing 'you should be on your second wife by now'?"

"It's not a secret. The Bach's don't do marriages very well. I told you that."

"Are you planning to do marriage well?"

"For us, it's different." Jonathan folded Lisa into his arms.

"Different how?" Lisa needed some assurance. She had said yes. And yes for her was for the rest of her life.

"I feel like they've all gone through their first spouses, in some cases two, and I've seen their mistakes. The difference is that I know what I want. It's not a shot in the dark. I manifested the girl I wanted. And here you are. If I screw this up, then the last four years were an exercise in futility."

"And what if I turn out to be better than Melissa?" Lisa teased. "Will you dump me to find someone, uh, less than perfect?"

"Of course," Jonathan said. "It's your job to fit into that niche; no better, no worse."

Lisa grabbed her pillow from under her head and swung it at him. "You're impossible."

"Yeah, and you love me." He clutched her wrists and pulled her to him. "And I love you. And yes, we can head back toward Seattle tomorrow. Believe it or not, between Rob and James, I've had enough of the Bach's at this point."

"Really?" Lisa loved that Jonathan was listening and doing something about her frustrations. She appreciated he listened to her and made decisions to ease her discomfort. "Now, I really love you." She curled into his arms and settled in to his accommodating embrace.

CHAPTER 31

A few days after Lisa and Jonathan returned to Seattle, Jonathan went on his book tour. What started as a three week, ten-city tour had been whittled down to a week and three cities. The Larry King Show appearance with his dad never materialized. The book was not exactly a hit. Back at school and Jillian's, Lisa showcased her plastic straw ring to friends and co-workers. Everyone ahhed at the romantic proposal. Lisa had said nothing to Cathy yet.

The Sunday after Jonathan's return from his tour, they were playing chess at his apartment —Jonathan was teaching her—when Lisa announced, "You know, you're going to have to call my dad."

"Call your dad for what?"

"To ask his permission."

"Ask his permission for what?"

Lisa looked at him curiously. "Permission for my hand in marriage."

"Are you serious?"

"Of course. I'm serious."

"That's not even a thing anymore, is it?"

"To my dad it is. To my parents it is. Remember they've been married over forty years. All my brothers-in-law did it."

"Really?"

"Yes, really."

"Let's call him."

"Not now," Lisa replied.

"Why not now?"

"Because you don't even have a ring for me yet." Lisa held up her hand with the Jack-in-the-Box straw. "I mean, this is cute and all, but I'm sure you want to get me a real ring, right?" She nudged Jonathan in his side.

"Yup, let's go." Jonathan stood up from the couch and pulled Lisa with him.

"Go? Go where?"

"To the mall. We're going to go pick your ring out right now."

"You want me to go with you?"

"Yes. I want you to get one that you want. I have no idea about these kinds of things."

"I don't either. How do I know what I want?" Lisa was pulling on her coat.

"I guess you'll know when you see it."

"And we just get it right now?"

"Why not?"

"I guess so. Why not?"

Jonathan was right. Lisa knew right when she saw it. It was white gold with a low set Marquise diamond surrounded by smaller diamonds. It fit perfectly. They were in and out of the store in less than thirty minutes.

"You know, that's another thing I love about you." Jonathan grabbed her outside the shop and hugged her. "I should have put that on the Melissa list."

"Put what on the Melissa list?" Lisa held out her hand to admire the ring.

"Doesn't take forever to make a decision."

"See, I told you. I'm going to end up being better than her." Lisa grabbed his hand. "I guess I am a lot like you. I know what I want." Lisa paused. "Although I didn't write out a list of what my ring had to be before finding it," she said.

"Now *that* would've been weird," Jonathan replied.

Back at Jonathan's, Lisa dialed her old home number. She was nervous. Her parents had only spoken with Jonathan a handful of times. Hell, *she'd* only known him for two months. She still didn't know how this had happened so fast. How would her parents understand it? How would Jonathan make them understand it?

"Hey, Pops."

"Hey, what's up?"

"Not much. Is mom home?"

"Yeah, she's right here."

"Can she get on the other line?"

"Ella," my dad called, "It's Lisa. Get the other phone."

"Is everything okay?" It was always her mom's first question.

"Everything's okay. Everything's good."

"How was Jonathan's tour?" Even her mom showed more interest in Jonathan's life than his own brother did, Lisa noted.

"Oh, good, great. He had a good time. Actually we have some news."

Her parents remained silent.

"Just a sec. Jonathan wants to say hi." Lisa handed the phone to Jonathan.

Jonathan grabbed it and greeted them. "Hello. Hello."

"Hi, Jonathan."

"Hello...sir." Jonathan raised his eyebrows in confusion at Lisa. She nodded. That was good. Sir. "I wanted to ask, or I wanted to tell. No I wanted to ask. For your permission. Your permission to marry your daughter."

She opened her eyes wide and turned her hands up in a question to Jonathan, but he shook his head.

"Yes, sir. Of course. Of course, I'll take care of her. Yes. Yes, I will. I know. Okay, here she is." Jonathan handed the phone back to Lisa and took her other hand with a smile.

"So?" She questioned her parents.

"Congratulations," they said simultaneously.

"You're okay with this?"

"You're the one who has to be okay," her dad said. "We're just here to support you."

"Mom?"

"Lisa, it's exciting. We want you to be happy. It's quick. But you know what you're doing. We're happy for you."

"Thank you. I love you guys. We just got the ring. It's gorgeous." Lisa held it out as if they could see it.

"You already got a ring? Have you set a date?" Her mom asked.

"We just got it tonight. Before calling. And no, no date yet. We haven't even talked about that yet." She watched Jonathan get up from the couch and pull the calendar from the wall.

"Keep in touch and we'll talk to you soon." As an afterthought, her mom asked, "Does Lynn know?"

"No, not yet. You're the first." Lisa omitted that they had told James. He didn't really seem to care anyway.

"Okay, well, love you. We'll talk later. Congratulations, again."

Hanging up the phone, Lisa said, "See that wasn't so bad."

"I'm sure neither of my two brothers did that for any of their wives."

"That's shocking. They're both so courteous. Hard to believe."

"Ah, I'm sensing sarcasm, Lisa."

"You're getting to know me so well."

"How about September 3rd?"

"September 3rd for what?"

"September 3rd for our wedding? Or have you forgotten already?"

"Like this September 3rd? This year? Like in—" Lisa quickly counted on her fingers; May, June, July, August, "four months?"

"Why not?"

"Do you know what goes in to planning a wedding? My sister planned hers for over a year."

"But you make things happen. Look how fast you picked your ring out. You don't need a year to plan a wedding." Jonathan pointed to the calendar. "September 3rd would be perfect. It's on a Saturday. And it's Labor Day weekend, so everyone has Monday off. What do you think?"

Lisa couldn't think of a reason why not. "Okay. September 3rd it is."

Jonathan was on Cloud Nine. Even if some other people thought it was fast, it wasn't. Really, he had known Lisa for over four years. Now, they were going to plan their wedding and then it would be complete. He would have his Melissa. He got tired of Keith and Greg telling him to slow it down with her. So he stopped going to Jillian's. And he convinced Lisa to quit her job there with the goal of focusing more on school; he would take care of things. It helped that he got her away from Frank and his pursuits also. He didn't trust that guy.

Sometimes he stressed about how he would manage things, but Lisa didn't know this. He was a published author and the proof of it sat in physical form on his shelf. But he had received the last of his advance money, and an almost daily email to his agent revealed that no more copies had been ordered. He had no other book in the making. But he was a published author. Certainly, that would get him somewhere.

He tried to keep writing; had told Lisa he was working on the next book while she was at school. But he spent more time on CompuServe where he found forums of Richard Bach fans who were more than enthusiastic to have Richard's son join their chats. Jonathan knew they were all fanatics of his father, but it never hurt to promote his book and get a fan or two of his own. It was good for his ego. He anxiously awaited any ping from his computer that signaled he was important.

Lisa got the third degree from her friends about how fast this was moving. Even the ones who seemed excited about the whole proposal thing voiced their opinions about maybe waiting a year to plan the wedding. Cathy and Tammy were the most vocal about waiting.

"I don't understand why you are doing this so fast, little cousin. Just a few months ago you said you were never going to get married. And now you're moving out and planning a wedding." They were in the bedroom, where Lisa's bed was covered with her suitcases. She was moving in with Jonathan.

"I didn't say I was never getting married," Lisa corrected her. "I said I didn't like the whole dating thing of trying to find someone. I just wanted to find someone. Now I've found someone." She pulled clothes from the closet and placed them in an open suitcase.

Cathy flung herself on her own bed and draped her arm across her face moaning, "I have failed thee. I have failed."

"You haven't failed me. It's crazy. But it's good," Lisa said, zipping up the first of the suitcases.

"Cathy, leave her alone. Marriage isn't that bad." Tammy at least was not completely against it.

Lisa pulled another suitcase from the top shelf of the closet. "See, it isn't that bad." She was happy for an ally.

"I'm not saying it's bad. I'm just saying this is fast. You've known him for like, what? Three seconds?"

"I think it's more like five, but who's counting?" Lisa was emptying a drawer of T-shirts and shorts into a duffel bag.

"It's not funny. I'm being serious."

"Cathy, drop it. She's happy. Look." Tammy turned Lisa around by the shoulders to face Cathy. "Look."

Lisa couldn't hold back her smile. Cathy was sitting Indian-style on her bed with her quilt wrapped up around her head. "See, I'm happy." Lisa laughed. "But, God, how I'm going to miss that." Lisa jumped on the bed next to her. "Don't be sad. We'll still hang out together."

"No, we won't. You're moving to Tacoma. Why are you moving to Tacoma? Tacoma sucks."

"Only until I finish school. We'll be back. I love Seattle." Lisa was definitely fonder of Seattle than Tacoma, but Jonathan had rationalized they might as well be close to her school to save her the two-hour daily drive. In Tacoma, they had found 3-bedroom houses for the same price as his tiny Seattle apartment. She didn't like moving away from her family, but she'd made friends at school who lived in Tacoma. It seemed like the wisest choice for now.

"No, you won't," Cathy sulked. "And now there's no one here to play kitty games with." Cathy forced her lower lip out into an exaggerated pout.

"Pick up your lip before you step on it." Lisa reached out to flap Cathy's protruding lip.

"I'm gonna step on you." She threw her arms from out of the quilt and grabbed Lisa in a hug pushing her down on the bed. "Dog pile, dog pile."

Tammy obliged, landing on top of her, chanting along with her sister, "Dog pile, dog pile."

When they finally let her up, Lisa said, "I must be crazy to be leaving this."

"Yes, you are. Stupid, stupid girl." Cathy knocked Lisa on the top of her head. "Now. What am I supposed to wear to this wedding?"

"Black, of course." Lisa snapped another suitcase closed.

"Sweet. I got a whole closet of black."

"I'm kidding, you know," Lisa said.

"Oh." Cathy looked at her blankly, then said to Tammy, "Did you know she was kidding?"

"I assume you wouldn't wear black. It's a wedding, not a funeral," Tammy answered.

"Depends on who you ask," Cathy said. "Kidding. Just kidding. But I don't have anything but black."

"Then you better go shopping. You still have time." Lisa lifted both suitcases from her bed and set them on the floor.

"And what should I get? Tammy, we need to go shopping."

"It's on a cruise boat in Coeur d' Alene and it can get a little chilly at night. So a dress is fine, but bring a wrap," Lisa explained.

"A dress?" Cathy asked. "No black *and* a dress? You're dreaming, little cousin."

Lisa stared at her until Tammy cut in, "Don't worry, I'll make sure she's presentable. Unfortunately..."

Tammy and Cathy shared a look. Tammy was smiling; Cathy was not.

"Unfortunately what?" Lisa asked.

"Unfortunately," Tammy started slowly. "I won't be able to make it."

"What? Why?"

"Because...unfortunately...fat head here went and got herself knocked up," Cathy said.

"No."

"Yes," Tammy said. "And I'm due on your wedding date—"

"No way."

"—so we can't make it." Tammy pulled her baggy sweatshirt up to reveal her slightly protruding bulge.

"Oh my gosh. This is great." Lisa rubbed Tammy's belly. "Great about the baby; not great you can't make it. Congratulations."

"I know. We're excited."

"Who's 'we're'?" Cathy said. "I got one getting married and the other having babies. No bueno. No bueno." She hung her head so her hair fell over the top and she shook it back and forth.

Both Tammy and Lisa put their arm around Cathy. "It'll be okay," Lisa said. "You still got Pasha." On cue, Pasha sashayed at their feet intertwining amongst their legs.

"Great. I'm gonna be cat lady," Cathy said.

"Auntie Cat Lady," Tammy corrected.

"Oh, yeah," as if the thought just struck her, "I'm gonna be an Auntie. Auntie. Auntie. Auntie." Cathy jumped off her bed and hoisted the larger of the two suitcases. "Come on. I'll help you carry them out."

Jonathan exited the CompuServe Forum just as Lisa opened the door. "Hey, you're back early."

"It didn't take as long to pack as I thought," Lisa said. She looked toward the computer. "Were you working on the new book?"

"Yup, yup. Got some good ideas down." He reached for her suitcase and quickly changed the subject. "We're officially living in sin now, eh?"

"It's not for long. And I'm here all the time anyway." Lisa still struggled with living together, but the imminent wedding seemed justification enough.

"I'm teasing. It's going to be fine. You're not going to hell, or whatever it is you believe in." Jonathan brought the suitcase into the bedroom. "I got a call about the house in Tacoma."

"Which one?"

"The one down by the water. The duplex."

"And?"

"He said our references check out and we can move in September 15th. Right after we get back from our honeymoon."

Lisa hugged him. "That's awesome. I really like that one."

"Me too. It's just that we have to come up with first, last, and a deposit."

Lisa pulled back and looked at him. "And?"

"And. That's a lot of money." Jonathan was not surprised she was surprised. He'd assured her there was plenty of money.

"But we have it, right? You have it, right?"

"Of course. It's just cutting into our savings." Jonathan didn't tell her the savings were dangerously low.

"But, we're okay, right? I mean, why am I not working if we're not okay?"

"It's just with the wedding and everything, funds are getting low."

"We've bought the invitations. That's it so far. I thought we were okay."

"We are okay. Don't worry about it. I said I'd take care of things." He shouldn't have paid for his brother's tuxes. Or his family's plane tickets. "I'll get the guy the money tomorrow. The house is ours."

"Okay. But you'd tell me if I should be working, right? I'm okay to work."

"No, no. You just get through school. It's a man's job to provide." Jonathan stood on top of his chair and crossed one arm across his chest. In a deep voice, he announced, "I will provide."

"And you thought asking my dad's permission to marry me was old-fashioned," Lisa said. "Now get down off that chair before you fall and break something."

Jonathan was relieved they'd left the topic of money alone for now. He was banking on a wedding check from his dad; that would help. And the credit card he just applied for with the help of Lisa's perfect credit would definitely cover the honeymoon in Hawaii. By then, he was sure royalties would be coming in for his book.

CHAPTER 32

Four weeks before the wedding, Lisa and Jonathan sat on the floor sifting through RSVPs. They hadn't sent out many invites and were expecting maybe fifty at the wedding. Most of those were from Lisa's side.

"Look. Rob replied yes." Jonathan held up the cream-colored postcard.

"Oh, goody. I can't wait to see what he's selling this time." She looked at Jonathan and caught a slight twitch on his face. "What? What did you buy from him now?"

"I told him if he came, I would pay for his plane ticket."

"You what?" Lisa was careful. She knew it was his money, but she thought he should talk about these things with her first. Plus, the first and only time she'd met Rob, he had been a complete jerk to her and conned them out of fifty bucks.

"It'll be fine. I'm paying for my mom's ticket and my sister's also." Jonathan avoided her stare.

"Are we going to pay for my family's tickets, too?"

"Why would we do that?"

"Why wouldn't we? It seems if you're paying for your mom and sister and brother to come that we should pay for mine also."

"If you want to pay for them, you can." Jonathan turned to the box of RSVPs. He knew she had no money. Even though they could definitely use the money and he knew she was more than willing to work, he liked that she was dependent on him. He was the provider. Which meant he was the decision maker.

"What do you mean, *I* can? You mean, *we* can?" Lisa slowed her speech to remain calm. "Remember, you're the one who convinced me to quit my job because you would take care of things."

"Well, *we* can't pay for *everyone*."

"Just *your* family?"

"I guess so. Besides, your family would be making the trip up to Idaho anyway to visit your parents. So now they get to go to a wedding."

"*Our* wedding; not *a* wedding, Jonathan. *Our* wedding. Do you understand this? *We* are getting married. For forever." Lisa had been worried lately with Jonathan's blasé attitude toward the whole thing. Her sister had convinced her that's how men are. They don't want anything to do with the planning. But there was something different with Jonathan. He didn't seem to be taking this seriously at all and it was weighing on Lisa. She had overheard him talking to James when he commented, "Well, we'll see how it goes." She wanted to believe he wasn't talking about the marriage. But she wasn't sure.

"Lisa, don't be silly. Of course, it's our wedding. I've been going to those stupid classes at your church for the last month, haven't I? It's all about our wedding."

This reminded Lisa. "Don't forget we have that retreat this weekend."

"Are we really going to that?" Jonathan headed to the fridge. He pulled a box of Ding-Dongs from the top.

"What do you mean, are we really going to that? You know we have to in order to get married in the church." Lisa wasn't going to be the first in her family to not be married in the church. "Besides, some of it is helpful. You know, learning how to communicate and being kind to one another."

Jonathan unwrapped two of the Ding-Dongs, placed them one on top of the other and bit into the double decker. After a few chews, he mumbled, "Oh right, all that 'life-giving' crap."

"Now, that wasn't very life-giving to say." Lisa smiled to lighten the mood.

Jonathan had white filling smudged on one side of his mouth.

"It's just so stupid. I know how to communicate. Those people can't teach me anything."

"Everyone can learn something from everything," Lisa said.

He stuffed the remainder of the two Ding-Dongs in his mouth and opened the fridge for the milk. "Not me," he proclaimed. "I know everything I need to know."

Lisa guffawed. "Are you serious? You're twenty-five and you believe you know everything?"

"More than what those people can tell me this weekend." He set a glass on the counter and twisted the lid off the jug.

"How can you even say something so ridiculous? You really believe you will not learn one thing you can take with you? That's pretty pompous." He was sounding more like his brother every day.

"Not pompous. Just realistic." Jonathan slopped the milk, getting some in the glass, but pouring more onto the counter.

Lisa stared at this man she was to marry in four weeks. Maybe they moved things too fast. She knew she loved him. But more and more, his actions and comments sounded just like James. She rose and stepped across the living room to grab her coat. "I'm going out for a walk."

"Okay." Then, as though an afterthought, Jonathan added, "Besides if there is anything I need to learn, I can learn it from my brother."

Lisa watched as Jonathan bent to fire up his computer. *Great, the most arrogant man I've ever met*. Lisa closed the door, shutting out the scene. Although August, the night air was heavy with the damp Pacific Northwest. She walked briskly up Queen Anne Avenue to Highland Park where she sat admiring the view of downtown and contemplating what she had gotten herself into.

She listed the pros and cons in her head. Jonathan did not sit and ponder ideas with her anymore. Jonathan had stopped going to the gym. Jonathan had stopped going to Jillian's since she quit working there. She knew it was odd; he used to shoot pool there everyday. And now this latest; Jonathan revealing that at twenty-five he had learned everything.

On the other hand, he was kind enough. They didn't fight; to-night being an exception. He had supported her quitting work to focus on school, though she found it hard at times not to have her own money. He was willing to move to Tacoma so she would not have such a long commute. He was a published author. Jonathan spent all his days working on his second book while she was at school. He couldn't tell her what the book was about yet, but she knew the potential was there. But does one marry for potential? Her sister's warning echoed faintly.

And of course, she couldn't brush aside the Melissa coinci-dence. How do you walk away from someone who had created you in his head before meeting you? Something about this still nagged at the back of her mind, but she couldn't pinpoint what it was. She knew only that she fit into Jonathan's soul mate experiment; she *was* Jonathan's soul mate experiment. She was still dazzled by the notion that Jonathan had manifested exactly what he wanted. She was a major part of this fairytale idea of meeting and marrying someone you created long before they came into your life. It was a thrilling idea that was holding her captive even amidst the doubts.

Walking back to the apartment, she realized she was having a moment of cold feet. Things were going to be fine. They would get married, she would finish school, Jonathan would publish more books, they would have children, and they would live happily ever after. Completing the fairytale ending. Plus, the invitations had al-ready been sent and deposits were already cashed. How could she possibly cancel everything now that it was in motion? She didn't want to embarrass her parents or herself by calling it all off. These minor things would work themselves out.

CHAPTER 33

Weeks later, Lisa and Jonathan were in Coeur d' Alene for their wedding weekend. The afternoon of the wedding rehearsal, Jonathan prepared for the last obstacle to get Melissa through before she became his wife: Meeting the rest of his family.

The two families had started to converge on the front churchyard and Lisa would be here any minute. Jonathan had already spent several days with Lisa's parents. It was as he had predicted—Cracker Jack. The other two sisters and their husbands, the same—Cracker Jack. On the other side, in stark contrast, was his family.

If Lisa hadn't already bolted with the idiosyncrasies of his family, she would surely make a run for it tonight. He knew he had to keep Rob away from her; their first meeting had been horrendous. Also James was so blatantly arrogant walking in and taking center stage; why had Jonathan never noticed this before? He was shocked that his sisters even came; but he knew it was because he paid for their plane tickets.

Then there was his mom and stepdad. His mom he would try to keep far, far away. Just moments earlier he overheard his mom say to James, "Doesn't she think it's weird he made her all up before he met her?"

Of course, his dad and Leslie didn't come. They knew better than to get around this side of the family. But they were his family. Jonathan was basking in the attention that had never been bestowed upon him as the youngest sibling. He was finally having his time. James had complimented him in his own way. "Well done. Who would've thought this whole Melissa thing would really work?" He patted him heartily on the back.

Jonathan was also enjoying Liana's affection. As the flower girl, she followed him around everywhere. She'd even brought the Shamu he'd bought for her. He became cooler in his nephew's eyes as they both fought to be the next one he swung up on his shoulders. Jonathan liked his family saw how much these kids adored him. He lumbered across the grass as he saw Lisa and Cathy arrive. "Hey, you made it."

"Of course, I made it. Can't have a rehearsal without the bride, can you?" Lisa lifted Liana up and she wrapped her legs around her waist. "How's my beautiful little flower girl?"

"Good. Look." She held up her arm. "Shamu's getting married too." Her stuffed Shamu had a tiny wedding veil sewn to the top of his head.

"That's adorable. Who did that?" Lisa asked her.

"Mommy."

"Nice. I think you'll have to carry him down the aisle with you," Lisa said.

"Really?"

"Of course," Jonathan chimed in. "That would be perfect."

"Goody," Liana said.

"My whole family's made it." Jonathan motioned to his clan standing around the table Lisa's mom had decorated with flowers.

"Your mom, too? I thought they weren't getting here until tonight?" Lisa scanned the little gathering across the lawn.

"They got an earlier flight. Come on, I'll introduce you." Jonathan reached for Lisa's hand, but then turned toward her. "Remember, she's a bit awkward socially, so be forgiving."

"Please. I've met her sons. I know what to expect." Lisa turned to Cathy and whispered, "This means you keep quiet no matter what."

Cathy only smiled her reply.

Lisa put Liana on the ground and she ran off to join Jonathan's nephew, who was chasing a butterfly around the yard.

"They're getting along good. They're so cute," Jonathan commented as he watched the two kids join up in their pursuit. Then he looked back to Lisa. "Okay, let's fly." That sounded cool and he *was* man of the day. His family was not going to ruin it. He hoped they wouldn't ruin it.

They approached the group. Lisa and Jonathan's moms were talking. Correction: Jonathan's mom was talking and Lisa's mom and Lynn were looking at her confused. As they got closer, Jonathan's mom could be heard saying, "Best to get marriage one out of the way while you're young," and then what could only be described as a cackle.

"Hey, Mom. This is Lisa." Jonathan interrupted.

"Ah, Melissa. Jonathan's starter bride. Nice to meet you."

Lisa bristled. He had warned her. In fact, Jonathan had told her this very phrase. But still, she bristled. "It's Lisa. We're a little over the Melissa thing," she said.

"Of course. Lisa." His mom made no move toward her. Lisa crossed her arms and moved closer to her own mom. Cathy stared open-mouthed and didn't even offer a witty retort. Jonathan recognized immediately, this was not going well. Lisa always welcomed people with a hug, but clearly it was not going to happen.

Jonathan stepped in and quickly introduced Lisa to his sisters, and then addressed his mom, "Mom, you said you had a gift for Lisa? Why don't you give it to her now?"

"Yes. I picked this up for you. It's really special." Jonathan's mom handed Lisa a loosely wrapped something.

Lisa uncrossed her arms to accept it. "Thank you. Should I open it now?"

"Sure. It's your wedding gift, but I guess you can open it now. It's pretty special." She winked at her daughters.

Lisa caught that she mentioned it was special twice, so she figured it must be. She carefully clipped her finger under the tape and slid the paper apart. Unwrapped, the gift was a baby blue potholder. Lisa looked confused and Jonathan's mom quickly told her, "Turn it over."

On the opposite side was the same baby blue fabric with seagulls outlined in white. It was a potholder. But she had said it was special. So Lisa assumed and asked, "Did you make this?"

"Oh, good God, no. I don't sew," she huffed.

"Oh."

"I picked it up at a rummage sale. I thought it was perfect. *Jonathan Livingston Seagull*. See, they're seagulls."

"Yes, I see. Thank you."

Cathy grabbed Lisa's elbow abruptly. "We need to go, Lisa. Now. I need to fix your makeup before the priest is ready to start."

"Uh, huh." Lisa let Cathy lead her away from the group.

Jonathan watched them go and hoped he'd see her again. What was his mom thinking? So provincial.

"What the hell is that?" Cathy grabbed the potholder from Lisa. "Are you kidding me? Special, perfect, rummage sale? Is she loony?" She threw the potholder on the corner chair.

"Cathy, keep your voice down." Lisa was still a bit speechless after the whole thing.

"No, seriously, is she loony? That's her wedding gift to you? She's kidding, right? Did Jonathan say she had a sense of humor?"

"Actually, the opposite. No sense of humor. And full of bitterness."

"It shows. What nerve. The starter bride? What a bitch. I wanted to punch her. And I'm not violent."

Cathy was voicing everything Lisa was thinking, but couldn't quite put into words. She walked to the chair and picked up the strange potholder. "Like, is this for real? I don't get it."

"Of course, you don't get it. She's an idiot. Are you sure you want to marry into this family?"

Lisa was still confused. A potholder? But then she started laughing. And once she started, she couldn't stop.

"What's so funny? This is so not funny." But Cathy started laughing too.

Then they couldn't stop.

"Oh my gosh, get me a tissue. Now you're really going to have to fix my make up." Tears streamed down Lisa's face.

"Maybe, there's like a million dollars that she lined the inside with and it's a test." Cathy made her laugh harder.

"Or maybe it's got a bug in it so she can listen in on all our conversations."

"Maybe she's listening right now." Cathy grabbed the potholder and slowly enunciated, "You're an idiot."

"No, no wait. You should flush it down the toilet, so she can hear that," Lisa said.

Cathy started towards the stall.

"No, no. I'm kidding."

"What? You want to keep this thing?" Cathy flipped it up into the air.

"What about when she comes to visit for Christmas and she asks to see her *special potholder* and I don't have it. Then what?"

Cathy stared hard at Lisa. "I don't know what's more moronic about that statement; that you care what she thinks or that you're planning to have her for Christmas. Here," Cathy tossed her the potholder, "keep it in a safe place."

"Come on, let's go. And you stay away from her," Lisa warned.

"Oh sure, take away all my fun."

The weekend passed and Jonathan felt like he'd held his breath the whole time. During the rehearsal and actual wedding, especially during the "I Dos," and even into the reception where his family was in close proximity to everyone on the boat, he kept waiting for the chaos to unleash. But on Sunday, he let his breath out. It was over. Melissa was his. His experiment was complete. He marveled at the genius of creating a soul mate from scratch and having her walk into his life four years later and become his wife six months after that.

The drive to the airport was quiet. Lisa napped and Jonathan was lost in thoughts. It was his first day as a married man and he couldn't help but think, 'What now?' They were leaving this afternoon on their honeymoon. But after the honeymoon, what? It seemed so final to him. Was that it? What would he do with Melissa after this? Even his brother and dad had stopped asking about her? He felt a sudden loss.

Melissa would soon be forgotten unless he did something about it. Already, the shoeboxes were shoved away high in the back of the closet. Perhaps that was his next book: the journey of creating and finding his soul mate. The idea intrigued him, but the thought of the tireless work of writing and editing and re-editing another book discouraged him.

At a stop light, Jonathan looked over at the woman sitting beside him and pondered the thought, *What if...this isn't even...Melissa*? He pulled a notebook from his coat pocket and quickly jotted down one word across the top: *Samantha.*

CHAPTER 34

Lisa's exhaustion overtook her on the way to the airport. The wedding complete they could now settle in to their new life. Lisa was still perplexed by the behavior of Jonathan's mom and family. Even the poster that all the guests had signed for them with well wishes had been ruined by Jonathan's mom. When most people had put things like 'Happily Ever After' and 'Jonathan and Lisa Forever,' she mockingly had written 'Jonathan and Lisa ForNow.' When Lisa pointed it out to Jonathan, he just bowed and shook his head. "She doesn't get it."

"And now the whole thing is ruined. We can't keep this." Lisa had tossed it to the side of their pile of wedding gifts. She didn't care enough about his mom to get mad, but she didn't like the woman very much. She was grateful she lived on the other side of the country with no plans to visit anytime soon.

Shedding the nuances of the weekend, Lisa began to relax as they made it through airport security. Waiting to board the plane, she was filled again with excitement. They could now enjoy being alone together for their ten-day honeymoon in Hawaii. A first-class upgrade 'for the newlyweds' made her giddy.

"Hey, husband. Are you excited?" Lisa nudged Jonathan moments after settling in to their plush roomy seats.

"Huh?" He looked startled "Oh, yeah. Of course. You?"

"Yes." Lisa reached down into her purse. "Chess?" She set the travel board on the tray. He was always up for a game.

"Huh? Oh, no."

"No? Really?"

"I think I'm going to write some ideas." Jonathan pulled a notepad from his carryon.

"Okay." Lisa was surprised—he hadn't written anything for months—but also encouraged that he was getting back to it. "Do you have some ideas for your book?"

"What? Oh, no. Yeah, maybe."

"Now that we're married, can you share with me what it's about? Or would you have to kill me?" Lisa said.

Jonathan turned to her. His eyes were blank and he removed a pen from inside his coat pocket. He was already miles away. "You know that's not it," he replied. "I'm not sure where it's going yet."

"Is everything okay?" Lisa was surprised by the dullness in his voice.

"Of course. I just have some thoughts I want to get down. Didn't you bring anything to read?"

"Yes." She'd been dismissed. "We'll play later."

Jonathan grunted out an acknowledgment and began scribbling on his notepad.

I guess the honeymoon's over, Lisa jokingly thought, grabbing her book.

Exhaustion quickly overtook her and she awoke to Jonathan scratching words across the page. She leaned toward him and glanced at his notepad. In capital letters centered at the top of the page was one word:

SAMANTHA

She could see bullets forming a list:

- Blond and short
- No college education
- Computer software tester

"What are you writing?"

Jonathan quickly flipped his notepad over. "Nothing."

"It didn't look like nothing. What is it?" The elevation was making Lisa nauseous. Looking at Jonathan was making her nauseous. Suddenly, the thought that had been nagging at her for months came rushing forward, *What if Jonathan is not right for me? If I had written a list, would he have even been close?* Lisa never thought about it; she was so consumed by being the perfect one for him, she had not taken one moment to evaluate if he was the perfect one for her.

"I'm going to be sick." Lisa stretched out across Jonathan and raced up the aisle to the toilet. She barely reached it before she began to purge the truth. It came in dry-heaving waves. She was not special to this man. She was his experiment. She was his Melissa. And Melissa was now dead. Therefore, Lisa was dead to him. Did... not...exist.

By the time Lisa returned to her seat, Jonathan was deep in sleep. She sunk into her window seat and watched miles and miles of water spread out beneath her. The sparkling reflection and expanse of ocean calmed her until her thoughts were clear. She was in this for the long haul. No matter where Jonathan was going with another experiment, they were now husband and wife. She would not be threatened by a fictitious idea played out in Jonathan's head. She was his reality now and he was going to have to learn to live in reality.

When he woke, Lisa softly demanded rather than asked, "Chess."

"Let's do it," Jonathan said.

The honeymoon in Hawaii was split between five days in Waikiki and five days in Kaanapali. After trying body surfing for about twenty minutes the first day, Jonathan did not want to go outside anymore. Too many people, too hot, too much sand. "We're in Hawaii. What'd you expect?" Lisa asked him.

"It's just cooler in here," Jonathan answered, sweeping his hand around the tiny hotel room.

Lisa explored on her own. She took the bus to the Dole Plantation and ate breakfast at North Beach. She took a surf lesson and went to Hilo Hattie's. On the city bus tour, the guide asked, "Who here is on their honeymoon?" Lisa raised her hand and looked around at all the other couples together enjoying Hawaii. The guide raised his eyebrow toward her in question and she shrugged her reply.

That afternoon, Lisa persuaded Jonathan to leave the hotel room and come sit poolside. "There's no sand, we can sit in the shade, and there are hardly any people out there right now. Come on. I don't want to spend my entire honeymoon alone."

Jonathan reluctantly acquiesced.

Sitting poolside, Lisa ordered a Mai Tai, complete with an umbrella. "You're going to have a drink?" Jonathan asked.

"Yup. You want one?"

"You know I don't drink," Jonathan said.

"I don't know anything about you. I certainly didn't think you'd sit inside all day in a hotel room while we were in Hawaii," she said.

"It's just so hot," Jonathan complained.

"Get in the pool," she suggested.

"I don't want to get wet. Maybe it will be cooler in Kaanapali."

"Maybe." Lisa finished her Mai Tai and jumped in the pool. "Come on. It's refreshing."

"Nah. I'm good here. I don't want to get in the sun," Jonathan said.

"Suit yourself."

Kaanapali was cooler and Jonathan sat poolside a bit more, even playing chess with her. But Lisa felt a distance between them that hadn't been there just days before. They were physical once and he complained about how uncomfortably hot he was immediately after. Still, she ignored it and continued to enjoy every bit of Hawaii she could. It was her first time traveling to such a beautiful place and she loved playing in the surf and the warmth of the tropical sunshine. Although it wasn't her vision of a dream honeymoon—she had assumed they would explore together as a newlywed couple—she soaked in as much of the experience as she could.

CHAPTER 35

A few weeks after returning to Tacoma, Lisa learned they were broke.

"What do you mean, we can't pay rent?" she asked.

"I've paid through October and then we have no cash left," Jonathan stated matter-of-factly.

"When were you going to tell me this?"

"I'm telling you now," he said, still eating the grilled chicken and corn on the cob Lisa had fixed for dinner.

Her meal sat untouched. "Why have we not been working? You said I didn't need to work."

"I *have* been working. On my next book." Jonathan slid through a whole row of corn, leaving remnants smothered on his chin.

"I mean working to earn money now," she said. "What about the credit card you got?"

"Maxed."

"Maxed. I thought it was $8000."

"It was. It paid for Hawaii. You remember. The honeymoon?"

"Oh, and your family's plane tickets, and tuxes and probably their hotel rooms also," Lisa added. "We'll just have to get jobs. I can waitress."

"When will I write my second book if I'm working? Plus, I have my CompuServe Forums that I need to keep up with," Jonathan said.

"CompuServe Forums?" Lisa could not believe this. She knew these forums were chat rooms where he and his brother trolled for fans of Richard Bach and then chimed in to offer their tidbits as his sons. She thought it had been cool at first, but Jonathan had become obsessed with it. "Well, you better keep that up. I'll fill out applications tomorrow when I get done with school." Lisa tried sarcasm to get her point across. It didn't work.

"Sounds good." Jonathan shoved the last bit of chicken in his mouth and got up from the table leaving his plate as he returned to his 'office.'

Lisa started work within the week at The Old Spaghetti Factory in Tacoma. Five nights a week plus her tips covered the bills while Jonathan continued working on his book.

The marriage lulled into a day-after-day tedium. Jonathan stayed home to write and Lisa went to school and worked. Her school progress slowed considerably because she no longer had evenings to practice. She'd been stuck at 120 words per minute for three months. The state test was 180 wpm, so she had figured another year, but now it looked more like a year and a half, maybe even two years. She enjoyed waitressing, though. It was fast-paced and her coworkers were fun. They knew she was married. She felt proud saying she was married to an author. Some even responded to the whole son of Richard Bach thing.

Jonathan would come in to eat often while she was working: Fifty percent discount for employees and spouses. One night, one of her coworkers returned to the workstation with a plate and held it up. "Look at this," he said. "I've never seen a customer clean a plate this well. It's like he licked it."

"Guaranteed, that's my husband," Lisa said.

"No way. Dude on table 33."

Lisa went out to the restaurant. Table 33. Jonathan sat finishing his spumoni; some of which had made its way to his shirt, just missing his schoolbus tie. She went over to him. "You're making quite an impression," she said leaning over to kiss him.

"What?"

"Your waiter couldn't believe how clean your plate was," Lisa said.

"Member of the Clean Plate Club. That's me." Jonathan held up his spoon.

Back in the kitchen, Lisa confirmed to the waiter and he responded, "That's your husband? Richard Bach's son?"

"Yeah. Why?"

"Just had a different picture in my head. Much different than the reality."

"I know what you mean," Lisa replied. "Here, I'll pay for his check."

A few months into the job, her wrists started bothering her while she practiced on her steno machine. Mostly her left one. She knew it had to do with carrying the food tray at work. Someone told her making her body strong and practicing better posture would help. So she began to run. A lot. Mornings before school and weekends. And during her lunch break at school, she would walk the hills of Tacoma with her classmate. She told herself it was to help her wrists, but she also ran to perhaps become more attractive to Jonathan. He had lost interest in anything physical with her and she figured if she got in shape he would want her more. It didn't help.

CHAPTER 36

Lisa observed as her marriage played out in similar fashion to a basketball or football game. The anticipation of a big game dulls as soon as the first tip off or kick off, and players fall into a methodical rhythm as the game plays out. The first quarter is essentially spent establishing the tempo. Lisa and Jonathan's marriage tempo had already emerged as an unexciting matchup. However, even unexciting matchups still continue for four quarters. And by the end of the first quarter, there comes a feeling of how the game will play out.

The end of their first quarter came three and a half months into the marriage: Christmas. It was their first as husband and wife. It was their first ever. They had plans to go to Cathy's later in the afternoon to celebrate. Jonathan was less than thrilled telling Lisa he didn't want to drive that far, he didn't want to be social, he had writing to do. But he finally agreed and said he'd go.

Christmas morning, Lisa awoke to streams of sunshine peeking through the curtains. She rolled toward Jonathan. "Merry Christmas, husband." She slipped her arm across his chest and up to his hairline, leaning in to kiss him on the cheek. To her surprise, he turned and kissed her back. "Merry Christmas, wife." He pulled her close and for the second time since their I Dos they were intimate.

After, she curled in his arms as long as she could. She wasn't going to be the one to end it. Eventually, Jonathan pulled apart and asked, "You want your Christmas present?"

All she wanted to do was stay there in her husband's arms and enjoy the physical contact. It felt so wonderful to be wrapped together. She didn't realize how much she had been craving this.

Jonathan had had very little interest in being physical until this morning. He had repeatedly quelled her advances the past few months, saying, 'I'm too tired,' 'I don't have time,' and one time even revealing, 'It takes too much effort.' Lisa hoped this was going to reenergize his interest.

"Well, do you?" Jonathan repeated and sat up.

"Of course." Lisa slowly rolled to her back. She grabbed his hand wanting to keep the contact as long as possible.

"Okay. Get up." He was already pulling his T-shirt over his head and putting his robe on. "It's in the garage."

"The garage?" Lisa was curious now. She had her robe around her shoulders and her feet slid in her slippers as Jonathan came to her side.

"Come on. Come on."

"I haven't seen you this excited since, well, I don't know if I have seen you this excited," Lisa said.

"I love Christmas morning. Come on."

This was news to Lisa. But then again, last year at this time, they hadn't even known one another.

"It's kind of for you. But it's kind of for me, too," Jonathan explained. Leading her through the kitchen and out the garage door, he flipped on the light and punched the garage door opener.

Sunlight poured in. In the middle of the garage was a bicycle. It was adorned with a lofty red bow and silver tinsel twinkling from the handlebars. Lisa paused in her spot. She wasn't a bike rider. In fact, she tried to remember if she had ever ridden one since they'd known each other. She hadn't. She looked at Jonathan confused, but walked the few steps toward the bike. It was a man's bike; the top tube was parallel to the ground. "Oh," was all she could say.

"Like I said, it's kind of for both of us. I'm going to ride next to you while you run," Jonathan said excitedly.

"Really?" This Lisa was thrilled about. "Really?" She had been trying to get him back into being active with her and this would be perfect.

"Yeah. I thought we could even go for a little ride right now," he said.

"Absolutely." She threw her arms around Jonathan.

"You like it?"

"It's perfect. You're really going to go with me?" She was already planning the route she would run this morning with her husband riding along side of her. It was a six-mile loop that was mostly flat; just a slight upgrade at the three-mile mark before the turn around. Her mind was already racing with future outings they could do. Point Defiance Loop. Point Ruston. They could even load the bike up and tackle the Burke-Gillman trail one afternoon. "This is great. I love it!"

Jonathan started complaining at about the two-mile mark. "How much farther?"

"Not much. Another mile and we'll turn around."

He couldn't make it up the grade and dismounted. "I'll wait for you here."

"It's okay. We can turn back," Lisa said. "I shouldn't have gone so far for your first time."

"Just a little out of shape." Jonathan climbed back on and let the bike coast for the quarter mile back down. "This is much better." But as the grade became level, Jonathan struggled. Lisa slowed her jog and began walking.

"Let's walk for awhile," she suggested.

Jonathan dismounted his bike.

"It'll get easier," Lisa said. "I only ran a mile my first day. It takes awhile to build up."

"Yeah," Jonathan responded.

It was the last day he rode the bike.

After showering and a blueberry pancake breakfast, Jonathan got up and went to his computer. Lisa could hear the dial up as she washed the dishes. “We’ll leave in about thirty minutes,” she called to him.

“We’re still doing that?” Jonathan replied.

Lisa stepped into the doorway of his office. “What’d you say?”

“I said, we’re still doing that?”

“Still doing what?” Lisa was confused. “Still going to my cousin’s for Christmas?”

“Yeah,” he said.

“I’m not sure what you’re asking. Of course, we’re ‘doing this.’ It’s Christmas. Why would you think we wouldn’t?”

“I don’t know. I’m just so tired.”

“You’ll be fine.” Lisa stood behind Jonathan and rubbed his shoulders.

“It’s so far to drive,” he offered another reason.

“I used to drive it every single day. It’ll be fine.”

“I don’t even know these people,” Jonathan said as he waited for his dial up to get him in. The screeching tone overtook the room.

“You know Cathy. And you’ve met Tammy.”

“Once.”

“Well, now you’re going to meet her again,” Lisa said. “And her husband. It’ll be a small gathering. Cathy’s making a turkey. We’ll eat, open presents, and be back here in time for you to watch David Letterman.”

Jonathan continued tapping away at his keyboard. She could see he was in CompuServe and some forum with Richard’s name on it. She backed out of the room and reminded him, “We’ll leave in twenty-five minutes.”

Getting ready, she could hear him furiously pounding out some response to some stranger to some obscure question about the universe and its parallel dimension. She didn’t understand his obsession with this forum. Night after night he chatted with people connected through invisible wires around the universe. He said once he even had a conversation with a lady in Norway. Many mornings as she got up for school, he was shutting down and getting ready for bed. Then when she returned from school or work, he would be waking up and firing up his connection. Their schedules had become completely opposite.

He could take Christmas off. She would let him finish up, but in twenty minutes, they were getting in the car and heading to Seattle. She laid out his clothes for him so he could get ready quickly. It was always the same. She finished up her hair and makeup and called, "Five minutes."

The tapping continued. Lisa pulled on her slacks and sweater. The tapping continued. She added earrings and a necklace. The tapping continued. She decided on a pair of red flats. The tapping continued.

"It's time to go." Lisa entered his office.

"I've got some work to do on the book. I think I'll stay here," Jonathan said, not breaking his cyber communication.

"That's not an option," Lisa said.

Jonathan continued.

"Please, Jonathan. It's Christmas."

"You'll be okay. Go spend time with your family. I'll stay here."

"It's our first Christmas. Can't you put that aside for one afternoon? You can come back and be on it all night," Lisa begged. "It's our *first* Christmas."

"Fine," Jonathan said.

"I'll be in the car."

Lisa got in the driver's seat and waited. Jonathan was out within three minutes. He was pouting, but he was going. "Thank you," Lisa said, patting his hand.

"I don't know why I have to go. It's not my family," he started.

"It *is* your family."

"I hardly know them."

"That's why you go spend time; to get to know them."

"It's just stupid."

"It's not stupid. It's Christmas and you spend Christmas with family."

"My family never did."

"That's a shock," Lisa said.

"I don't see why we have to."

"It's not that we *have* to. You should *want* to. It's part of having family."

"But we're married now. We should just be able to stay home and not have to do all the social crap," Jonathan said.

They had gone about four blocks from their home and Lisa pulled to the side of the road. "What'd you say?" she asked softly.

"We don't have to do all this," Jonathan waved his arm around, "stuff."

"Stuff. Like hang out with friends? With family? Go out together? Go shoot pool? See movies? Go to the park?" Lisa listed all the things he had refused to do over the past few months.

"Exactly," Jonathan said.

Lisa pulled a U-turn in the road.

"What're you doing?" Jonathan asked.

"Taking you home. You don't have to do this *stuff,*" she emphasized the last word.

"Really?" Jonathan's voice filled with excitement.

The four blocks home was quiet. She pulled in the driveway. Jonathan threw open his door and leaned back in quickly to kiss her. "You're the best. Merry Christmas." He bounced out of the car, ran up the front steps and was in the house and out of sight before Lisa even started backing out of the driveway. Merry Christmas.

"What do you mean, he didn't want to come?" Cathy started in right away.

"Not that he didn't want to come," Lisa covered for Jonathan. "He just had a lot of work to do." She didn't know why, but she threw in, "Working on his book."

"The life of the wife of an author." As soon as Lisa set down the packages she had carried in, Cathy pulled her into one of her bear hugs. "Oh, my," she exclaimed. "Does the wife of an author not eat? Where'd you go?" She pulled off Lisa's coat and let it drop to the floor. "Oy, vey, get this kid a donut."

"Stop," Lisa said. Although it did feel good that someone noticed her weight loss. "I've been running a lot."

"I'd say. Tammy," she yelled, "bring the tray of fattening appetizers and meet us in the living room." To Lisa she said, "The boys are finishing the rest of the meal, the baby's sleeping and we're going to sit and eat nibbles while we can." Then again she yelled to Tammy, "And bring her a drink."

As they entered the living room from one side, Tammy appeared from the kitchen, her hands full. She had a tray of bite-sized stuffed mushrooms in one and in the other, two wine glasses held upside down by the stem. Under her arm was a bottle of wine and in her mouth was a wine opener. Lisa rushed to her and grabbed the wine and the opener. Cathy grabbed a mushroom and popped it in her mouth. "Oh, thanks," Tammy said to her.

"What?" Cathy said. "I'm hungry."

Tammy set the plate on the table and hugged Lisa. "Oh, she wasn't kidding. Have you eaten in the last three months?"

"Yes, yes. I've been running a lot. I haven't lost that much, just toned up," Lisa said.

"I don't know," Cathy said. "From my experience, weight loss is usually a sign of depression. Are you depressed, little cousin?"

"No," she said.

"It wouldn't surprise me if you were. Tacoma is no place to stay for very long." Cathy stuffed another mushroom in her mouth, then plucked one from the tray and put it to Lisa's lips. "Open wide. These'll fatten you up." Lisa let her put the whole mushroom in her mouth and the juices of sausage and seasonings filled it. Tammy placed a glass of wine in front of her.

"Here. My favorite. Sangiovese."

Lisa took a sip and wrinkled her nose not having yet acquired a taste for red wine. "Sangio what?"

"Vese. Keep drinking. You'll start to like it."

"Or," Cathy put another mushroom to her lips, "you can forget the wine and eat more of these."

Lisa accepted another mushroom and set the wine down. "I think I do like the mushrooms much better."

Cathy handed her a napkin. "So, spill. Are you happy?"

"Of course, I'm happy," Lisa said.

"You don't seem happy. Does she seem happy to you, fat head?" Cathy asked Tammy.

Tammy remained quiet but Lisa could feel her studying her. "I'm happy. Why would I not be happy?"

"You tell us," Cathy said.

"There's nothing to tell. I'm happy."

"So, how come you're here on Christmas and your husband of what, three months, isn't?"

"I told you, he's working."

"Bullshit."

"Cathy, let it rest," Tammy said.

Lisa was grateful to have Tammy end the inquisition. But she noticed the pained look in Tammy's eyes as she watched her. *Do I really look that unhappy*? Lisa didn't think she was unhappy. In her day-to-day, she didn't feel unhappy. She went to school where she was learning something she loved even though her wrists were bothering her all the time now. She really liked working at The Old Spaghetti Factory and the people she had met there. A group of them had gone out dancing and to karaoke a few times and had a blast. Jonathan never minded. Of course, he never wanted to join them. But he never minded. She was proud to be the married one in the group and the ring on her finger shielded her from awkward advances and devastating rejections.

Sure, her marriage wasn't exactly what she had envisioned. She would rather have had her partner here at her side with her on their first Christmas. She would rather have had her partner join her to go out with friends. She would rather not go to movies by herself. But, he also didn't mind that she kept living. He didn't tell her she couldn't do these things. He just didn't want to do them with her.

He wanted to stay home and write and be on his computer. They were finding a way to make it work and they both still enjoyed the things they enjoyed. Unfortunately, it wasn't together.

"Everything's fine. I'm happy. I'm just fine," Lisa said to no one in particular.

During dinner, Lisa felt herself forcing smiles more than once. She realized quickly she did not like spending Christmas without her husband. Watching Tammy and her husband laughing and enjoying one another's company like a couple should reinforced her aloneness. When she was single, she never felt this alone. It wasn't fair to be feeling it now. She shouldn't be feeling this now.

She wanted to get home and she excused herself soon after dessert was done.

"What? Little cousin. I want you to stay and play," Cathy said.

"You didn't even get to see the baby wake up," Tammy joined in.

"I know. I know. I have a long drive though and I should get home to Jonathan."

"You tell that stupid boy to come with you next time or I will send the goblins out to get him," Cathy said. She had entwined Lisa in her gruff hug. For once, Lisa wanted her to squeeze tighter and longer.

"I will. He will," she said. "You guys come and visit us soon."

"Tacoma? No way!" Cathy put her finger to her mouth, stuck her tongue out and engaged in a fake barfing action.

"Thank you for the gift." Lisa held up an unopened package. Cathy would not let her open it in front of the others. She said she didn't want her to be too embarrassed. Which Lisa knew Cathy thrived on, so it must really be a doozy.

"For those lonely nights." Cathy winked. She hugged her tight again and then shoved her out the door saying, "Be gone with you, little cousin. Be gone."

Jonathan was still tapping away at his computer when she got home. He barely looked up as she came behind him and kissed him on the cheek. "You're home earlier than I thought." He kept on tapping. She could see he was in his CompuServe Forum.

"Tired." Lisa went to the bedroom and crawled into her thick comforter.

The first quarter ended with the realization that unless a shift in the game plan occurred, the result was going to be a devastating loss.

CHAPTER 37

The second quarter in a game is basically filler. Teams continue to mimic the set tempo and ride it out until halftime when the coach reassesses the situation and revamps the offense and defense for the important remaining quarters in the game. Occasionally, a last minute play at the end of the second quarter can send a team to the locker room in a tailspin.

After the New Year, Jonathan got a job working part time at Borders Books. They pretty much hired him on the spot: Bachelor's Degree, wearing a tie, and published author. He thrived even though it was entry level book selling and stocking shelves. He got a thrill when his coworkers would bring customers over to meet the author and show off his book. Of the very few copies sold around the nation, probably ninety-five percent were sold at the Tacoma Borders. But it was a good boost for his ego and Lisa enjoyed seeing him passionate about something.

It didn't change the fact that they never did anything together. The bike was forgotten. He spent all night on the computer. She spent all day at school. It was a rare evening they sat down together on the living room couch and watched TV.

One such night, they were watching Seinfeld. It was the one with the ugly baby. At commercial, Lisa said, "When do you think we'll start having babies?"

"I'm not having babies," Jonathan said immediately.

Lisa had been laying in his lap and sat up. "Why would you say that?"

"Because I mean it. Not gonna be like my dad and have a slew of babies and then realize I don't want them. Better to not start."

"You're not being serious right now, are you?"

"Yes, Lisa. I'm being serious," Jonathan said.

"You just feel that way now. But in a few years, maybe—" Lisa waited for him to finish her thought.

"Nope. Never gonna happen."

"You didn't think this was important to mention to me?" Lisa asked.

"You didn't think it was important to ask?" Jonathan fired back nonchalantly.

"I just assumed. I mean you're so good with Liana and you actually said you'd make a good dad." Lisa recalled the day at Sea World. He and Liana had been inseparable. He carried her on his shoulders and knelt down to listen to her stories. He taught her cute sayings and read all the signs to her. He was going to be a great dad.

"I know I'd make a good dad," Jonathan said. "Doesn't mean I want to be one." He got up from the couch.

"Where are you going?"

"I'm going to go do some writing and work on the book."

"So, that's it? End of discussion?" Lisa asked.

"What more is there to discuss? I said I don't want kids. I don't want kids. You can't make my mind change."

Lisa sat staring blankly at the TV and listened to the damn dial up mock her from Jonathan's computer. Heading into halftime after the other team has scored a game-changer at the buzzer shifts the entire momentum of the second half.

CHAPTER 38

In the first minutes of the third quarter, teams rally to try their new strategies discussed at halftime. It's determined pretty quickly who will take over at this point. And a surge late in the third quarter seals the outcome of many a game.

The marriage didn't get any better. It didn't get any worse. Jonathan and Lisa coexisted, but it reminded Lisa more of having a roommate than what she thought having a husband would be like. They no longer had mutual friends. Jonathan had a few friends at Borders; none that he would spend time with outside of work, but friends. Lisa had friends from school and work and her running partner that she spent an hour with every morning, and more on weekends.

Lisa stopped visiting Cathy and Tammy. She knew they knew and she was embarrassed. She still believed she and Jonathan just had to get through a transition phase and then the marriage would start. It wasn't like they fought or exchanged harsh words. Many times she just got the feeling he put up with her. One word answers as he continuously tapped out something on his computer or a dismissive 'thanks' when she would bring his dinner to him at his desk. They never ate together anymore.

Lisa's strategy involved trying to engage Jonathan in conversations like they used to have. But usually it ended with her hearing things she didn't want to hear, certainly didn't understand. It was frustrating for her to talk with him. He didn't appear to care about her ideas or opinions anymore. One evening, she pulled a chair into his office, sat down, and asked him, "Are you happy?"

"Of course. You?"

"I'm happy," she paused and looked to the floor. "But I wish sometimes you would make plans for us to do something together. I want to do things with my husband."

"We're together everyday," Jonathan said.

"You don't talk to me like you used to. Remember when we would exchange ideas and talk about what we would do if?"

"That's what I do in my forums."

"But I want you to do that with me," Lisa said.

"We've already discussed all that."

"No, we haven't, Jonathan. You can make up more questions like you used to and we could talk forever."

Jonathan reached to the side of his computer and fetched a bag of Doritos. He pulled the bag apart and retrieved a handful of chips. He put one in his mouth and started the slow methodical crunch.

"Are you dismissing me?" Lisa asked.

"I just have a lot of messages to answer and want to get a start on them."

"Can you think about what I said and can we make some kind of plan?"

"Sure."

Lisa stood. Over his back, she could see the title of the Forum he had been furiously attending to when she interrupted him. "The Soul Mate Forum?" She leaned in for a closer look. "Jonathan, what are you doing?"

"Nothing." He closed his screen.

"Let me see it," she said.

"It's nothing. James and I started a thread about the whole Melissa thing. It's getting feedback on the idea."

"But the idea is right here, Jonathan. Standing right here. Living right here with you. And yet you...Are you looking for your next soul mate? Am I your starter wife?"

"Don't be ridiculous."

"I'm not being ridiculous. What's the truth? Am I not Melissa? Are you still searching for her?"

Jonathan grabbed another handful of Doritos. Lisa stood and

waited for him to answer the question. When a full minute passed and she realized he was not going to answer, she removed her chair from his office and went to bed. Alone. Lonely. The end of the third-quarter surge was going to be almost impossible to overcome.

CHAPTER 39

A lot of games should end after the third quarter. The score is insurmountable and the outcome is inevitable. However, the fourth quarter must always be played regardless. The losing team—however futile—tries to make plays and put a few more points on the board in order to save face. The winning team rides out their victory urging the game clock to tick off the seconds faster so they can begin their celebration.

Not long after their second Christmas—she spent it with her parents and sisters in Idaho, Jonathan stayed home—Lisa joined her friends from school for a night out dancing to the hits of the '70s. They went to a dance club just north of Tacoma in Fife where a popular disc jockey from Seattle was deejaying. One of her school friends was dating him, so they all got in for free and had a table front and center.

Their group spent the night dominating the dance floor and belting out popular tunes like "Dancing Queen" and "Play that Funky Music White Boy." The only down time came when a slow song was played, much to the dismay of most of their group. Lisa would never slow dance with anyone, quickly quelling any invitation with, "I'm married," and displaying her ring.

When the first few strums of Clapton's "Wonderful Tonight," started, the majority of them playfully booed and moved off the dance floor. There was only one married couple with them: Sharon, a fellow classmate, and her husband, who had announced, "Our song." They remained on the floor where he skillfully guided her into a soft pirouette and then wrapped his arm lovingly around her waist. Sharon cocked her head to one side and looked up at him.

For one moment, Lisa caught a snapshot into their relationship. His eyes were filled with complete adoration for his wife and she looked at him with a deep love.

Lisa looked down, embarrassed she had intruded into their intimate moment. She tried to focus on the others at the table who were quenching their thirst and chattering about what songs they hoped would be played next. It wasn't until Lisa heard, "You just don't realize how much I love you" that she snuck a look at Sharon and her husband again. He was holding her close and Lisa could see him mouthing the words smoothly into his wife's ear. As they turned, Sharon's face carried a serene, peaceful smile. She slowly lifted her head to her husband and wrapped an arm tight up into the base of his neck as she sang with Clapton, "It's time to go home now." He nodded slightly and kissed her, then led her off the dance floor to the table for goodbyes.

The tingling of emotion was threatening to flow and Lisa excused herself to the bathroom where the tears stumbled effortlessly. She sat in the stall and tried to catch her breath. It was coming in short gasps. She was never going to have someone look at her like that. She would never have a song. She would never be led home with longing. Things needed to change and change quickly if this marriage was to be salvaged.

She waved dismissively to her dancing group as she grabbed her coat to leave. A few put their palms up and lifted their shoulders in a questioning motion—no one wanted to resign the "YMCA" routine. Lisa placed her hand on her stomach and mouthed to them, "not feeling well."

When she got home, Jonathan was in his office typing away. She grabbed the chair and pulled it in the room setting it next to him. He continued tapping a few more lines, and then acknowledged Lisa's presence, "What's up?"

"Can you tell me? Is this how it's always going to be?"

"What do you mean?" Jonathan asked.

"You, up all night writing, then sleeping during the day?"

"You knew I was a writer when you married me."

"You're messaging strangers. That's not writing."

"It's not just the Forums. I'm working on my second book also."

"You should be pretty much done with that book, the time you've spent on it." Lisa was done hinting around about the second book progress and decided to be more direct.

"You have no idea how long it takes to write a book. Are you questioning my work?"

"No, no. That's not it. But can you at least tell me what it's about?" she asked.

"I haven't told anybody what it's about. And my dad and brother will be the first to know. Once I tell them, I'll let you know."

"Jonathan, I'm your wife. Why wouldn't you tell me first?"

His hmphh was clearly audible as his answer.

"Again, is this how it's going to be? We don't do anything together. Are you ever going to go out with me? You've stopped seeing your friends, or those I thought were your friends. Greg and Keith have even given up calling you. God, we haven't even spent one holiday together since we've been married."

Jonathan sat and listened. It was all true. "I'm married. I've told you I don't have to do those things anymore. I want to stay home, write, chat. You're capable of doing whatever you want. I should be allowed to do what I want."

"I thought you decided you were going to get a job," Lisa continued. "A career. That you needed to get a job." The part-time hours at Borders weren't really covering any of the bills.

"I'm an author. When will I write if I start working full time?"

Lisa knew Jonathan was more concerned about how it would look rather than the lack of writing time. He felt he was to become a famous author. Even though his book tanked and William Morrow would never bank on him again, that was who he was—an author. An author who wrote for free. There would be no more money from his book. He was lucky he didn't have to pay back the advance. Besides, she knew he worried more about if he had a full-time job, he wouldn't have time to answer all his fans on CompuServe.

Lisa stood and walked behind him, putting her hands on his shoulders. "Come on. Come to bed." Lisa tried to get his attention. "It's late. You can finish this up tomorrow."

He lightly kissed Lisa's hand on his shoulder and told her, "I'll be in in a little bit. I just have one more thing I want to write."

Lisa sat back down and waited. She would wait for him to finish his 'one more thing.' But Jonathan would not continue while she was there. This solidified for her that what he was doing on the computer had nothing to do with working on a second book. She knew in her gut there was a great possibility he was grooming a relationship thousands of miles—figuratively and literally—away from their marriage.

Minutes passed with them sitting there doing nothing, saying nothing. "So this is really how it's going to always be, isn't it? You doing your thing, me mine. This is marriage for you?" Lisa asked.

"Yeah, this is marriage for me."

"Do you understand that marriage for me is spending time together, shooting pool, playing racquetball, riding bikes, seeing movies. Together. What happened to the Jonathan that started out doing those things with me?" There was a deep sigh in her voice. It wasn't anger; only disappointment.

Jonathan mumbled, "I'm sorry you feel that way. I can have my stuff out by tomorrow."

"What?" Lisa looked at him in disbelief. And repeated, "What?"

"You're right," he said. "This isn't working. And I know you'll never be the one to say it because your family doesn't divorce," he mocked her with the last word. "I can pack up and be out by tomorrow. I'll stay with my brother."

Lisa sat staring at him. James had moved to Seattle only last month. Had they already discussed Jonathan staying with him? She stood. She had no words. She turned and walked out of the room. Immediately, she heard Jonathan click to trigger his computer back up.

In the bedroom alone, Lisa sprawled on the bed. She was stunned. This was obviously something Jonathan had been thinking about. How could he already have a plan in place? She contemplated how to handle this. She was not getting divorced. How could they make this work? They got along fine enough, never fought. But it made her sad they did nothing together. Their ideas of marriage were so opposite. Why had they not talked about this before? They could talk about it now. This was fixable. There could be compromises.

She walked down the hall and before entering the office could hear the tap, tap, tap of energy pouring through Jonathan's fingers to his computer. It was fast and furious. It was not the tapping of a man who had just said the words to end his marriage. Lisa paused, *is this the man I want to fight for*? One who cares so little about me that he's already on to his next task moments after destroying me? She returned to her room knowing there would be no discussion; content in the fact there would be no discussion. Game over.

As the final buzzer sounds in a game, realization settles in. All the pre-planning, all the strategizing, all the execution is over. The result is all that's left. Some are thrilled. Some are devastated. Some—who never really had their heart in it—are not even affected. There was no one thrilled in this outcome.

Even though the game is officially over, there's always the obligatory handshakes and locker room summations that occur securing the final nail in the coffin.

CHAPTER 40

True to his word Jonathan was out the next day. Lisa returned home from school as he and his brother were loading up the last of it. James was curt as always. "Hey." Lisa didn't feel the need to answer him.

Jonathan came around the corner, all business. "I took the TV since it was mine before and some other things. I think it was fair."

"Sure." Lisa had no energy to fight.

"I called your sister to let her know."

"You called my sister?" Lisa had talked to no one about what happened, what was happening. It had been less than twenty-four hours since the proclamation had even been made. She had made no phone calls. At school, her muscle memory carried her through the motions of drills. Her mind was numb to the fact a divorce was looming. It wasn't quite believable yet, but Jonathan had sealed the fate informing Lynn it was happening.

"Well, yeah," he answered as if it was the only reasonable thing he could have done.

"Why? Why would you do that?"

"She was basically my sister, too."

It angered Lisa that he seemed to be enjoying he was the one able to announce this; treating it as the climax of their relationship. "You arrogant man," she hissed. "You knew this would devastate my family. Yet, you took it upon yourself to—"

James flew in the door interrupting, "Hey, man come on. You're gonna miss your flight if we don't leave now."

"Your flight to where?" Lisa took the bait.

James looked at Jonathan, then Lisa, then back to Jonathan. "Bro, you didn't tell her?"

She didn't want to know what he was going to say. She didn't want James to have the satisfaction of her asking him anything. But, of course, he gave her the answer. "He's going to Connecticut." He got to be the one to deliver the dagger. "To meet Samantha."

Jonathan shrugged to Lisa as James cast her an arrogant smirk and grabbed Jonathan to lead him out the door. Post-game summation finished.

CHAPTER 41

Months passed and Lisa was well beyond the anger stage. She had moved in to acceptance, realizing that the eighteen months of marriage had been her depression stage having naïvely fostered thoughts that things were bound to get better. Acceptance had not been easy. She carried a lot of guilt because of the divorce, but her family had been supportive and helpful.

Through counseling, she learned many mistakes she had made. But more importantly she learned to accept this as a piece of her life. She wasn't regretful. She formed a belief that you could only truly be regretful about something if you didn't learn anything from it. So, she focused on things she learned from the experience.

First and foremost, she learned that fitting into somebody else's 'plan' is all well and good but it's also important you make sure they fit into yours. Melissa was Jonathan's fictional mold that intertwined into Lisa's world. She had found it fascinating to exchange biographies and notes with her, but if she had to do it over again, she would take a step back and ask herself, "Does Jonathan fulfill what I want in a relationship and a partner?"

Although she knew he would not have matched most things had she had a list, she also knew there were things he offered that would not have been on her original list. Her list would be much more complete having met Jonathan. Early in the relationship, he had taught her to think more deeply about subjects and to contemplate things in the universe. She had also learned to be more independent, having to do many things on her own during their marriage if she wanted to do them at all. She would never feel uncomfortable going to a movie or dining alone again. Although she would be much happier sharing the experience with someone, she was comfortable going it alone if she had to.

Working through several sessions, she could focus on positives that came out of the relationship and she knew she was going to be okay. She did voice many times she wished Jonathan would acknowledge his part. Perhaps realizing how unfair his approach at getting his Melissa, and then so easily discarding the idea once it became reality. She thought someday she may get an apology. But her counselor preached, “You can’t control how other people behave. Only focus on yourself.”

She did focus on herself. She spent lots of evenings at home reading and listening to music. She didn’t go out much. The irony of it was, she had holed up in her apartment and become Jonathan. However, she never felt lonely. Not like she had many nights while she was sleeping in a bed with Jonathan right next to her.

One evening, Lisa secured herself from the storm that raged outside her window. Bundled in a tattered quilt, hands wrapped around a hot cup of cocoa, and stockinged feet curled warm beneath her, she opened the latest article from her counselor: “Moving on From Divorce.” The telephone ring echoed through her sparse apartment.

“Hello.”

“Hey. It’s Jonathan.”

Lisa paused long enough to let him know his call was not welcome, although she had anticipated it. “Yeah?” Lisa had nothing to say. This was his purging. Even though Lisa had been waiting patiently for an apology, she would be shocked if this is what his call was about.

“How are you?”

Lisa did not respond. She waited.

“Are things going well?”

She focused on the familiar branch tapping lonely on her window as the wind coerced it into a melancholy dance.

“Lisa?”

Patience. It was coming. Tap tap tap swirl tap tap.

"Are you there?"

Safe question. "I'm here."

"Oh, I thought you hung up."

No way. Lisa had waited six months, thinking maybe an apology was coming. She heard a crinkling of wrapper on the other end. *Was he preparing to shove something in his mouth*?

The crackling stopped. "You need to send me a check for sixty-seven dollars and three cents." The reason for his call.

Three cents. The branch snapped harshly outside. She knew exactly what it was for. The Pier One credit card she used to purchase forks and knives and spoons, replacing the ones he'd taken when he moved out. "You're not getting another dime from me," Lisa finally answered. She had been more than fair in the split—taking on half the debt he ran up on credit cards with her name—and writing him a check for $3400 on the day of the divorce. There were no assets.

Without hesitation, Jonathan announced, "I'll just have my lawyer call you."

Lisa huffed.

"Is that what you want?" He questioned her laughter, missing the exasperation.

"Sure, Jonathan. Have him call me." She was pretty confident a lawyer was not going to deal with an issue of sixty-seven dollars and three *cents;* especially after reading the terms of the divorce where she had paid him and not pursued spousal maintenance payments. She also knew Jonathan didn't have a lawyer. Had he forgotten they were married? Sounded like a James threat. They were perfect for one another. More than a moment of awkward silence passed. The tree branch whipped to a crescendo and the wind emitted an ear-piercing shrill.

"I guess I'll have him call you then."

Lisa was floating between the idea of hanging up or hanging on. Hanging up would end it. But she would always wonder, what if? What if I had stayed on the line? Would he have offered an explanation or an apology of recognition? Had he realized anything wrong in what he had done? Did he even view her as someone real, or was she just an idea to him stuffed neatly into a shoebox? She hung on in silence.

"Are you still there?"

"Yes, Jonathan. I'm still here." The cold seeped through the single-paned sill. "Anything else you want to say?"

"No. Is there something you want me to say?"

"Only if you want to say something." Outside, the storm had become eerily silent, as if waiting with her, not wanting to miss a hint of sorrow from the other end of the line.

"Well, uh, how have you been?"

Silence.

"What have you been doing?" He tried again.

Small talk?

"Really, Lisa. I do care about you. What have you been doing?"

Lisa did not know what she wanted to tell him. She had not planned for him to ask about her. She was only hoping for an apology or explanation on his part. That's all she wanted. The tapping at the window had begun again, slowly, slowly egging her on.

"I've been working and going to school and practicing my machine. My wrists are still giving me a lot of trouble." Was she hoping for sympathy?

"Is that it?" His voice already sounded bored.

Is that it? What did he want from her? What great and wondrous thing had he been doing for the past half year? The tapping accelerated and the wind became frenzied, forcing Lisa to pull the quilt tight around her. A fleeting thought crossed her mind; if he could hear she was trying to learn something from all this, he might see the need to get a grip about his own character flaws. "Actually, I've been to a couple of counseling groups."

In the quiet pause, she heard him chewing on something, and she could picture the crumbs littering his belly. Now, she felt the chill of the wind and heard the prodding branch filling her with life and she continued with one last shred of hope for this man who would always be her 'starter husband.' "I've also been meeting one-on-one with a therapist to work through some things."

She waited, hoping he'd echo that he had done some self-reflection about their relationship also. A large crack of thunder shook the window and tightened Lisa's core, heightening her awareness of both storms converging in the night.

Lisa heard the remnants of whatever Jonathan had been shoving in his mouth gulp down his throat and he spoke the last words she would ever hear from him, "That's good, Lisa. I think counseling is a good thing for you. You'll probably get a lot out of that."

The first harsh drops of rain pounded outside, promising to purify the environment. A shift of awareness streamed through her entire body. It was not anger. It was no longer resentment. It was a release. Enlightenment pulsed through her. She realized it was pity she felt for this man. He would never be happy. He would always be chasing his next figment of Melissa or Samantha or whomever. And the moment he found her, he'd be on to the next list of his new and improved requirements.

Serenely, as the rain echoed outside her door, Lisa hung up the phone and whispered, "Goodbye Melissa."

ACKNOWLEDGEMENTS

The Truth About Melissa: A Soul Mate Experiment has been in my head for over 20 years.

Thank you...

Friends and family who generously contributed by placing orders well in advance of publication. Your copies are on their way.

The World Famous Coffee Cup in Boulder City for the best BLTs, pork chili verde, and peanut butter/pecan/banana waffles in the world. Nothing to do with the book; but everything to do with sustenance and life and love!

Lisa Luma, Deborah Steiner, Lynn Wilson, Leslie Parrish and Julie Christine Johnson for being my first readers and contributing valuable feedback to the overall story. I appreciate the time and encouragement you gave to a friend struggling through this whole process.

Sequim Writers Group—Jon, Patrick, Sarah, Mike, and Alana—for listening to yet another 'Melissa piece' and adding depth to sections and deleting out all those overused words. (Like the word 'out' in the previous sentence.)

LuAnne Meissen—proofreader extraordinaire. Just when I thought I had caught all the errors...Your the best! I know, I know. You're.

And mostly, Mark Textor for believing in me and gifting me the time to get *Melissa* finished and published. You know I have five more in the works after this, right? I love you.

CPSIA information can be obtained
at www.ICGtesting.com
Printed in the USA
FSOW01n0724291017
40468FS